SACRED BUFFALO

The Lakota Way for a New Beginning

James G. Durham and Virginia Thomas
Photographs by David Bjorkman · Drawings by James G. Durham

Sycamore Island Books · Boulder, Colorado

Sacred Buffalo:
The Lakota Way for a New Beginning
by James G. Durham and Virginia E. Thomas

Copyright © 1996 by Buffalo LLC and Virginia E. Thomas
Photographs Copyright © 1996 by Buffalo LLC and David C. Bjorkman
Original Drawings Copyright © 1996 by James G. Durham and Buffalo LLC

ISBN 0-87364-868-4
Printed in the United States of America

Durham, James G. and Thomas, Virginia E.
   Sacred buffalo : the Lakota way for a new beginning / by
James G. Durham and Virginia E. Thomas.
   p. cm.
   ISBN 0-87364-868-4

   1. Teton Indians--Rights and ceremonies. 2. Durham, James G. 3.
Scrimshaws. 4. Indian art--North America. 5. Vietnamese Conflict,
1961-1975--Veterans.   I. Title

E99.T34T46 1996   299'.78'5
                           QBI95-20583

Published by Sycamore Island Books,
a division of Paladin Enterprises, Inc.,
P.O. Box 1307,
Boulder, Colorado 80306, USA.
(303) 443-7250

Direct inquiries and/or orders to the above address.

All rights reserved. Except for use in a review, no portion
of this book may be reproduced in any form without the
express written permission of the publisher and Buffalo LLC.

Neither the authors, the publisher, nor Buffalo LLC assumes
any responsibility for the use or misuse of
information contained in this book.

Cover photos and book design by David Bjorkman.
Black and white photographs custom printed by Paula David
and Diana Anderson, Photo Craft Laboratories, Boulder, Colorado.

Contents

Preface		xi
Chapter 1:	Introduction	1
Chapter 2:	The Vision	5
Chapter 3:	Carving the Buffalo	21
Chapter 4:	The Chanunpa, the Sacred Pipe	31
Chapter 5:	The End of Time	45
Chapter 6:	Carving the Buffalo	53
Chapter 7:	Inipi, Making Yourself Pure Again	65
Chapter 8:	Hunkapi, Making of Relatives	75
Chapter 9:	Carving the Buffalo	81
Chapter 10:	Keeping and Releasing of a Soul and the Yuwipi Ceremony	93
Chapter 11:	Tapa Wanka Yap, Throwing of the Ball and Making of a Woman	101
Chapter 12:	Carving the Buffalo	109
Chapter 13:	Hanbleceya, Crying for a Vision	123
Chapter 14:	Wiwanyag Wachipi, Sundance	137
Chapter 15:	Carving the Buffalo	157
Chapter 16:	Beginning of Time	169
Glossary		175
References		177
Acknowledgments		178
Drawings		179

I dedicate this Sacred Buffalo to my dad.
"These are the footprints you said could never be left behind."
Thank you.

To my son, Nick.
"With these words, your Buffalo now speaks."

To my daughter, Crystal.
"I give you all my love."
—JGD

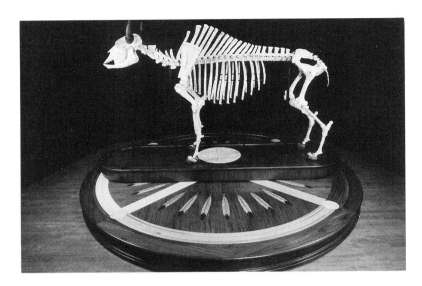

Special Thanks

To my friend, James Dubray, spiritual leader of the Oglala tribe
of the Lakota Nation;

To Verdell "Big Red" Red Cloud and the Red Cloud family, for always
being there for me;

To all the dancers at the Frank Fools Crow International Sundance;

To my brother Dick Baker, one of the Vietnam veteran dancers at
Arvol Looking Horse's Sundance grounds;

To my friends Don Ruleaux and Rose;

To the Lakota People;

To my Vietnam Vets Motorcycle Club brothers—I am forever L.O.S.T.;

To Ohio State University, William Richeimer, and his staff, Barb Shardy,
Jacque Shepherd, and Shane Donley;

To Peder Lund and Rick Rippberger for believing in the dream;

To Bill Escobar and Donna DuVall;

To Matt, my gratitude and undying love.

I dedicate this book to my dad
for giving me the desire to know.
—VET

Preface

VERY EARLY IN THE making of the Sacred Buffalo, it became apparent that a book should be written and photographs taken to document the process of its being carved and to interpret the Lakota sacred rites depicted on its bones. As a result, this writer and photographer spent more than a year compiling a record of the Sacred Buffalo's journey from a bare-bones skeleton to a living tribute to the ancient wisdom and ceremony of the Lakota people.

The intent of the words and photos that follow is to provide a guide and a memento to those people who see the Buffalo in person and to those who will come to know it through these stories and images.

Hundreds of hours were spent in conversation with the artist and coauthor, Jim Durham; with the spiritual leader of the Oglala tribe of the Lakota Nation, Jimmy Dubray—a gifted teacher; and with those who worked on the Buffalo and its stand: Beemer (Harry Lindsay), Teri Krukowski, Tommy Dubray, Mike Riss, and Steve Riss.

Jim Durham and Jimmy Dubray are the main sources for the descriptions of the sacred rites—along with countless historical references that helped to provide context. This writer's account in chapters 3, 6, 9, 12, and 15 endeavor to give you a sense of the texture of daily life during the carving of the Buffalo, while the other chapters tell the story of the vision that brought the Buffalo to life, as well as the sacred ceremonies.

Before we began the journey that would result in this book, we all smoked Jimmy Dubray's Chanunpa, his Sacred Pipe. Throughout the year, we constantly relived that singular privilege—letting it guide us day by day. Months later, when Jimmy and his wife, Florine, were sitting in their living room, Jimmy recalled that day. "A person prays, 'Bless me, Father,' and who does it help?" he said. "Just he who asks? But in the Lakota Way, we pray for everyone, and the blessings just keep coming in. Wisdom comes in that way, too. Remember this: what I call the Indian Holy Ghost might come to you. You might see something beautiful. I hope and pray hard that you do. If only we could make people see it, they would understand why our belief is so strong."

"Through a little boy's vision a Buffalo and this book were begun—they each have a beginning and no end," he continued. "Maybe this book is how my prayer has been answered. Whatever is written, always remember that little *hokshila*, that boy. Only Tunkashila will get credit for this book, but we'll all get our blessing. Maybe two or three million people will read it and benefit. The blessings will roll in. Because when we bless someone, they will bless us."

"Even if it helps save one person, Tunkashila will bless you," Florine added. "Just in the writing of this book, Almighty God will help. Then, maybe an idea (from it) will come over a person like a fog, and he'll think about it, and say, 'Maybe I should do this, maybe it is the good way.' Do you realize what you are doing?"

In truth, the text and photos that follow chronicle the love and unselfish labor of everyone involved in the Sacred Buffalo project.

—*Virginia Thomas*

Chapter 1

Introduction

"The spirit of the Sacred Buffalo will touch you if you'll let it."
—BIG JIM DURHAM

IN MY DREAM ABOUT the Sacred Buffalo, I simply walked away at the end without saying a word.

I can recall the details of the scene before I woke up as if it happened last night: I was standing alone in the back of a big, bright room crowded with smiling people. Standing beyond the glare of the lights, I could look over the crowd to the far end of the room to where the Sacred Buffalo stood in all its glory and power. Men in penguin suits and their fancy women talked and nodded and drank from stemmed glasses as they admired the Sacred Buffalo and deciphered the stories carved onto its bleached bones. I looked down at my clothes—my worn jeans and shabby size fourteen-and-a-half cowboy boots—and at the chapped hands that had lived those sacred rites and carved them. I planned then never to tell this story. I opened a side door and walked away.

In the past, the deer and buffalo hides I've painted have always spoken for me, and if people saw them and remembered the name James G. Durham—Big Jim as some of my friends call me—it was because my passion had cut through their defenses to pierce their very souls. I knew the Sacred Buffalo would speak to people according to their ability to hear it. I had seen it happen time and time again in the studio while I was in the process of carving it. You see, it pulls people to it like a magnet pulls iron. If it wants you, its force is irresistible. I can say that without fear of bragging because I never set out to create it. It chose me. All I did was to bring the vision of a seven-year-old boy to the people of the world. I just did what I was told: I transformed his vision into reality.

I like to watch the Sacred Buffalo hook up with people and take them where they need to go.

INTRODUCTION

"Boy, it's *huge*!" you might say, looking from a distance at its ten-foot-long frame. But I see behind your eyes as its power grabs you. You feel the tug of some primal memory of an ancient hunt stirring in your cells—of heaving a spear at a charging, wild-eyed animal and the smell of hot blood and hot breath as the wounded animal comes close. There's a flurry of horns and hooves and you turn to run. But then the animal drops. In giving its life, it gives you life. Your family will survive the winter on its meat. That is the gift of the buffalo spirit.

Or you might step closer to the Sacred Buffalo to study the details of the seven sacred rites of the Lakota people—the Sioux—carved on its bones: the Chanunpa, the Rite of Purification, Making of Relatives, the Keeping and Releasing of a Soul, Throwing of the Ball, Crying for a Vision, and Sundance. "What a lot of work," you might exclaim. Every single leg bone has more than 6,500 lines scratched into it to show the stories—not counting the hundreds of little lines that make the shading. You ask, "How did you have the patience?"

It's been a labor of love. For seven years, I lived those sacred ceremonies of the Lakota—which may be why I was chosen for the dream. Me, a breed—the term some full-bloods use to describe those of us with white ancestry in our DNA. I suffered seven years to learn the seven sacred rites shown on the Buffalo.

Or maybe you're one of those people who can sense the spirits around the Sacred Buffalo. The spirit of the buffalo itself will touch you if you let it—as will the spirits of each of the figures carved onto its bones. When I asked my friend Old Man Jimmy Dubray, spiritual leader of the Oglala tribe of the Lakota people, to bless the skeleton before I began to work on it, he warned at the ceremony that the spirit of the animal would walk the studio at night, and that the spirit of each of the figures carved on it would come to life. "Don't eat in front of it," he cautioned. "Treat it with respect." The *wopila* bowl inside the circle where the Buffalo stands has never been without food as an offering to spirit. Cigarettes and tobacco offerings are always there, and toward the end, someone began to offer the simple gift of water.

These spirits live. On the right front leg, a man carries his dying daughter from the Sundance tree where he has pleaded with Tunkashila, the Creator, to save her. He holds her wasted body, hoping for a miracle. Perhaps in response to that scene, a Catholic couple from Wyoming brought their dying only son to pray with us beside the Sacred Buffalo.

On the left front leg, a man drags three heavy buffalo skulls attached to piercing sticks pushed through the skin on his back. Their weight pulls hard against his skin. He's in agony, but he offers his pain to the Creator as he prays to leave his ignorance behind. A woman who came fresh from a whiskey bottle to pray with us found the strength to go on without alcohol.

Those of us who worked on the Sacred Buffalo lived for a year in the old, cold, drafty South Dakota schoolhouse where we set up our studio. We slept barracks-style in cubbyholes and sucked comfort from the telephone wire—our only contact with our wives and children. Our hearts broke at their long-distance tears of loneliness. The Chanunpa, the prayer pipe, carved on the back left leg has been our source of strength as we've walked the Sacred Red Road.

At the blessing ceremony the Old Man warned us that no one with bad intentions would be able to stand in front of the Sacred Buffalo. During the carving of it, promoters and artists who only wanted to make money—not to serve—eliminated themselves

INTRODUCTION

through alcohol or other problems. Lies and threats aimed at stopping our progress caused us some sleepless nights, but little more. Someone who tried to steal photographs of the Buffalo didn't get away with them. And at one point, a front window in the schoolhouse was shattered by gunfire, but the project persevered.

I planned never to stand in the spotlight. I figured to walk away and let the Sacred Buffalo speak for itself. As my dad always tells me, "Let people see the dog hunt." In other words, let people know you by your actions, not your words. But the Sacred Buffalo must have wanted words, too, because the day its bones were blessed I began to tell my story to the reporter.

I dreamed as a child that I was walking on a big wall and talking to millions of people. Maybe that dream is coming true now.

The Buffalo People sacrificed themselves so that their brothers, the Lakota, could survive.

Chapter 2
The Vision

"What I can see in my mind, I can touch."
—BIG JIM DURHAM

I GUESS THE STORY of the Sacred Buffalo really began in 1988 at the Wall [the Vietnam Veterans Memorial] in Washington, D.C. A bunch of us veterans from the Vietnam Vets Motorcycle Club had gone there to honor our fallen and missing brothers when someone came over to me. "See that guy over there handing out fliers?" he said. "He has an eagle feather on his hat."

"Oh, yeah?" I looked in the direction he was pointing. I know that only Native Americans are permitted by federal law to carry an eagle feather. "Well, I'm going to take it if he's not Indian."

* * *

I raise my voice over the sound of tires slapping the pavement and direct my words into a tape recorder the reporter points toward my mouth. I'm behind the wheel of my black Chevy pickup truck heading East across South Dakota from my studio near Sturgis where I've been working a year on the Sacred Buffalo, an enormous bull buffalo skeleton on which I'm carving the seven sacred rites of the Lakota Indians. With several months of work still ahead of me, I just have to get away for a break, and the reporter has decided to ride a few hours with me. My fishing pole bounces in the bed of the truck, and my red-and-black, soft-tail low-rider Harley rides on a trailer behind.

It's late afternoon in February, and the winter sun is helpless against the cold. Out the driver's window Matopaha—Bear Butte—where people go on their vision quests, looms silent and proud over the prairie. Ahead lie the wind-swept plains that are the winter playground of hawks and eagles.

I light a cigarette and resume my story.

* * *

When I found the man with the eagle feather, I watched for a minute before I walked up to him. "What's this flier thing about?" I asked.

"It's about a POW/MIA Sundance," he said, handing me the piece of paper. "We're going to dance to bring home our missing brothers—this summer in Green Grass, South Dakota."

"Green Grass?" I repeated. I knew that the tribal Chanunpa Wakan of the Lakota—their Sacred Pipe—is kept at Green Grass. Sundance is a sacred ceremony for both thanking the Creator for your life and offering yourself up to him for the good of your family and your people.

"You have to be a full-blood to dance there?" I asked. Anyone can tell from my hair that I'm not full-blooded Indian.

"No," came the reply. "You decide you want to dance there, you can dance. Just call the number on the flier."

I stuffed the paper in my pocket. What impressed me about it was the drawing of the prisoner of war. Until then, all the posters and flags I'd seen showed a soldier with his head bowed. But the flier showed him looking up, proud and full of hope, like he was looking for an eagle. Or someone to come and get him. I figured to go dance.

It was a week before I dialed the number on the flier. A man answered, and I asked him if he knew Dr. Bob, code for asking if he had been to Alcoholics Anonymous. He did, and I knew then I was talking to a man like me—a Vietnam vet and a sober man. I told him I figured to come out and dance, and he gave me instructions for what I would need—a kilt and an eagle bone whistle. He told me to fast and pray.

"Only us Vietnam vets are going to dance," he said.

"I'll be there," I said.

> **Seven Sacred Rites of the Lakota**
> 1. Chanunpa
> 2. Rite of Purification
> 3. Making of Relatives
> 4. The Keeping and Releasing of a Soul
> 5. Throwing of the Ball
> 6. Crying for a Vision
> 7. Sundance

I did a lot of thinking and praying after that conversation. I asked my friend John to go with me. He was searching for God. His God had left him standing knee-deep in mud and blood in Vietnam, and he had given up on the whole idea of the Almighty. My wife, Beth, decided to drive on out, too, and bring my seven-year-old son, Nick.

As it happened, I left for South Dakota before they did. I jumped on my motorcycle one morning and headed West across America. By the time I hit the South Dakota border, it was hailing and sleeting—even though it was summer—and I rode a hundred miles through the pounding ice. It was torture. But as a child, I had learned to deal with pain—to make a friend of it. I learned how to get next to it and use it as a power source. So the more the hail beat down on me, the harder I rode. I remember screaming at the Creator: "If you think I'm going to turn around and go home on account of this, you're crazy. Make it rain harder. Come on, give me some more."

I had a rag on my face, and I jerked it off and lifted my face to the sky. I rode that way for about eighty miles. I touched my fingers to my cheeks and saw that I was bleeding. But I wouldn't hide from the pain for a minute. I figured I'd take it as long as the Creator wanted to dish it out. I had made the decision to dance, and nothing was going to stop me.

THE VISION

By the time I got near Green Grass, the sun was shining and it was about 85 degrees. It was summertime full-blown. I rode up over the crest of a hill and stopped short at the scene below. The Sundance tree stood majestic in the center of a circular arbor.

"This is what I came for," I said, "to bring the boys home."

Down on the Sundance grounds, I found the man I had talked to on the phone. He was carving two piercing sticks—sticks that are pushed under the skin on a man's chest during Sundance and then hooked by a rope to the tree.

"These are for you," he said, "to bring the boys home."

Then he helped me make sage wreaths for my wrists in preparation for Sundance the next day.

I was really hungry from my ride, but he told me, "You only need to eat this *ohanpi*—soup."

My memories of the sweat lodge there are vivid. I'm claustrophobic, and a sweat lodge is dark and close inside, so always before, I struggled to find a little leak of light to focus on. When we went into that sweat at Green Grass and they closed the door, I looked around until I spotted a little hole by the door where light shown in. I felt a wave of relief. But all of a sudden someone said, "Hey, there's light over there. Somebody fix that." Someone did, and I freaked. I was holding on the best I could, when my rock, a *wotah*, a friend, struck my chest. I grabbed it and started praying real hard, and finally I calmed down.

The next morning only four of us veterans went into the center to dance and pray, and we danced all day. The feeling among us was so strong that it was like we had known each other all our lives. The POW flag was flying high, and we were praying together for one common cause—that even one prisoner of war still left in Vietnam might come home. There is supposedly power among the Lakota, and I went to Sundance to suffer and sacrifice myself so that one bone, one piece, one little finger of a POW would come back to America; that if one POW is still living he would be relieved of his suffering. I remember thinking, "No matter how bad piercing would hurt, I only have to suffer these four days, but some of my brothers have endured twenty years of pain." I kept seeing POWs' faces staring at me from cages. I saw them being bitten by rats and tortured. I kept thinking, This is a small price to pay for those men in Vietnam. It was a very special time for me because our prayers were so strong.

I caught a glimpse of my wife and John praying in the arbor. Nick was smiling wide, and I was really proud.

Suddenly, toward the end of the day, two eagles swooped down into the arbor and then flew all the way to the top and back out. They had taken our prayers to the Creator. Sundance was declared over in just one day.

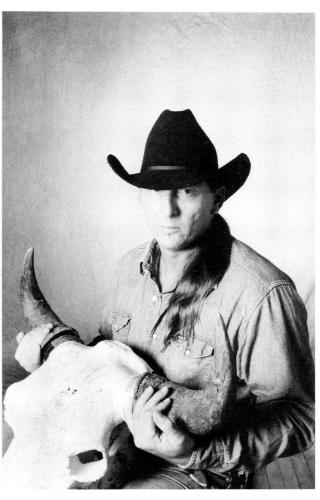

James G. Durham—Big Jim—holds the scrimshawed skull of the Sacred Buffalo. The Buffalo told him in a dream where to place on its bones the carvings of the seven sacred rites of the Lakota.

* * *

Suddenly, as if to agree with my account of that Sundance, an enormous bird swoops across the highway in front of the pickup truck like he controls the sky.

"See that?" I tell the reporter. "It's a golden eagle."

I hand her a cigarette from my pack. "Here, throw this out the window and say, 'Mitakuye Oyasin.'"

"Say what?" she asks.

"Just say, 'For all my relations.'"

With this gift of tobacco, the magnificent bird is honored.

A melancholy descends on me like a cloud, and I'm reminded of an event that happened earlier in the day. "People lie to themselves," I say suddenly. "They think they can control things. But really, the Creator controls our lives. Life is a constant prayer, whether or not you admit it."

I look at the reporter to see if she's with me.

"Take today, for example. I was planning to take this trip next week, but today I looked up in the sky and saw an eagle and a red-tailed hawk fighting. The eagle rolled over, talons up. It came down, talons down. The birds circled and fought each other. These two children of the Creator were locked in battle. Most people would look at them and think, Hmmm, they must not like each other.

"But, I thought, that battle is going on in me right now. I want to go East and visit my family, and here I am trying to hold myself in South Dakota. I saw it as a sign from the Creator that there's a conflict in me.

"As I watched, the eagle went East and the hawk went another way, and that's when I decided to leave right away.

"You see, everything in life is a gift from God if you view things spiritually. Most people don't see things that way. What a shallow world they must live in!"

I look out the window toward the blazing sunset. The sun is sitting on the horizon, its golden rays giving a moment of glory to the brittle, broken, winter-ravaged grass.

"Nothing is more beautiful than what you're presented with each day. You just have to take notice of it."

I take another cigarette and speak again toward the tape recorder.

* * *

A few months after that Sundance, a group of us Vietnam vets decided to hold a sweat lodge ceremony near where we lived back East. The sweat lodge is one of the sacred rites of the Lakota, the rite of purification. We brought along our wives and children and a few friends.

It was a nice warm day in fall. I had gotten a few live rabbits from a neighbor, and we were going to make soup from them. I had brought a little .22 pistol, and I commenced to kill the rabbits. My son was standing with a friend watching me.

"Let me shoot one of those rabbits," he said.

I told him, no, that I'd take care of it, and I killed another one.

Nick and the other boy were laughing, and I thought, Hmmm, they haven't learned to respect life yet.

"Is this funny?" I asked Nick.

THE VISION

He giggled.

"You want to kill one of these rabbits?" I said.

"Oh, yeah," he said, eager for the experience.

"Okay," I told him. "Grab him by the neck and pray with him and for him. Because he's going to give his life up for you so you can eat."

Nick grabbed the rabbit real tight and started praying to the four directions. He finished and said, "Give me the gun."

"Oh, no. You're not going to kill that rabbit with a gun. You're going to kill him with your hands."

Nick's eyes got really big. "You mean choke him? I can't do that."

"Yes, you can. If you're going to respect life, you've got to understand death. If you're going to amuse yourself with the death of these pitiful little *mastincala*, these rabbits, you have to understand that to take a life—no matter whose life it is, whether human or animal or bird—you must take it responsibly. To learn understanding, you have to kill it with your hands. To learn respect, you have to suffer like you're going to make this animal suffer. So kill the rabbit."

The boy just stood there. Finally, he asked, "Can I pray again?"

He prayed with the rabbit again, and then he choked it to death. As he choked it, he started to cry. When the rabbit was still, he handed it to me.

"Did you feel him kick because he wanted to live? That's how precious life is. This rabbit gave its life so we can eat. You remember this.

"Now, do you want to kill another one?" I asked.

Nick shook his head.

That's the kind of day it was when we took that fateful sweat.

All of us who were going into the sweat lodge together were Vietnam vets. I should tell you this: in that particular sweat lodge, we had a sacred rock from Hawaii. A girl and man I knew went to Hawaii and brought me back one of those volcano rocks to sweat with. The girl convinced someone to ask a holy man for a rock for me. She told him she wanted it for a friend who prayed for Vietnam veterans. I heard the holy man had never before given his permission for anyone to take a rock from the island, but he let the girl have one with this instruction: "This is a special thing. Tell her to take one rock, and make sure that someday—after her friend has prayed with it—part of the rock comes home." That rock was the last one onto the fire that day. Later, we sent a little piece of it back to Hawaii.

Also, it probably made a difference that Frank Fools Crow's buffalo skull was the skull on the altar that day. The old skull had come out of a pond with a few other ones, and I had it then.

I knew that sweat was going to be really hot. We were all veterans, and a lot of people had brought prayer ties and put them on the altar. We were going to be doing a lot of hard prayers, and hard prayers make a hard sweat.

Nick asked me, "Can I sweat with you?"

"No, you're just a *hokshila*, a boy," I told him. "You can't sweat with combat veterans. It's going to be too hot."

But he kept on with his pleading. "No, Dad, I have to come in with you. I do."

Finally, I let him in. "Okay, tough guy, but sit next to me."

Midway through the sweat he passed out, and we opened the flap and set him outside. The women took him and rubbed him and fanned him. He was out a pretty good while, I guess.

After he passed out, one of the veterans inside who had been a dog handler in 'Nam saw himself dead. He suffered from survivor's guilt. He couldn't figure out why his name wasn't on the Wall. Like I say, it was a really powerful sweat.

The next day Beth and I had Nick and my daughter, Crystal, in the truck with us.

"Dad, I had a dream while I was passed out," he said after awhile.

I figured I had better listen. Children are sacred to us because they are innocent. They don't make dreams up to make themselves seem powerful. "Go on and tell me."

"It was really clear," he began. "I saw you standing out in a big, green field. You were wearing buckskin clothes. Your hair was way down to your belt, and your eyebrows were really bushy."

That surprised me because my hair was short then and I have almost no eyebrows.

"You had your Pipe with you," he added.

"Really? Which hand?" I asked.

Nick pointed to his own left hand. That meant a lot to me. When you hold a Chanunpa in your left hand, the one closest to your heart, it means something special. But I didn't comment.

Nick went on. "You were standing out on the prairie looking at millions of buffaloes. They began to move. They sort of walked to both sides and left an open path in the center of the herd, and this one great big bull buffalo walked out. He walked right up to you. And you and the buffalo started talking."

I was really interested. "What did the buffalo say? Could you hear the words?"

"I couldn't understand any of it," the boy said. "It was another language. The words were, like, jumbled. But you talked for a long time, and then every once in a while you'd point with the Pipe. You kept waving the other hand like you were talking to a human being. The buffalo just kept talking.

"And then, finally, he turned and started to walk away, but then he stopped. He turned his head back and looked at you. He said something to you, and you nodded. Then he walked back into the herd and just disappeared into the millions of them."

I was really choked up. I told him, "That's a pretty big dream. It will carry you the rest of your life."

I've always had a lot of dreams—even when I was a child. Some people say they see a place and feel like they've been there before. But from the time I was little, I would dream about a place and know I'd go there someday. Sometimes it took a few years for things to happen, but they always came true.

But riding in the truck that day, Nick pressed me for an answer. "But what do you think it means?"

I just shook my head. "It'll be a long time before we understand it. The Creator will teach us about it."

About four years after Nick had his vision in the sweat lodge, my wife and I drove with a couple of friends to a buffalo ranch out in South Dakota. For a long time I had a secret desire to lie down on the ground and feel buffalo stampeding all around me. I could imagine the sensation of the earth moving under their hooves. I wanted to experience for myself the power that could make the earth jump. I talked the owner of the ranch into letting me drive the van down into the pasture where a herd of buffalo was

THE VISION

grazing. Of course, I didn't tell him what I was planning. Buffalo—especially the bulls—are infamous for their aggressive, dangerous behavior toward humans.

It was hot down in the pasture, and the wind that almost always blows over the prairie was unusually quiet. Several hundred buffalo were slowly grazing their way across the grassland like an organic lawnmower. A lone tree stood in the direction they were heading.

"This is my chance," I told my wife. "I'm going to climb that tree and wait for the herd to get to it."

I got up in the tree and waited until five hundred or so buffalo had moved into a little gully close by. If they knew I was there, they gave no sign. When some of them had walked a little beyond the tree, I jumped down into the middle of them and hollered. They started to stampede. I quick laid face down on the ground. As they ran, I could feel their hooves striking the earth, and the vibration echoed in my chest. It felt like a trampoline of thunder. I marveled at their power. But I hadn't counted on the dust. I almost choked to death on the dirt they stirred up.

I walked back to the van, and we all had a good laugh about it.

I drove on, and we were a little way out onto the prairie when the woman with us wanted to stop and look for agates. I wasn't too happy about it, but I stopped. We piled out of the van, and the woman and my wife started searching around in a wash for rocks.

I walked on a little way alone when my attention was drawn to a hill. There was a little opening near the top, like a tiny cave or a shrine. I went up to have a look. Just inside the opening was a long, flat rock with a flesh-colored rock slightly bigger than a walnut on top of it. I had never seen a rock that color.

I prayed and threw down an offering of four cigarettes, then I reached into the hole. The rock was ice cold even though the day was hot. I turned it over in my hand, and it reminded me of a human embryo. I felt my stomach knot. I clamped my fingers around it, and in a minute or two, it got so hot I got scared. I set it on the ground. When it had cooled down again, I stuck it in my pocket.

I looked at those cigarettes I had thrown down. This is a great gift, I thought. Did I pray enough?

I prayed again.

I showed my wife the rock—I knew it was sacred so I only held it in my left hand. The elders say that when the holy men of old got ready to die, they would take their special *inyan*—stones—out into the wilderness and give them back to the Creator. A geologist at the South Dakota School of Mines later told me that the rock I found had been in the stomach of a dinosaur.

We got back into the van, and I drove across the grassland toward the road. I had just come up over a ridge when I saw a hundred buffalo grazing below. They all seemed to be cows, so I slowly nosed the van into the herd. Then I saw him—the tallest, most magnificent bull buffalo I had ever seen.

"Wouldn't it be beautiful if his bones were all scrimshawed?" I said.

The bull started toward the van. He looked at me through the open window, fixing me in his wild, dark gaze.

"I'm not afraid of you," I told him.

But I felt a chill. He seemed to look inside me. He looked at me like a man who's going to kill you looks at you.

"Give me my knife," I told my wife. "I can kill him."

THE VISION

"You're crazy," she said.

"Just give me the knife. If I can jump on his back, I can take him."

"No, let's go," she said, fear in her voice. "He's going to ram the van."

"Give me my knife," I commanded. "He wants me."

But no knife was placed in my outstretched hand.

The buffalo looked at me, and I stared at him. It felt to me like combat. Like man to man.

Then he snorted and walked away as if I were nothing. That made me mad.

A couple of years after I'd seen that big buffalo, I was down on the Pine Ridge Reservation visiting Old Man Jimmy Dubray, spiritual leader of the Oglala tribe of the Lakota Nation. He motioned me to follow him into his room where he started pulling stuff out of a drawer. He handed me two eagle spikes.

"I want you to dance for me at Sundance," he said. "I don't have the legs for it anymore."

I guess he was more than seventy then and had heart trouble. I took the feathers.

Then he handed me a piercing stick.

About that time, his wife, Florine, came into the room. She squealed. "Did he give you that stuff?"

"Yeah," I told her.

"Oh, no. He wants you to pierce for him. Give it back to him. Just wipe it off and give it back to him!" she said.

Jimmy Dubray, spiritual leader of the Oglala tribe of the Lakota Nation, ponders a thought in his home in Allen, South Dakota, on the Pine Ridge Reservation.

But I shook my head. "I already shook his hand."

Some time later, we all went up on Bear Butte for Hanbleceya, vision quest. We had set up the *hochoka*, circle, and got out the Chanunpas when Jimmy looked at me.

"Why don't you pray for some art?" he said.

"What do you mean?" I asked.

Jimmy's truly a holy man. He has one foot in God's world and one foot here. He gave his life to the Creator a long time ago.

"Pray for your own art," he said.

"I *do* my own art," I told him.

"No, like pictures," he said. "Pray for some pictures."

I didn't understand what he meant, but I went ahead and did it. I went up to the top of Bear Butte, and I fasted and prayed like he had told me to. None of it made any sense to me.

Later, at Sundance, I danced for him.

About that time, my wife got orders to go to California. The Navy wanted her to go to school there, and she wanted me to go with her. I didn't know how I could live around so many people. But she wanted me to try it, so I left the Black Hills and went with her.

12 SACRED BUFFALO

THE VISION

In California, I was taken to the lowest point of my whole life. I had never been so depressed. I felt like a number there. In South Dakota, I was a warrior, a Sundancer, a friend. But in the Navy compound for dependent housing, I felt like a prisoner. I remember sitting on the front step of our apartment, tears in my eyes, thinking, What's happened to me?

All I did in California was sit and wait for my wife to come home. There was no place I could go to get away from people. Being around so many people sapped my strength. I tried to do my artwork, but nothing I did panned out. I couldn't think, I couldn't draw, I couldn't do anything. So I just sat.

I fell asleep one afternoon, and I had a dream. I dreamed I saw a buffalo skeleton standing tall in the middle of a big room with a high ceiling and a bare wood floor. The animal stood on a wooden stand. A single, strong light shone on it.

I was sitting in a metal chair in the dream, looking at the buffalo skeleton. I was wearing my straw cowboy hat in the dream and my old boots—I remember looking down and thinking, What lousy boots. There was a funny little curved window at one end of the room with light streaming through it.

At first I was completely struck by the beauty of the magnificent skeleton in front of me. Then I noticed: pictures had been carved onto all of the buffalo's bones—the skull, the legs, even the hump bones. I was in awe.

"This is a beautiful, beautiful thing," I said.

Just then, the buffalo skeleton turned its head toward me as if it were about to speak. "*Pilamayapelo*," it said. "Thank you."

I smiled and nodded my head. "You're welcome."

I woke with a start and looked at the clock. My wife was supposed to come back at five, and as soon as she walked in the door, I grabbed her.

"It was that bull buffalo we saw," I told her. "He came and he looked inside me."

We went to the art store to buy a sketch pad, and I started drawing that night.

In my mind's eye, I could picture all the bones of the skeleton, and I drew the scenes on them exactly as I had dreamed them. I drew the seven sacred rites of the Lakota. I drew the Wounded Knee Massacre and the Battle of the Little Bighorn—all of them from that dream. I tried to change the placement of drawings a couple of times, but I always ended up right back at the dream.

Suddenly it all made sense to me: I was meant to scrimshaw all the pictures I had dreamed onto the skeleton of a buffalo. I got excited. Life had meaning for me again.

As soon as I could, I telephoned back to the buffalo ranch we had visited in South Dakota.

Pray Like There's Someone Listening

YOU ASK, WHAT is the biggest obstacle in learning to pray? Fear. It's the fear that you're not sure there's someone who cares. You ask yourself, is there really a God? The more you fail in the things you do, the more you have doubts. You run into those obstacles, and you think there is no God. You think, he didn't answer me. Fear has a lot to do with it. But when you pray and you believe, things change for you.

Whatever you're praying for, if you believe it, so be it. It's done. If you have faith and you believe it, your answer is there.

It's like waiting for the mail. If you think you're going to get a letter tomorrow, you wait for it because you know it's coming. When you pray, the minute you believe, you receive. That's what I believe.

Say you go to the doctor because you're sick. The doctor is a good one, and he—or maybe she—tells you what to do to get better. He says, "Eat right for four days, get up at four o'clock and walk a mile, and drink plenty of water." You follow his instructions the first day, and you begin to improve. Then you follow them the three extra days as insurance.

That first day is what changes you because you believe it will.

—Jimmy Dubray

"You know that really big buffalo bull down in the pasture?" I asked the rancher.
"Yeah, I know the one you mean," he said.
"How old is he?" I asked.
"Seven years old."
Hmmm, I thought. Seven years old, seven sacred rites, my son was seven when he had the vision.
"I've got to have that buffalo," I said.
"Sorry, you can't have that one," the rancher said. "He's killed a couple of other bulls, and I have him penned up in a horse trailer. He's going to slaughter in the morning."
"You can't," I told him. "I have to have that bull."
"I've got to," he said.
"You're sure we're talking about the same animal?" I pressed. "The one that has eyes like a man's."
"Yeah, that's the one," he said. "But I have another bull down here you'll like."
"No, it's gotta be that one."
There was nothing left to do, so I hung up.
I called the buffalo ranch again the next day.
"You're not going to believe what that buffalo did," the rancher said. "You know, he crashed his way out of the horse trailer and escaped."
"You mean he kicked the gate out?" I asked.
There was a laugh. "No, he rammed his way through the front of the trailer. He's loose on the prairie somewhere."
"I've got to have him," I said.
"Well, okay. If we can round him up."
I left California for South Dakota. My wife knew the buffalo was going to separate us for many months, but she also knew it was something I had to do. That child's dream connected us spiritually. Before we had been connected physically, but our connection had become spiritual.
It was hard to leave her standing there on the porch. I remember telling her, "If you love something so much, and you know it's dying day by day, you have to let it go."
She agreed. She knew I had to go.

Back in South Dakota, I went to see Verdell Red Cloud, son of Chief Red Cloud. I asked him to pray about the buffalo, and he asked me for the stomach because it's a spiritual food. On the ranch, they recaptured the buffalo and smudged it with sage and killed it the right way.
I asked a Vietnam vet, Les Lutz, to go on over and skin it for me.
I also asked that half the meat be saved for distribution at Sundance and the other be put aside for my family.
Three days after that I got an unexpected phone call.
"This meat's green," the slaughterer told me. "I don't know how it happened."
"Green?" I didn't comprehend. "Like how?"
"It's no good," he explained. "We put it in the locker, and it was all right. When

---

Mitakuye Oyasin

SINCE GOD HAS created all things—man and animals, birds and reptiles, insects and plants—we are related. We are brothers and sisters. The air, the earth, the trees, the water—everything is our relatives. The trees sing. Have you heard them? Sit under a pine tree or a cottonwood and listen. When the wind comes through, the tree will sing. Or go to a creek and listen to the music it makes when the water hits those little rocks. It will make you happy. This is what we mean when we pray and say, "Mitakuye Oyasin"—all my relations. That doesn't mean just your cousins or your friends. It means everything on earth—even in the universe.

—Jimmy Dubray

THE VISION

we pulled it out, it was bad."

"Mine and how many others?" I asked.

"We killed about ten animals the day we killed yours. Every other piece of meat in there is fine."

I immediately told my dad, who often gives me advice, what had happened. "That meat was never meant for people to eat," he said. "It came here for one reason only."

There was only one thing to do: I had the slaughterer cut the meat away from the bones and bury it. I returned it to the earth as *wopila*—as a food offering given out of respect. I knew then the buffalo was sacred.

* * *

The buffalo's skeleton was shipped to Ohio State University (OSU) to be prepared for carving. A Vietnam Vets Motorcycle Club member, Irish, had made a connection for me there. I went to Ohio to visit with it. You see, its spirit will always stay with the skeleton. No matter where it goes.

I showed Beemer, another friend who had served in Vietnam, my drawings and explained how the bones would need high-grade sanding before they could be carved. Right away he asked to be considered for that job. I told him to talk to his wife about it because I figured it would take him away from home for a year.

I returned to South Dakota. I searched all spring for the perfect work space to carve the buffalo skeleton. I even went to Wyoming and Colorado. But nothing I saw matched my dream—the big room with the little window and a metal chair. Beemer came out in April for Hanbleceya on Bear Butte. At Hanbleceya, I took the flesh offerings from everyone who wanted to give them, and I pierced a couple of men who wanted to pierce.

Nick came out, too, and we shared a lot of things about his vision. We prayed a lot together, and we went to the sweat lodge a lot. We prayed for a place, and someone told us about an old schoolhouse in Whitewood, near Sturgis, that might make a good studio. We went to look at it.

As soon as I saw its bare, wooden floors, I recalled my dream about the buffalo.

This is good, I thought.

Then we walked down a long, dark hallway that opened into a cavernous gym. I paused at the door: bare-bulb lights lit the center of the room, and at one end, light streamed through a little curved window.

"I'll take it," I said.

Later, a thought began to nag at me. The setup seemed perfect except for one thing—I couldn't recall seeing the metal chair I had sat on in the dream.

"Don't you remember, Dad?" Nick said. "It was in the gym, and you sat down on it."

I looked at him, puzzled. "What color was it?"

Beemer—Harry Lindsay—holds the left front leg of the Sacred Buffalo, which details the sacred rite of Sundance and the Yuwipi ceremony. During the making of the Buffalo, he sanded the skeleton in preparation for carving, washed it, rewired it, built its traveling cases, and kept the checkbook for the project in balance.

"Brown."

"*Washte*," I said. "Good. It's the place in the dream."

* * *

I moved with Beemer into the schoolhouse at the first of June, and we set up the studio. We didn't have much at first—my drawing table and chair and our personal gear mostly. We had no refrigerator—only a Coleman cooler to keep our food cool. We had nothing to cook with—just a small microwave and a coffee pot. But it was okay for awhile because we didn't have the buffalo either. It was still in the process of being cleaned and assembled at Ohio State University.

The buffalo still hadn't come by mid-July, and I began to worry that something was wrong. But Sundance was coming at the end of the month, and I figured maybe the Creator was holding it for some reason till then. Beemer and I took a good sweat and prayed on it and decided to just wait on the Creator. We set up a hochoka of sage in the studio and put out prayer ties for the four directions to get ready for when it would come.

One night when I was feeling really depressed about the delay, I got out my Chanunpa and prayed with all my heart to be able to give the Sacred Buffalo what it deserved in its creation. I prayed that all the talent of my grandfathers and my dad would come into my hands just this once so I could complete this project. I prayed that all the best parts of the Creator's power would come forward—the power of prayer, the power of a child's innocence, the power of having ancient talent in my hands. I knew full well what I was asking for—my dad taught me well to be careful what you ask for because you may get it.

A few months later Beth came for a visit, and we went out for a ride in the truck. Suddenly, she cried out in a scared voice.

"What's wrong with your hands?" she asked.

She reached over and touched my right hand where it gripped the steering wheel.

I looked at my hands. They were all wrinkled. Suddenly it occurred to me: I had gotten my grandpa's hands. Now, I'm self-conscious about how dry and wrinkled my hands are, and when I'm around people, I try to keep them hidden.

Sundance came and went and still the buffalo wasn't ready to come West. I was practically climbing the walls with impatience and worry.

One day in August, my friend Bill from Ohio died. Bill's family called: "Please come over and pray with us." I didn't have much choice about whether or not to make that 2,800-mile round trip. I've been given permission to pray for others with my Chanunpa, and because of that I'm duty bound to honor any request—no matter how hard it is. The family called me at two in the afternoon, and by four, Beemer and I had loaded the truck and were ready to drive twenty hours to pray with Bill's children.

I met with the kids in the sweat lodge, and I told them, "You have a bunch of dads now. Us veterans are going to take care of you now. Any time you feel you have to talk to your dad, you just call one of us, and

---

On Being Drawn In

WHEN I HEARD myself tell Jim that I could sand the buffalo bones to get them ready for carving, I was completely surprised. He had been telling me about the project, and I suddenly heard myself offering to work on it. I had no idea at that time.

Working on the Sacred Buffalo has filled me with a sense of awe. I realize now that there really is a Creator—I had denied it for a long time. To be this close to the people and to an object that are the instruments of that power is very awe-inspiring. I'm just another simple human being, but there has to be some kind of reason for my involvement. It's not just a random kind of thing.

Since I don't count my chickens before they're hatched, I don't know what will be required of me in the long run. I only hope that there will be good come from it for me and my family. We've had our trials over the years. Maybe this will be the turning point.

—Beemer

THE VISION

Burning sage purifies the studio of negativity, and it is used several times a day during the carving of the Buffalo. To attract good, sweet grass and dried cedar are burned, too.

THE VISION

we'll do whatever we can to help you. You're our kids now. You belong to us."

Now the kids call me on the phone. "Dad?" they say, and sometimes I mistake them for Nick.

While we were in Ohio, we heard news that a white buffalo calf had been born in Janesville, Wisconsin. We listened with great interest as the news spread like wild-fire and thousands of Native Americans and others began streaming to Janesville to pray with that baby buffalo. Most people don't know that the Buffalo Calf Woman who brought the Chanunpa to the Lakota people promised to return.

Since we were in Ohio, we stopped by the university to see how work was going on the buffalo skeleton. It wasn't quite ready, but it was close enough to being done that we decided to wait around for the last few details to be finished.

Later, when the skeleton had been reassembled, Beemer and I loaded it into the back of my pickup and took off West with it. We didn't know it at the time, but we discovered later that we passed through Janesville, Wisconsin, with the Sacred Buffalo in about the same period of time that the sire of the white buffalo baby dropped dead. Apparently, he had been given a clean bill of health, but then he suddenly died.

I can't say what the connection is between the Sacred Buffalo and that white buffalo calf. I can tell you this: when I dreamed the drawings that were to be carved onto the skeleton, I saw the end of time. But I couldn't stand the horror of what I was shown. I told the Creator that I couldn't burden my son or my family with the responsibility of presenting that horrendous scene to the people of the world. I prayed to the Creator to show me an alternative. About a year later, I felt compelled to carve the white buffalo calf inside the pelvis of the Sacred Buffalo as the beginning of time—a new beginning if we choose to follow it.

All I can say is what I said about my son's vision when he first told me: "It'll be a long time before we understand it. The Creator will teach us."

* * *

With the Sacred Buffalo in Whitewood, I just sat in total awe of its magnificence. It was so huge, so beautiful. I often crawled out of bed at two in the morning and visited with it until four or five o'clock. I kept imagining how powerful it would be with all the drawings scrimshawed on it. I knew that as I carved the seven sacred ceremonies of the Lakota onto the bones each carved figure would spring to life.

I know now that the spirit of each person on the Sacred Buffalo has a power of its own. The power is the power of humble, prayerful people offering their suffering to the Creator.

The spirit of the buffalo has power, too. For centuries, the buffalo

---

A Mystery Called Miracle

THE WHITE BABY buffalo's name is Miracle. She was born in Janesville, Wisconsin, on August 20, 1994. I went up there to Janesville to pray with that young lady buffalo. I set a fire, and knowing I was supposed to feed it, I set a whole wooden plate down next to it. The fire jumped out and got hold of me. Florine fought with the fire, and luckily she won.

That done, someone said, "Grandpa's going to go see the young lady now," and everyone started moving back. I don't know what they were afraid of. I walked toward the pasture where the little white buffalo was.

At the gate I could see two young buffalo standing there, the white one and her older sister. Suddenly, the people behind me started singing Sundance songs, and as they did the little white buffalo began to dance. She danced to the sound of the singing. Then she ran up the hill. I went on into the pasture and started up the hill. I was barefoot out of respect for the baby buffalo, and there were lots of cactus out there. But I just walked on without thinking much about them; it was as though someone had lifted me up.

That little white buffalo ran from tree to tree. It spooked me. She was like a little child, playing tree to tree. After a while, I grew to feel like that calf—innocent. My mind became clear, and I was with her. Silently I prayed.

I didn't even think about the presence of the other buffalo in the pasture. They can move from zero to forty miles per hour pretty quickly. Unless I could move zero to sixty, I couldn't outrun them. But I was barefoot, and I was part of that buffalo family then. I pictured how we came to be and how we go back. But I keep all that to myself.

An odd thing happened: Miracle's dad, Marvin, died a few days after she was born, even though he seemed to be in perfect health. An Oneida medicine man prayed for the old buffalo when they buried him.

—Jimmy Dubray

THE VISION

spirit fed the Indian people on this continent. It gave its body so they would have food and clothes and tools. It gave them life. It sacrificed itself so that the people would survive and thank the Creator for their lives. It taught them about the great circle of life and their connectedness to the Creator.

I often thank the Sacred Buffalo for coming now. I have never questioned why it came—or why it came to me. I know the Creator has touched it.

At first, I was a little afraid of its power. I knew we were crossing over into a place I had never been before. The fear of that responsibility—of knowing what the buffalo was going to mean to the people of the world when it was done—scared me.

During the carving, we kept the project pretty much a secret. I knew that many Lakota people would believe the sacred rites shouldn't be revealed to non-Indians, and I didn't want protesters outside the studio disrupting the work. Even so, we suffered from some chaos. Lies were told about us. Threats were made. I developed a contingency plan so that in case of my death all the drawings from the dream would be preserved and the Sacred Buffalo could be finished. Remember, I had vowed to the Creator that if he'd give me the talent, I'd complete the project. I had to make good on my word.

But gradually, I let go of the fear. I figured the project had all been set up a long time ago by a force far more powerful than my enemies. It was out of my control. I just surrendered to it.

Jimmy Dubray blesses the Sacred Buffalo before it is drawn on or carved. He says that the Buffalo spirit will always stay with the bones and that those who appreciate it will be blessed.

* * *

I stop talking for several minutes. Night has claimed the sky, and a rising full moon casts its frigid light over the prairie. The only sound is the soft whir of the truck's heater trying to overpower the cold.

The little red eye of the reporter's recorder urges me on. When I speak again, my voice is strangely husky.

* * *

I have never questioned why the Sacred Buffalo came into the world now. It sprang from a child's vision. That vision was born of innocence. I figure the Sacred Buffalo is meant for the children of the world.

I remember when I was waiting for the skeleton to arrive in Whitewood so I could get started on it. I had done everything I could to make it happen, but it just wasn't ready. On Memorial Day of that year I went to the Black Hills national cemetery to honor the veterans. I walked among the headstones, reading the names of the men who had fought for our great country in the Spanish-American War, World War I, World War II, Korea, and Vietnam. I started weeping. I thought, We have failed you, you grandfathers who have gone before us, you *akicita wichasa*, you veteran men. We have failed you who have paid with your lives. We're turning our old people out and putting them in nursing homes, we're beating our wives, we're abusing our children. We're without conscience.

I felt the horror of living in a world where everyone is taking, taking, taking. People are grabbing everything from everyone else and giving nothing back to the earth, to the people, to their families. Take something as simple as a pot of soup: if everyone who goes by takes a big bowl of it for themselves—and then reaches in and grabs some extra meat—there will be no soup left for the others unless a grandmother comes along and adds more water. That's what's happening in the world. Everyone is taking. We have to learn to give back something besides hollow promises.

My prayer is that the Sacred Buffalo will cause people to care for one another. My prayer is that little kids won't have to live hard like their parents have—in anger and hatred and violence.

Do you remember when you were a kid and you'd crawl up onto your dad's or your grandpa's lap and they'd pull you in close and rub your head and tell you how everything's okay? That's how I feel the Creator has me now. That's what I wish for kids all over the world. Maybe then they'll be able to realize early on the greatness that's in them, and they'll have time to walk in the beauty of the light.

I don't really know why the Sacred Buffalo came now. Maybe it came because people are sick with viruses and allergies and cancer. They're sick physically, and they're sick spiritually. They're discouraged and depressed and distanced from their family and their people. Maybe it came now to help people understand themselves and each other. The prayer ties that mark the four directions of the hochoka where it stands are black, red, yellow, and white. Some people claim these colors represent the races of man. Maybe the Sacred Buffalo will bring people together to do something so humble as to pray together.

I guess the Creator knows we need a way to fix our lives.

Chapter 3

Carving the Buffalo

"An artist without heart is nothing more than a Xerox machine."

—BIG JIM DURHAM

BIG JIM DURHAM RIDES the stool behind his oak draftsman's table like a horseman astride his mount. His eyes are riveted on the Sacred Buffalo that dominates the front of the room. A sketchpad that holds the drawings from his dream lies closed on the tabletop cluttered with pencils and erasers and X-acto knives—the stuff of an artist. It's late afternoon in winter, and the fluorescent lights struggle against the inky dusk outside a row of tall windows. The bitter smell of too-old coffee hangs in the air. A radio-tape player broadcasts Aaron Neville's crystal voice from his *Yellow Moon* album: "Will the circle be unbroken...."

The studio occupies a large, square, high-ceilinged room on the second floor of what used to be the elementary school in the little town of Whitewood, South Dakota, near the Wyoming border. You might already be familiar with it: the school's interior was made to look like a Catholic boarding school for the filming of *Lakota Woman*.

Flanking Big Jim's desk are three workstations—makeshift tables of plywood on sawhorse legs. Beemer's desk faces the windows. A longtime friend of Jim's, he has worked on the project since the men first moved into the studio. He sanded the Buffalo's bones in preparation for their carving, and he assembles and disassembles the skeleton as Jim needs the bones. So far, his record time for disassembly is twenty-nine minutes. Tommy Dubray, second son of Jimmy Dubray, faces the wall opposite the windows. He's quilling covers for the Buffalo's hooves. Next to a door to the hall, Steve from Ohio has been helping copy Jim's original drawings onto the bones. A woman Jim has dreamed will come to help—a brown-eyed woman with a light spot in the iris of one eye—has not yet appeared on the scene.

The room shows few signs of the restless fourth-graders that passed through it. Green chalkboards that once held spelling words and math problems have been covered for the most part with cork. Thumbtacks hold news clippings about the birth of the baby white buffalo in Janesville, Wisconsin, an announcement about an upcoming motorcycle rally, and cards from home. There's a poster honoring Vietnam-era veterans (Jim and Beemer both are Vietnam vets), a banner from the Vietnam Vets Motorcycle Club, and a POW/MIA flag. A "Bound and Gagged" cartoon by Dana Summers shows a scientist examining a tiny buffalo through a magnifying glass; its caption reads, "So this is where microchips come from."

A makeshift counter behind Big Jim's desk holds a jumble of electrical appliances—a microwave, blender, rice cooker, and crockpot used for heat-and-eat meals. The men spend their time between the studio and a similar-size room across the hall that has a television and their beds.

Every surface save the floor is strewn with art supplies: babyfood jars full of beads, acrylic paints, sinew, a tanned deer hide, books on the Plains Indians and Walt Disney—Jim's hero. Everything is covered with fine, chalky bone dust from sanding the Sacred Buffalo's bones.

There's no mistaking the studio's reason for being: the Sacred Buffalo stands bigger than life on a raised platform center front of the room, facing the windows. Its massive head is lifted high, as though it's surveying the world outside, and for an instant you can sense the force of the mighty bull Buffalo racing across the frigid plains, head thrown back, gulping air and exhaling steam. The lift of the skull is unusual; buffalo are normally portrayed with their heads low. But seeing it, you can't help but remember the proud, hopeful prisoner of war on the flag that lured Big Jim to his first Sundance. Even in the confines of the studio, the proud, mighty Buffalo—head high, horns pointed to the sky—seems ever-watchful, ever-alert to its mission.

Marking the sacred circle where the Buffalo stands is a twelve-foot diameter ring of dried sage. The four directions are honored by prayer ties on chokecherry sticks stuck in coffee cans full of dirt. A black semicircle has been painted on the wall, and in contrast, the Buffalo's bleached bones reflect light in a way that makes it seem to shine from some internal power.

At this point, most of the drawings from Jim's dream have been penciled onto the bones in preparation for the next step: the carving and inking process of scrimshaw. Only the skull is still bare. Big Jim scrutinizes it through eyes narrowed to slits.

"Take a look at this," Beemer says. He hands Jim a magazine open to a photo showing a detailed tattoo of an eagle. The men are planning to get identical tattoos

The Sacred Buffalo skeleton was prepared at Ohio State University's Department of Veterinary Biosciences in Columbus before it came to stand on a simple plywood platform in Big Jim's studio in Whitewood, South Dakota. It stands six feet tall and is ten feet long.

as an outward reminder of time spent working on the Sacred Buffalo.

"That artist's good," Jim says.

"We could go to Albuquerque to get ours," Beemer suggests. "I know of a guy there who is the best in the country."

Jim laughs. "I remember at the fiftieth anniversary of the motorcycle rally at Sturgis, some guys were getting tattoos to mark the occasion. A buddy from Michigan had one done, and he came up to me and said, 'Doesn't this look great?' I looked at it. 'Yeah,' I told him, 'but they spelled Sturgis wrong.'

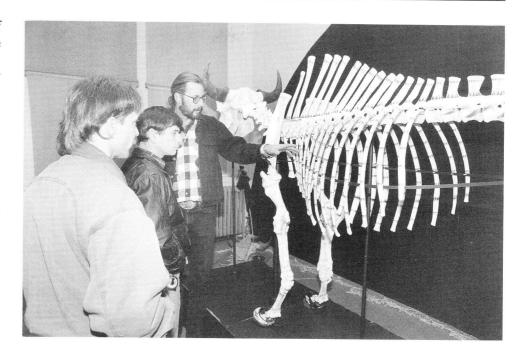

Beemer shows the Sacred Buffalo to Mike Riss (center) and his assistant Guy before Mike tackles the job of building a rotating platform on which to display it.

"The guy laughed. He thought I was joking. But the artist had written S-T-U-G-I-S—without the r. The guy was real bummed. He went back and got a big rose tattooed over it."

Footsteps sound on the bare stairs, and Big Jim turns sharply. Two men walk into the studio. They introduce themselves as Mike Riss, one of the owners of a custom cabinet shop, and Guy, a shop employee. Mike has expressed interest in making the base the Sacred Buffalo will stand on when it goes on tour.

"Smudge 'em," Jim tells Beemer.

"What?" Mike asks.

"*Wazilya*," Jim says. "Incense. You use the smoke of sage to get rid of any bad influences you might have on you."

Beemer grabs a stalk of sage from the *hochoka,* the circle, ringing the Sacred Buffalo. He touches his lighter to it, and when its spicy smoke begins to rise, he puts the smoldering leaves in an abalone shell and tells Mike and Guy to fan the smoke onto their faces. Mike looks a little uncertain.

"If you're going to work with us, it's time to go to school," Jim says. "There's a big difference between the world outside and the sacred."

Beemer opens the sage "gate" of the hochoka and takes the men into the circle for a brief tour of the skeleton.

"It's just magnificent," Mike says. He's in his early forties, with dark hair and small blue eyes. He's dwarfed by the massive skeleton.

"It's nearly ten feet from nose to tail," Beemer says. "It's more than six feet from the ground to the top of the tallest hump bone."

Mike registers surprise. "That long, huh? I had an idea what it might look like, but I never thought it would be so beautiful."

Beemer nods. "That's why we wanted you to drive up here and see it."

Beemer and Mike discuss some preliminary plans for a stand for the Buffalo. Beemer

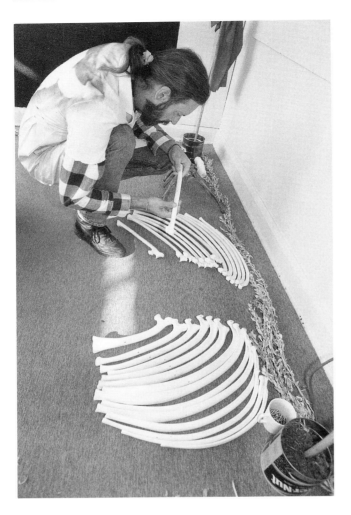

Beemer chooses a rib bone, which he will sand smooth in preparation for the feathers and spirits that will be scrimshawed onto it. The prayer flags and sage mark the hochoka, circle, that protect the Sacred Buffalo bones.

talks size; Mike suggests types of wood.

Jim sits silent, watching. His worn size fourteen-and-a-half alligator boots are propped up on his desk next to a red telephone. When the men exit the circle, Jim walks clockwise around the Buffalo as if clearing the space. He's tall—well over six feet, with shoulders hard from lifting weights. Fourteen long, stripelike scars earned during a ceremony mark his biceps. He closes the sage gate as he exits the circle and returns to the chair behind his desk.

"What I want to know," Mike says, "is what's going to go on the skull. Or do you know yet?"

Big Jim smiles. "Oh, yeah, I know. A dream I had more than a year ago dictated exactly where each ceremony would go on the bones."

"Really? You don't say," Mike says.

"There is a Pipe here in this room," Jim continues, "which to me, being Indian, means you can't lie or something bad will happen to you or your family. So the things we speak here are the truth."

"Where's the Pipe?" Mike looks around.

"Over there in the hochoka," Jim says. "That's my family Pipe."

His long Chanunpa leans against a weathered buffalo skull in front of the Sacred Buffalo, a knot of red cloth plugging the opening in its stone bowl. The skull and the Pipe have been placed on a red cloth laid out on the floor. A wooden wopila bowl holds an offering for Spirit—a hunk of glazed donut, a rectangle of Frosted Shredded Wheat, a meat chunk—whatever the men offered from their own food. Another bowl holds cigarettes.

"If you really look at the Buffalo, you'll notice that the Chanunpa appears on all four of its legs," Jim says. "This is because nothing of importance is ever begun without the Chanunpa. The Pipe drives all of the seven sacred ceremonies that are the foundation of right living in the Lakota tradition. It's the force that drives our lives.

"This Sacred Buffalo holds the most sacred ceremonies in the history of Indian people. The Lakota spiritual leader claims that people will come to it looking for help. That's how much power he thinks it has. And all of it began from a child's vision. During a sweat lodge where there was a Pipe."

Mike blinks. "I've got a lump in my throat."

"We've seen people cry in here," Beemer says.

Jim points at the skull. "The skull is going to show the coming of the Chanunpa. It's going to tell the story of how Buffalo Calf Woman brought the Pipe to the people. And the warning she gave."

"What was her warning?" Mike asks.

"About the end of time," Jim says. "But we'll visit on that later."

* * *

CARVING THE BUFFALO

Tommy

TOMMY DUBRAY SITS at a plywood table opposite the windows in Jim Durham's studio quilling covers for the Sacred Buffalo's hooves. He's just finishing the white one, with its center design of red and yellow blocks and a feather motif. In making the hoof covers, he has sorted through thousands of black, red, yellow, and white porcupine quills looking for those he needs. It's exacting work and painful. The quill tips are half an inch long and as strong and sharp as a needle. A tip that breaks off in the skin can "travel" in the body doing damage.

"I learned to respect the quills because no matter where you go, they'll want to go with you," Tommy says. "If you go to bed, they'll want to wake you up. If you walk around barefoot, they'll remind you, 'Here I am.'"

Tommy is fortyish, with black hair pulled back into a short braid. Behind thick glasses, his eyes are the grayish-green of rocks under fast water. He's the second son of Jimmy Dubray.

Tommy gathered the quills he uses especially for the hoof covers. He left a tobacco offering to Spirit in respect for the porcupine that gave its life. Before he could begin work, he boiled the quills twice to clean them. Traditionally, quills were boiled with the cleansing root of the yucca plant and dyed with roots and berries, but Tommy uses Dawn detergent and chlorine bleach to degrease and whiten quills. Rit dye provides the color.

Tommy searches through the quills for the straightest, longest specimens.

"But in the Lakota Way," he says, "we recognize that nothing is perfect. Life isn't perfect. So if there's a little color difference between the quills, a difference in shape, those qualities are respected."

He pulls each quill through his teeth a couple of times to flatten and moisten it before he weaves it into the design. It takes about a dozen quills to do an inch. The quills make a smooth, durable, glossy surface.

The hoof covers are black, red, yellow, and white. Black goes on the Buffalo's right front hoof and stands for West and the Thunder-Beings. Red covers the right back hoof and stands for North and the buffalo and the Sacred Pipe. Yellow covers the left back hoof and stands for East and the deer. White goes on the left front hoof for South and the eagle.

"The design is plain and simple," he says. "That's the Lakota Way."

When he's done, he will offer those not used back to the earth, except perhaps for enough to make a bag for his Pipe.

"I know a lot of my people have some fear about this project," he reflects. They question the wisdom of depicting the Lakota's seven sacred rites. "People have felt for a long time that the stories should stay within the tribe. Out of respect for the stories, people didn't repeat them, and sometimes they died without passing them on. But now on the reservation, the children are maybe one-half, one-quarter, one-eighth Indian. And so if the stories aren't passed on, they will die out."

He says he understands their concern.

"This Buffalo shows the story of my people, so working on it has taken a toll on me. But it makes me happy, too."

The hooves each wear a cover made from porcupine quills.

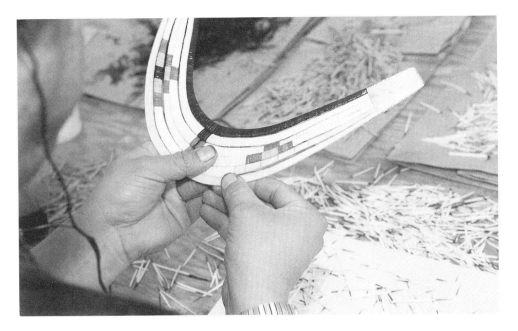

Quilling the covers for each of the four hooves is exacting work performed by Tommy Dubray. He quills the covers in black, red, yellow, and white for the four directions.

Big Jim pulls a cigarette from a box of Marlboro Mediums. He lights it, takes a couple of long drags, and props it in an ashtray where, forgotten, it sends up a swirl of smoke. Beemer sits on the torn, green, plastic-covered secretary chair at his table. Mike and Guy stand.

"There's something I have to tell you," Jim begins. "Before you can work on this project, you've got to come to my church. I have a sweat lodge about five miles from here, and before you start on the stand, we as men need to take a sweat together. First we pray together, then we talk."

Mike nods. "I'd be honored."

"This is our way," Jim explains. "You have your Christian ways and I respect and love your ways. But you're working now as part of this hochoka. So to complete the circle you have to come inside the sweat lodge with me. It'll be good. You'll enjoy it."

"Gladly," Mike agrees.

"Inside the sweat lodge there can be no lies," Jim warns. "Only the truth can be spoken there."

"Sure." Mike looks a little puzzled. "That stands to reason."

"By the way," Beemer interrupts, "one more bit of business. Whatever goes on in this room that concerns the Buffalo is strictly confidential. No leaks to the news, and certainly no photos. Steve and I have both signed a contract to that effect."

"But I can tell my wife?"

"Yes. But we want to keep this under wraps until it's done and we can present it with the dignity it deserves."

"Mike, do you drink?" Jim's eyes are piercing.

"I'm a recovering alcoholic," Mike says.

"Washte," Jim says. "I've known Dr. Bob myself for twelve years now."

"I've been sober for months," Mike says. "I took the step."

"Beemer doesn't drink, either," Jim says. "I ask because it's important. Never come here or go to anything that has to do with spirituality or work on the stand for the Buffalo if you've had anything to drink—or if you've used marijuana. Show that respect. Because if you don't, it will reflect on what we're doing here. If you drink, maybe you'll touch something that someone else'll touch later, and maybe he'll be weak and he'll drink because of it and it'll kill him. This is what we believe. Maybe you think it's superstitious or something, but we call it respect. There's a prayer, 'All the people look up, look up, always look up.' Pray that way and remember that. You're in a hochoka, a circle, now with us. That's what you crossed into when you came down the road today.

CARVING THE BUFFALO

You have to have respect."

Beyond the windows, the moonless sky is dark.

Jim levels his gaze on Mike. "I saw you last night when I was in the sweat lodge," he says.

Mike's eyes widen.

"We took a sweat and prayed about whether to ask you to come up here," Jim says. "I saw your face. I described you as the 'crooked-faced' man. And I saw a man with soft eyes. That's Guy."

Mike takes out a cigarette and lights it.

"Is a crooked face bad?" he asks.

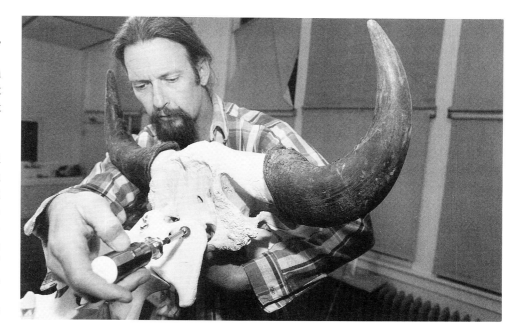

Beemer adjusts the screws in the vertebrae as he attaches the Sacred Buffalo skull. The skull weighs upward of thirty pounds.

"When you told me you've gone five months without drinking, I knew then why your face seemed crooked," Jim says. "You're having a tough time. You're learning about who you are. That's what you learn as you get sober. So sometimes your face is tense because you're confused about how you can deal with all the emotions you feel. You think, I'm too eager for this, or I'm madder than hell about this. You think, My kids are driving me crazy, and then the next minute you love them more than anything you can explain as a man. They call that the crooked face. A lot of things are happening in your life.

"I told Beemer this morning, 'The crooked face man will show himself today.' We prayed on this last night with the Red Clouds. They brought the Red Cloud Pipe out, and we prayed to make sure you're the right people. Because that phone call you made to me the other night was unusual. So we had to ask Tunkashila, is this man a good man? And here you are today."

"How was my phone call unusual?" Mike asks.

Jim laughs. "Not very many people call up and say, 'I really want to build a stand for your Buffalo just because I want to be a part of it and I don't want any money for it.' This coming from a man in business? I know there's something else in your head, but that's okay. You're the right guy."

"Well, thanks," Mike says.

"We've found," Beemer says, "that from the beginning, this project has brought the right people to it and eliminated those who don't belong here without any effort on our parts. It just happens."

Jim agrees. "The Buffalo brings out the best and the worst of what people have in their hearts. Jimmy Dubray said at the blessing ceremony that only the true of heart will be able to stand in the hochoka with the Buffalo. I credit it with telling me what people will do."

He pauses to glance at Steve, who is sitting with his back to the room, hunched over his table penciling curlicues onto a tablet.

"Let me tell you about the day I found Steve," Jim says.

"Early on, I began the task of hiring an artist to help me do the scrimshaw. I already had Beemer on board. I had showed him the drawings and explained how the bones would need high-grade sanding before they could be carved. Right away he asked to be considered for that job. I told him to talk to his wife about it because I figured it would take him away from home for a year.

"But I knew I also needed someone to help me copy my original drawings onto the bones before I could carve them. I could have done it myself, but I wanted to be fresh for the carving. Steve here was one of the people who came in for an interview. He showed me some good work he had done.

"'Talk to your fiancée and mom and dad about it—pray with them,' I told him. 'Then come back in a week and we'll take a sweat. We'll let the Creator decide. You've got the talent, but do you have the stamina? If God says you're the one, during the next twelve months you'll be subjected to every extreme of emotion—hate, love, and the whole gamut of other feelings.'

"Later, when we were in the sweat lodge, he told me his parents felt this was a great opportunity for him. 'I can be your hands,' he said.

"'Be careful what you say,' I warned him. 'In order to do what you're about to do, you have to stop looking at the world with your eyes and learn to see with your fingertips and your heart.' That's what my grandpa taught me. There can be no art without heart."

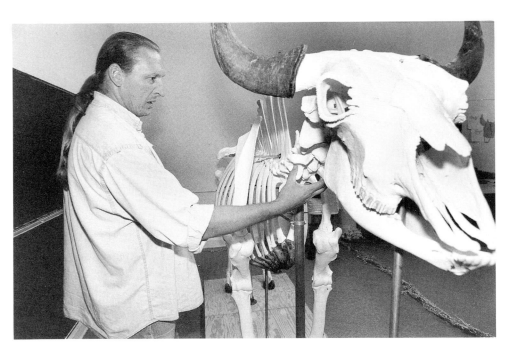

Big Jim checks the alignment of the skull.

Jim stands and walks to the corkboard. His eyes settle on a paper thumbtacked there and he reads: "'When the spirit does not work with the hand, there is no art.' That's what Leonardo Da Vinci had to say about it."

The red phone rings. Jim's wife Beth is calling from Virginia, and he talks to her for several minutes. The telephone is the men's families' life line, and calls are a priority. Beth calls every evening, Beemer's wife, Mair, several times a week. The phone bill runs between two and three hundred dollars a month.

Mike turns toward Beemer. "My brothers told me before I came up here that the shop is too busy to do anything like this. That we don't have the time. At that point, I went out and sat in the break room. My thought was, 'I don't want to do it to make money; I just want to do it for the challenge, the meaning.'"

Beemer nods. "We had the same reaction from the people at OSU. The bones were transferred there early because of OSU's expertise in assembling skeletons for museums. When the bones arrived there, they went through a four-step process—cleaning, degreasing, bleaching, and rebleaching—before the people there could even start to assemble them. They spent a total of 780 hours on the job. Until the day we had the skeleton crated and ready to load on the truck to come out here, we didn't know what the bill was going to be. But the people told us, 'We don't want anything for this. Our hours, our work are our gifts to the project.' So while your phone call was unusual, it wasn't unique. Things like that have happened all along. It's amazing to sit here and watch people's reactions to it. It has a profound effect on everyone who comes in contact with it."

"I see it as one heck of a challenge," Mike says. "I've always wanted the challenges no one else wants."

Jim puts the receiver back on the phone. He seemingly hasn't missed a beat of the conversation in the studio.

"Bill Richeimer, who was supervising the work at the OSU Department of Veterinary Biosciences lab, took me into his office that day we were moving the Buffalo to South Dakota. He said to me, 'What was that story you told me about how time doesn't mean anything?'

"I had told him about the time a few years back when me and some men were sitting outside Jimmy Dubray's house on the Pine Ridge Reservation. It was a bunch of us ranging from eighty years old down to about fifteen. We were visiting, and we'd just move our chairs around the house each day as the day wore on, staying in the shade.

"We had moved to the north side, when someone asked, 'What day is it?' Someone answered, 'Summertime.' Another person said it was Thursday. 'No, it can't be Thursday,' someone else said. I figured it had to be Tuesday. Someone said maybe it was Wednesday. We went back and forth. Finally, Jimmy's wife hollered out the kitchen window, 'You foolish men, it's Monday.'

"None of us knew what day it was. Because we didn't care. All we knew was that it was summertime. The day of the week had no significance.

"'What a beautiful thing that must be,' Richeimer said.

"Then he donated a chunk of money toward the expenses, and the people on his staff donated their labor."

Mike smiles. "I guess most people would give an arm and a leg not to have their every minute scheduled."

"It's called Indian time," Jim says. "Doing things when the spirit moves you. I'm going to design a watch face, and all it'll have on it is 'spring,' ' summer,' 'fall,' and 'winter.'"

The men laugh.

"But on the other hand, some people have ruled themselves out of the project completely," Beemer adds.

Jim picks a quarter out of a drawer in his drafting table and holds it up, turning it over and over in his fingers.

"The people who weed themselves out of this project, the first thing they ask is, 'How much money am I going to make?' As soon as those words are out of their mouth, they get rid of themselves somehow." He tosses the coin back into the drawer where it lands with a clink. "They drink too much, they have family problems, they have conflicts. All they saw here was the money.

"But the Sacred Buffalo is about people's suffering—about giving your life to God.

CARVING THE BUFFALO

Beemer rewires the skeleton with aluminum and steel wire to replace the less durable original copper wire.

You can't put a price on that. If people come to take, not give, it pushes them out. But if a man's supposed to be here, it draws him in. It spits out the takers and sucks the givers in. People who get involved in it say to me, 'I don't know why I'm doing this.' I tell them, 'Well, just pray on it.'

"In dreams, it tells me about people—and what they're going to do. People who aren't what they say they are—especially people who say they're medicine men—are so afraid of its power they can't even stand in front of it.

"But we don't worry about that. We know it has God's power."

Chapter 4

The Chanunpa, the Sacred Pipe

"The Chanunpa is the force that drives our lives."

—BIG JIM DURHAM

THIS I KNOW TO be true: I've never misused my Chanunpa, my Sacred Pipe. It's real strong.

I also know this: you can tell no lies when you hold the Chanunpa in your hands. Buffalo Calf Woman told us this when she brought the Chanunpa, and Native American people solemnly believe that if you knowingly and willingly lie when you smoke it, you or your family will pay in four ways. The Sacred Buffalo has the coming of the Chanunpa on its skull and on its jaws. For this reason, everything it says is the truth. I've lived that life. I know how many footsteps it takes to walk the Sacred Red Road. When you walk the Sacred Red Road, you live by way of the Chanunpa.

I was nine years old when I got my first Chanunpa. I used to trap for a man my brothers and I called Muskrat because he smelled like muskrats. We used to trap muskrats and skin them, and he'd buy the skins from us for fifty cents apiece.

Then one day Muskrat gave me a Chanunpa. It was a pretty unusual gift for a boy of nine, but now I figure that the Creator must have been working through old Muskrat. I had that Pipe for twenty years until I felt I needed a new one. That one had been through just too many hard times. I was living hard while I had it, and I did plenty of things that weren't on the Sacred Red Road, like they should be when you carry a Pipe. The Sacred Red Road means you give your life to the Creator. It's a path of compassion and service. There's a difference between it and the Red Road. I've seen people take part in the ceremonies of traditional Native American religion and then live their daily lives in a way that you wouldn't consider sacred. The sacred part comes when you serve the Creator.

THE CHANUNPA, THE SACRED PIPE

Sacred Buffalo Ribs

MAN AND BUFFALO are related; we are brothers. The buffalo used to feed the people. He was spiritually bound to us. For a while, now, that's been reversed. The buffalo has become dependent on the people for food. People shot them until almost none were left, and only through our protection has he reemerged. He helped us, and now we've helped him. Mitakye Oyasin. For all my relatives. We're all related.

On the Sacred Buffalo, the ribs tell this story. Once the spirit of buffalo was inside the people because he fed them—he gave them life. Now, people are inside the buffalo because we feed him. So many people have asked me: "Who are those people?" All I can tell you, is go to the Badlands some time and look up at the tops of the mountains there—it's said that no one lives in the Badlands but spirits. Or make a prayer tie and see if you notice any resemblance. Or go to the top of a mountain on a cold morning, and look down at the people in camp below all wrapped up in their blankets. Then tell me who those 163 people inside the ribs are.

The Wanbli Gleska wiyaka, the spotted eagle feathers, on the outside of the ribs are spirits. Each of them represents a person. The 163 feathers each have individuality and personality—they are fat or thin or crooked; each one is unique.

—Jim Durham

After I'd had that first Pipe for twenty years, I let it go. I thought about saving it for my son, Nick, but it had too many bad things attached to it. I needed to give it to someone spiritually in need, so I gave it to my friend Irish. Once someone wanted to give me a black pipe of the Heyoka, the contrary man who goes counter to nature. But I didn't want to go down that path. I didn't want to have to say, "I hate you," to mean "I love you" or go into the sweat lodge counterclockwise instead of the right way. That just didn't suit me, so I turned that Pipe down.

I was about thirty when I got the Chanunpa I use now. The bowl is T-shaped, and I made the stem myself. I think a Pipe should be kept simple. Many people go for fancy decorations on their Pipe—carvings of animals or inlaid designs, but they probably don't understand what each thing means. For example, if you slide a mallard's neck over your Pipe, it means you've taken one mate for life, and that promise is secured to God. Would you be willing to live with that pledge no matter what? Anything you put on your Pipe should have long-standing meaning in your life and a huge, personal story connected to it.

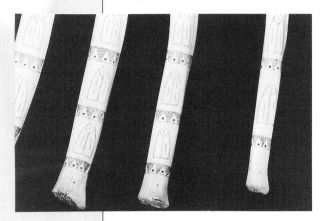

There are 163 spirits on the ribs.

The Chanunpa represents the power and mystery of the universe. During the Pipe ceremony, we sing, "People look this way, it's a beautiful thing." The Pipe is the breath you breathe on Tunkashila. You inhale from it and its smoke purifies your body; it takes the prayer into you. You exhale and it's the breath you breathe on Tunkashila to ask that your prayers be answered.

Tunkashila is the spirit of the grandfathers. It's the wisdom and comfort of a grandfather—the calmness. Tunkashila is the knowledge that came before us and will last after we're gone. Those men who have gone on to the Spirit World—your grandfather, my grandfather, and all the grandfathers before them—are Tunkashila. It's a source of strength and help in our everyday lives.

The grandfathers are different from some other spirits because they've lived on earth. They seem to me to be someone who sits and listens to you as he paints an elk hide. He doesn't necessarily speak to you. Some people come here seeking power and they say, "Oh, Tunkashila," and think that Crazy Horse's spirit is going to come to them. I tell them, "Talk to your own ancestors. Say Tunkashila, but spiritually mean your people. Ask them for help. Ask for them to hear you." I think there's a huge council on the other side of people from all earthly backgrounds. Each time there's a call from earth, they find out if it's one of their relatives, and they connect to their own people. It's silly to believe that Crazy Horse, Sitting Bull, Sequoia, or Swimmer are going to come back and help someone who's not related to them. Pray to your own grandfathers. When I prayed for my grandpa's hands to

THE CHANUNPA, THE SACRED PIPE

come into me and give me the ability to finish this Sacred Buffalo, I didn't pray for Red Cloud's family to show up. I prayed to my own grandfathers.

You can pray to Tunkashila to help you find the guidance to run your life, but you have a brain and the ability to make choices; if you make a bad decision, it's you, not Tunkashila. Nothing bothers me more than to hear people say, "Look what life has done to me." I'd like to be able to review the options they've had and the gifts the Creator has given them. Then I'd ask, "Why did you make the choice not to see what your little son was up to, so he tried to slice a piece of watermelon and he ended up cutting all the tendons in his hand?" The answer: "Because it was football Sunday, and I couldn't leave the game." Or "I was drinking with my buddies." Or "I was busy." You see, they chose the road that led to disaster. You're connected to the spiritual world, and you can choose to live your life with awareness or carelessness. You can make the choice to feel the Creator's gift or reject it. You can embrace the ability to suffer for the beauty of something, or steel your heart against it. It's that simple

Sometimes, though, something comes into your life that you just have to live with. Then I say, "Smudge off and pray on it." No lesson is without its blessings. No path of suffering is without its rewards.

A new Chanunpa is fresh and young and innocent like a child, and it has to be taken into the sweat lodge and blessed and purified just like you purify yourself. It has no history, and so you have to go slow with it and be very careful what you use it for. Some people feel that the more people you have smoke your Pipe, the more powerful it is. But no Chanunpa is any more powerful than any other. Your Pipe is only as powerful as your prayers. I have a little stick—a twig, really—that my son carved. He was little at the time, and he carved it uneven. He was going to make a turtle rattle out of it, but then one of the forks at the top broke. It's so pitiful. It's ugly to anyone else, but I've kept it all these years because it's powerful good medicine to me.

Out of respect for the Pipe, you should never pray for unworthy things. You should never pray for money; what a huge misuse of that gift that would be! Some people have asked why I don't pray for the lottery numbers. Out of respect, I'd never do that. What if I got a million dollars but both of my children died? But when people ask me to pray for their mom who has cancer or their unborn child, I pray with all my heart.

The responsibility of the Chanunpa becomes great when you're given permission by a holy man to use it to help people outside your family. I carry this responsibility, and whenever people call on me in need, I have to go, like when my friend Bill in Ohio died and his relatives called me to come pray with them. No matter how hard it is or how bad you feel, you go because you're duty bound to honor any request. When you accept the responsibility of praying for suffering people, you're on a one-lane road built by the Creator. When you pray in a ceremony, you open a door on power.

Your can only use your Chanunpa for yourself and your family until you've learned enough not to hurt yourself or someone else. You wouldn't want to carve your Pipe over a four-year period and then jump in and hand it to someone who wants to pray for a job

Beemer's Chanunpa

MY CHANUNPA IS for my family. I can't bring it out for anyone, so I don't. I've had it about three years; I carved the bowl myself, and Big Jim gave me the stem. I made the pipe bag in my spare time while I was working on the Sacred Buffalo. My beaded lighter was given to me at Sundance, and I cut the chokecherry tamping stick at Sundance. The rest of the stick was used as piercing pegs.

It took a while before I used my Chanunpa at all. I had respect for it, and I didn't want to use it until I was ready. I've approached my Chanunpa the way I've approached all of these natural ways: I haven't rushed into it, and I haven't started to apply the limited knowledge I have until I feel comfortable with it and/or worthy of it. I've watched other people jump into this and treat it like a show—like they just got a new car so they have to drive it all over the place and show it off.

I'm more sure of myself with my Chanunpa now. I know the songs. My spirituality has developed to the point where I'm comfortable enough to teach my wife, Mair, what I know, although I wouldn't presume to do that with anyone else. Mair's ready, now, too. And my Chanunpa has been purified in the sweat lodge. The time is right.

—*Beemer*

THE CHANUNPA, THE SACRED PIPE

> ### Lies
>
> DON'T LIE. DON'T lie to yourself or to anyone else. Because if you lie, you'll steal. If you lie to others, you'll lie to yourself so you can trick yourself into doing what you know isn't right. In lying, you become nothing. You become no one.
>
> —*Jimmy Dubray*

with it. You have to learn to pray first. You have to learn to use the Chanunpa. Tunkashila has his own time frame, and you'll know when—if ever—you're strong enough to pray with it for other people. So if someone's dying and he asks for a Pipe to be brought forward, I would be real reluctant to step forward if I wasn't totally secure with my Chanunpa and had permission from someone close to Tunkashila to use it for other people. That's what I mean by its being young.

A Chanunpa should be properly kept in its special pipe bag with the bowl and the stem apart. They are too powerful once they're joined to be left together. The bowl should be plugged with sage and a red cloth. The word *cha* means wood or tree, and *nunpa* means two. It's not a "peace" pipe, as the uninformed say, but a Sacred Pipe. It's the force that drives our lives, and it's the basis of all the seven sacred rites practiced by spiritual people.

During a ceremony, the Chanunpa is handled with the greatest respect because it's the door to the power of the Creator. There are strict rules for loading it with *cansasa*, a native tobacco of red willow, passing it around the circle of people, and depositing the unfinished ash. The Pipe is smoked and pointed stem first in a clockwise direction to the powers of the West, the North, the East, and the South, to the One Who Is Everything, and to Grandmother Earth.

In the same breath that people ask about the Chanunpa, they often ask, "How can I become more spiritual?" In turn, I ask them what they're after. If it's power, I can't help. If it's knowledge they want, only life experiences can give that. Words can't. The search for knowledge is not a journey for weekend warriors. It starts and it never ends. It's a decision to visit with God for a lifetime. If people want others to look up to them and make them powerful in a spiritual way, that's wrong thinking. But if you learn to pray every day—really pray—the rest of it will come.

But the search for knowledge carries a heavy price. It's a long road. And it doesn't end when you die. Most people relate that price to money: "How much do I have to pay for that?" But you have to pay for spiritual growth not with dollars and cents but with enlightened emotions—extreme emotions. Whether something is on the dark side or it's as simple as a baby's smile, you have to learn to feel it. That's the price. Some people tell me, "I've never really felt anything." That's a high price, too, when you think about it—living as an empty shell. When you see a dead skunk, do you say, "Oh, boy, that stinks!" or do you see all her babies going unfed? When you see a drawing of a POW in a cage, do you see the sad faces of his fatherless children? Do you look into the head of your friend and see his suffering and feel it along with him? That's the price you pay for the spiritual life. People glorify it. They think of being able to pierce people and take flesh from them. Let me tell you that when you do that you look at your own hands and say, "My God, what am I doing? I'm just a man."

I tell people who come seeking knowledge: calculate the price. I tell most of them, "Don't ever leave the realm of your own house." Because what you think you want, and what you get may be two totally different things.

> ### Seven Sacred Rites
>
> THE WAY I see it, the seven sacred rites of the Lakota are from the original circle of the Lakota people. They are a gift from the Creator. Buffalo Calf Woman brought them to us when she brought us the Chanunpa, the Sacred Pipe. They are equivalent to the Bible's Ten Commandments.
>
> The Lakota people aren't the owner of these ways, but the guardian. We must share our way of life with the innocent in the different races of man. At the same time, we must protect our ideals. We must have respect for them and fear them because they are the ways of the Creator.
>
> The seven rites of the Lakota are the force—the spiritual power—behind this Sacred Buffalo. If we live a life according to these, life is good. But many of us don't. We live two or three of them. We need to change that.
>
> —*Thomas Dubray*

THE CHANUNPA, THE SACRED PIPE

A lot of people come to my friend Old Man Jimmy Dubray looking for help. Over his lifetime, he's visited with the Creator a lot more than most people have.

* * *

I AM DEFENDS HIS PEOPLE, also James Dubray, the spiritual leader of the Oglala people and Sundance Chief of the Fools Crows International Sundance in Kyle, South Dakota. There are seven bands of Lakota—seven campfires, but I speak only for the Oglala.

I have to tell you a little joke before I get serious: For a long time, I prayed, "Almighty God, look down on me, this is Jim. Bless me today. I need this and I need that." And then I thought, How many Jims are there in this world? So I tried something different. Grandpa Fools Crow always told me that when people came to him with a problem, he'd tell them, "Well, you tried that, so now why don't you try something different?" So I prayed, "This is Defends His People. I need a little help today." I asked for understanding. I asked for health. I asked for help to move around. A little later, a little sack of potatoes came in the door, and the mail brought a five-dollar bill to buy gas for the car. And I thought, All that time, all those other Jims got that blessing.

A man should learn from the buffalo. Like the male buffalo protects the females and their calves, he should stand like a guard over the women and protect them and their offspring. We men are supposed to protect our people when evil comes in, yet the only weapon I have is the Chanunpa. I have a .22 rifle that I'm supposed to give to my grandson when he becomes a man—which in the Lakota Way means he has to be over forty years old. But protection isn't involved with a rifle. When you have the Chanunpa with you, you have everything you need. This wisdom was given to the chief of the people by Calf Pipe Woman and from the chief to the individual. The only weapon we need is the Chanunpa as given by her.

Some people say that the buffalo came from Wind Cave here in South Dakota. They say that man and the buffalo lived in the darkness below as brother and brother, and that the female buffalo and woman lived as sister and sister. When the buffalo comes up from beneath the surface, he becomes a man. And when he goes back into the ground, he becomes a buffalo again. It's a cycle. How did God create this? How did he create the Chanunpa, crying for a vision, sweat lodge, and Sundance? He created them for all people, but maybe the Lakota were better listeners in those days, and that's why they still have their culture. Other people are creating their God from silver and gold and possessions, and they believe in what they've created. But they will become nothing because of it. They will be dust. Maybe that's where that saying "ashes to ashes, dust to dust" comes from. But we come from the Spirit World, and we go back into it. The buffalo has much to do with that.

For a long time, man and buffalo have been connected. I myself know that without the buffalo in the ceremony, there is nothing. I have a buffalo skull altar that only I can pray with because I hooked it on my flesh to give it thanks. One reason the buffalo is so interrelated with man is because it has used itself to give us food, shelter, and clothing.

A Song to the Chanunpa

People you must look at me.
People you must look at me.
This Pipe before you is sacred.
People you must look at me.

People you must look at me.
People you must look at me.
This Pipe before you is sacred.
People you shall live.

—*A Traditional Song*

A Beautiful Woman Brings the Chanunpa

ONE DAY SO long ago that no one now can remember whether it was during the soft, growing heat of spring or the white-hot sun of summer or the raspy dryness of autumn, two young hunters were sent out from their people to track game. These two young men were chosen to go because they showed great bravery. You see, one of the elders had dreamed that something special was coming to the people, and for this reason the leaders decided that two of their best young men should go out to meet it. The hunters, being young, weren't told about the elder's vision. They were only told to look for signs of animals that might feed the people.

The two hunters walked far under the big sky. All they had were their legs to carry them, but they were strong and used to traveling great distances without seeing signs of another man. And so they walked with courage through valleys and over ridges noticing the fresh footprints and droppings of any four-leggeds that might serve to feed their people. For the people of their tribe were hungry. The hunger made them restless, and they were not content.

One day the two young men were walking up a high, steep ridge when they looked up and spotted a young buffalo alone on the crest of the hill. Perhaps they viewed it as meat for their people or a robe for their tipi floor. They paused to talk about how they could sneak up on it, but when they looked up again, a young woman stood where the buffalo had been. The men froze in their tracks. This was a mystery.

One of the hunters said, "Hey, look, we really found something. Maybe it's a *toka*, an enemy, but even so, she sure is a pretty girl."

But the other young man was suddenly cautious. He said, "Be careful, this looks like something sacred. She shouldn't be out here all by herself without anyone around."

The impatient hunter looked on the woman with lust, and he ran up and grabbed her. They say that a cloud covered them both, and when it lifted, he was only a pile of bones. He had no respect for the sacred.

The cautious hunter viewed the woman as one who represented his grandmother, his mother, and his sister, so he showed his respect.

But he was also frightened and started to run away.

The woman called to him. "Wait," she said, "I bring a message for your people. A good message. Go now and tell them to prepare."

The young hunter ran back to camp and told his people what he had seen. They were troubled and excited and frightened all at the same time to think that a sacred woman was coming to visit them. They made *ohanpi*, soup, out of the food they had on hand, and when a lookout spotted the woman coming, the people gathered to see her. She was beautiful, and she was singing a song. The people sing that song even now. In her hands, she carried a long bundle and a piece of sage.

It's said that the woman served soup to the men before she ate any of it herself. It's said she stayed in the camp for four days, but that was so long ago no one can speak for certain about these details.

THE CHANUNPA, THE SACRED PIPE

What they do know is this: the woman reached into the bundle she carried and drew out something that would change the people's lives forever. She drew out the Chanunpa, the Calf Pipe, and fitted the bowl and the stem together.

She drew one thing more from the bundle, a small pouch containing cansasa.

The woman built an altar to show the chief how it should be arranged and what should be placed on it. Then she fit the stem and bowl, placed the Chanunpa on the altar, and danced around it as a blessing.

Perhaps the first Chanunpa was made of a slender, hollowed-out piece of wood about as long as your arm and a stone bent like your elbow with two openings. Some people say it was made from a buffalo leg.

The woman reached into the tobacco pouch and took a pinch of the fine, dry tobacco and pushed it into the Sacred Pipe. When she had done this, she asked the chief of the people to step forward. She handed him the Sacred Pipe.

The woman told the chief to put the Chanunpa to his lips. She then touched a burning coal from the fire to the tobacco inside it. The chief inhaled the sacred smoke and breathed out a prayer that spiraled toward the sky. In this way, people learned to honor Wakan Tanka, the Great Mystery.

The chief called forth the spiritual leader, the healer, and the herald, and they also smoked the Chanunpa.

It's said that the woman stayed with the people until she had taught them many things. She taught the chief and his men how to pray with the Sacred Pipe for the good of their families and the people. She sang prayer songs for the women until they knew them by heart. She showed the leaders how to use the Sacred Pipe for sacred ceremonies that would help the people lead good lives. She talked to them about how their lives would be better and their prayers answered if they would pay the Chanunpa the respect it deserves. The people learned that when they smoked the Chanunpa in prayer they would find strength and help.

She told them, "Walk in peace."

But the woman warned them to be careful to pray only for worthy things and never to deceive people with lies while holding it. She warned them not to play with its power.

When the time came for the woman to leave the camp, the people gathered to watch her go. They realized that they had been hungry for Spirit, and the woman had seen their need and come to them in mercy. As she walked away toward the place where the earth meets the sky, she turned into a white buffalo, and in that form, she rolled on the ground. When she stood up, she was a different color. It is said that the people saw the buffalo change color three more times—to black, red, and yellow.

She told the people, "Some day I will come back. But in the meantime, I will always be with you."

The people were grateful to the woman for helping them. She had brought them the Chanunpa to use in prayer. In praying with the Chanunpa, the people and their children and their children's children—from then until forever—could be close to Wakan Tanka.

That's how the Chanunpa came to the people.

Mitakuye Oyasin.

Detail from jaw depicting the Buffalo Calf Woman.

THE CHANUNPA, THE SACRED PIPE

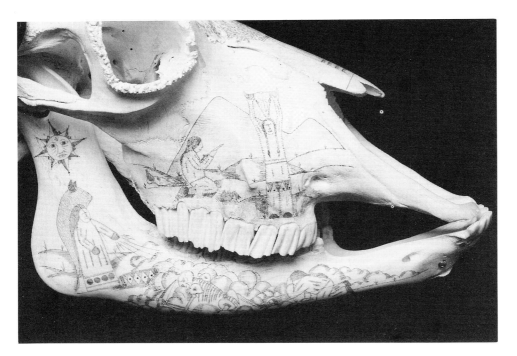

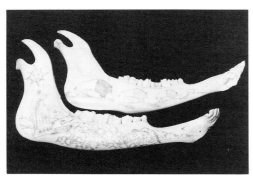

Two men pray on the sides of the skull, one with the Chanunpa and the other with a buffalo skull in an ancient tradition. On the jaws, Buffalo Calf Woman appears to two hunters. One looks on her with lust and is reduced to a pile of bones. Inside the jaw, white, red, black, and yellow buffalo go toward the Chanunpa.

The buffalo just minds its own business, grazing along on the grass, but when the time comes it sacrifices itself for the people. When the time comes, its spirit moves out (Animal killings traditionally happened in the fall of the year because there was no spirit in the animals then—just the flesh. By March, the spirit had moved back in—which is why you don't kill a buffalo in the summer.), and we eat its flesh. The bones have grease in them, and when they are boiled, they render fat that is mixed with dried meat and chokecherries to make *wasna*. The bones are used for tools, too, and broken up used for fire. The bladder is used to carry water. The big intestine is the cooking pot. The liver is good to cure gallstones. We use the hide to make clothing or bedding. We even make our house—our *tipi*—from the hide. Everything is used—even the hooves, sinew, and chips. Chips were the first baby Pampers. The women took buckskin and put a layer of crumbled chips on it and then another layer of soft buckskin and that's what they used for diapers. Because of all these things, the Indian became the buffalo. I don't eat buffalo though. I would feel guilty.

The buffalo and man are connected spiritually, too. Even before the Calf Pipe came to us, the buffalo chose a man and taught him to pray. He gave the man the power to ordain a medicine man, a spiritual leader, an advisor, and a herald or crier to take the news around camp. This is how close man and buffalo are.

Everyone always talks about a "white" buffalo: "White" Buffalo Calf Woman. But the old people say "Pte San Win", which means "the gray virgin bison." *San* means gray; *pte* is bison. Everyone went crazy when a little, white, female buffalo was born in Janesville, Wisconsin, on August 20, 1994. Several decades ago, a white albino calf was born, but the one in Janesville isn't albino—it's even more special. I went to see her, and I can picture her now. She's changing color as she grows older, and she's going to be a gray buffalo cow—going first through black and brown and red and yellow. Think of a color and then think of yesterday. You can't remember everything you did or said yesterday. It's gone, and a new day started at dawn this morning. Everything that comes, we become that.

We Indians respect gray. Look at the gray head of an old woman or man. Gray means knowledge or wisdom. That is what Pte San Win brought us. But she's not the gray virgin anymore. She was young when she brought the Calf Pipe, but she's the gray old woman now. She's the Grandmother.

Man and the buffalo have survived together since the beginning, and they will survive

THE CHANUNPA, THE SACRED PIPE

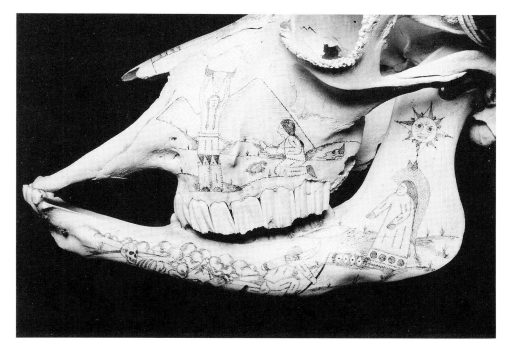

until the end of time. They will end up in the Spirit World together where they will become one. But as humans, we didn't know how to get to the Spirit World, and we needed guidance—a map for understanding. Pte San Win actually brought us a physical Calf Pipe to guide us. She brought us a hochoka, which means center or in the middle. She put the chief on the spot. She brought the Calf Pipe to him and said, "This is how you pray; this is what you sing. Pray to the four directions, and the Tunkashila, the Grandfather, will come. You'll see him, you'll feel him, he'll be there with you. He'll give all that you ask to you and your people if you pray with this sacred Calf Pipe."

I believe she put the Calf Pipe there on the altar, she put the tobacco there, and she put a little rock there to remind the chief that he was not alone. It says in the Christian Bible that if you have the faith of a mustard seed, anything is possible. If you have the faith of that rock, nothing is impossible. She placed roots there, too. That was the beginning between her and the people.

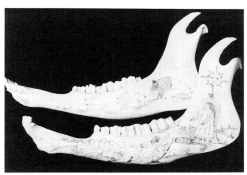

Why is it called the Calf Pipe? Because you're a little calf, and with faith and spirit, you will learn to survive. You'll learn to use the nipple and learn how to eat grass, and you'll grow. If you learn to use the Calf Pipe, you'll grow in spirit. It's as simple as that. The older you get, the teaching gets stronger. If you're wise, you hang onto the teaching.

I tell people, remember to pray four times during the day—morning, noon, evening, and midnight. And when you look up into the sky at night and see the seven sacred stars of the Dipper, think about the seven Sacred Rites the Calf Pipe Woman brought. When you pray, pray for understanding. Don't pray for wisdom, wisdom is not the same as understanding. In your prayer cloth, put understanding in first. Then, put in health. So now you have understanding and health, but stop and think, how are you going to move? Nowadays, we use the car, and you have to have a little money for gas. So ask for a little help to be able to move, ask for energy. Next, you need courage. And you must share. That's the Lakota Way. The buffalo shares everything it has with the people and you must do that, too.

The Calf Pipe Woman instructed the chief on how to use the Calf Pipe. She told us very plainly, "Use it wisely. Don't play with this power or try to fool me." How many of us have fooled her today? We must use our own mind and judgment to choose the right way to walk. This is the teaching of the Chanunpa. This teaching is sacred, and it must be said right. The Woman told us, "Use this carefully or it will destroy you, or you will destroy people."

Two men pray to Tunkashila, with Bear Butte standing behind them. On the jaw, Buffalo Calf Woman tells the hunter who respects her to go tell his people to prepare for the gift she brings. The buffalo inside the jaw show that the Sacred Buffalo speaks the truth.

THE CHANUNPA, THE SACRED PIPE

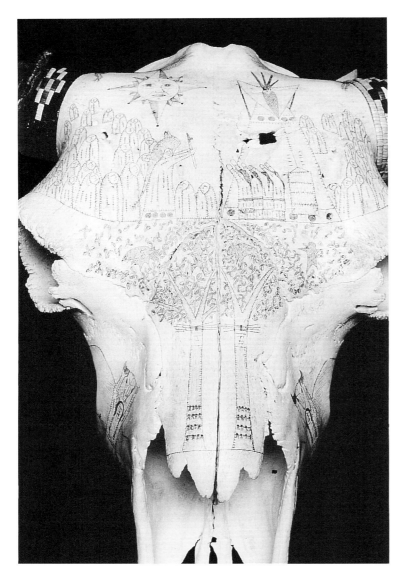

The skull bears the carving of the coming of the Chanunpa, where Buffalo Calf Woman presents the Sacred Pipe to the chief of the people. She tells him to use it wisely. "Walk in peace," she says. The Chanunpa is the foundation of all the Lakota's sacred rites. The sacred Sundance tree is shown on the front of the skull.

From the beginning, you're taught and trained in a belief. We believe in the four generations—ourselves and our fathers, our grandpas and the Great Grandfather—the Holy Grandfather, the Almighty One, the Awesome One. Nowadays, I scold people a little when they say Wakan Tanka, just because *tatanka*, the word for buffalo, came into popularity. God is awesome, so you say Wakaya Tanka. We pray to the Holy Grandfather.

I can explain it like this: one time my grandpa said, "You know, we grandpas are very close to Almighty God. Suppose you ask your dad for something and he doesn't give it to you. So you come to me, and I say, 'My grandchild, if your dad won't give it to you, I will. And if I forget, you can go to the Awesome One. How huge he is. And he's all ears.'"

The Calf Pipe has a stem and a stone bowl with a little circle on top. The stem is cedar or ash or oak or cherry. I like to use ash for the stem because it's very hard wood. They tell me you have to take it in the Fall, though; if you take it in the Spring, it will split. Cedar is beautiful, but it breaks easy. Cherry is good. But pray about it, and it will come to you which wood to use and which not to. Pray that you have that knowledge or wisdom to choose.

The hole inside the stem is a straight line from tip to tip. If you talk straight, you pray right and that smoke goes straight through it. You inhale some of it, and you put your own prayer on it. You can bless yourself with it, too. When we smoked the Chanunpa the other day, some of the people took the smoke and covered themselves with it like it was a shawl. That was neat. They blessed themselves. Hopefully those blessings won't end but will keep on going.

The original Pipe doesn't exist today. Some people try to date its coming at 800 or 1,200 years ago. But we're talking about nineteen generations ago that it came. Some Lakota elders now figure a generation at 1,000 years, but I really don't know how to judge it in terms of time. The pipestone (catlinite, named after early Western artist George Catlin) from Minnesota isn't the original material either. It's a symbol; it reminds people. Today, the Chanunpa of the Lakota Nation is cared for by Arvol Looking Horse near Green Grass, South Dakota. There was a black stone they used to make pipes out of, but then someone said that only the Heyoka carries a black stone Pipe. That's not a traditional belief, though. Man has made rules. He puts in easy parts and takes out the hard ones.

THE CHANUNPA, THE SACRED PIPE

As for the bowl, remember that it's a circle. The Calf Pipe Woman gave the Calf Pipe to the men to use. The women are there to see that it's used right. The woman constantly watches over that circle of love—the family. The circle is hers.

When we go into the buffalo, the next door we open is to the Spirit World. We're going through that black hole. There's no turning back—if you turn back, you're going to get lost. We're walking through that Pipe stem, that's the black hole I'm talking about. We're in the cave of the buffalo people now. We're getting deeper and deeper. We're going to be able to see things clearly. This is the Pipe bowl. Then when we come out of the bowl of the Pipe, we're inside a circle. That's where we are at Sundance time—we're standing there in that circle.

Buffalo Calf Woman presents the Sacred Pipe to the chief, who has summoned his spiritual leader, healer, and herald to honor it. Visible in the Sundance tree—a cottonwood—are images of a man and a buffalo.

If you learn how to pray, you may be given a Chanunpa. But not everyone should have one. Before you get a Chanunpa, you have to have a vision showing why: Why do you want to carry it? Is it because other people are doing it, or do you have a reason? Is a life on the line and you have to pray for health for someone? Do you want to give yourself for the people? Of course, today everyone buys one for about twenty dollars. People bring them to Sundance, but if I don't recognize them, they're out there on their own. They're just playing around, like they were told not to play. They come with heartaches, and they take them home with them. They bring nothing in, and they take nothing out.

When you decide to smoke the Calf Pipe, it's a special time. I only use my Chanunpa at the beginning of something that has no end. If we smoke and you fall along the wayside, that's your problem. If you don't believe all the way, you drop off and bloom where you fall. Or maybe you fall on a stony place and you don't bloom. It's like walking through the valley. Sometimes I walk alone, sometimes with many, many people. My wife is always there to help me and pray for me. She reminds me what I need to do. She helps me pray. So you can find peace with me in smoking the Pipe, or not. As you wish. If you believe what I believe, that's beautiful. If you don't, then believe what you will. I say walk with peace and love, and forgive others what they say about you.

In the Lakota Way you walk with your blessings—whatever they are. You've been blessed by God, so don't stand there and say, "I'm a

Pipestone

THE MOST WIDELY used material for making the Chanunpa is a distinctive orange-red stone mined in southwestern Minnesota. Some people say that the Pipe bowl stands for woman and the Pipe stem for man; that the bowl of the Pipe is the head and the stem is the backbone. Members of many Native American tribes visit the site yearly to quarry the pipestone for their Sacred Pipes. The area is now part of the national monument system; it is about five miles from the small town of Pipestone.

THE CHANUNPA, THE SACRED PIPE

In the art of scrimshaw, lines are carved into bone and then inked. Here Big Jim uses a razor-sharp knife to carve the coming of the Chanunpa into the skull. More than 10,000 individual lines comprise this one scene.

I Am the Buffalo

MY BELIEF IS that I am part of that buffalo. I am related to the Pte Oyate, the Buffalo People. I say people because Grandpa Fools Crow says that when he prays to the owls at night, he says, "Take care of us, watch us as we sleep and dream. Give us a good dream, a vision, so we can survive." He said that the Buffalo People are from the North. But I believe they are from the West. Almighty God brought life, and he brought good things from the West to give us a second chance to say, "Hey, you forgot this."

—Jimmy Dubray

poor individual, I have nothing in this world. I am so poor, and I am so sickly." Gee. It seems like that's all we hear. Every day you convince yourself that you're sick and you're helpless and you're poor. Before you know it, you condemn yourself to sleep. Why not count your blessings? You're standing there with that Chanunpa, so why not say, "This morning I saw the sun come up, and I thank you for it. I thank you for this, I thank you for that. I thank you." Many blessings will come from that. Pray with your arms outstretched to God, like friend to friend, like people who have come to hug one another. Maybe he will reward your faith by teaching you how to pray for your people.

Be careful what you pray for, though. I had a nephew who came over two days before Sundance and told me he wanted to pray with a big buffalo skull. I couldn't refuse him. The first day of Sundance, someone brought in a huge buffalo skull. My nephew came over and looked at it, and I told him, "There's no turning back now." He said, "How am I going to get through it?" I told him, "We'll pierce your back and put it there, and you'll drag it around and pray for all the people. Not for yourself. Forget about yourself. But be careful what you ask for. You might get more than you bargained for."

My first go with a buffalo skull, I got a medicine wheel on my back. I went to Sundance expecting to be there only one day, but it didn't work that way. A young man was putting up a skull I had prayed with and he kept adding skulls until there were seven. He called me and said, "Dad, it's time now."

I asked myself, "Time for what?"

I went and sat facing West.

He said, "I was told to put a medicine wheel on your back."

Each skull had a rope around it. They weren't tied together; they were separate. He tried to pierce my back, but he couldn't do it. I was in good shape in those days, and my skin was hard. He kept slicing my skin, but he couldn't get through it.

I said, "Last night I prayed for my brother Leonard Crow Dog to be here. I prayed he'd be here to help me."

THE CHANUNPA, THE SACRED PIPE

I looked up, and he was coming.

"What happened, big brother?" he said, and he took the cherry sticks and without any blade or pain killer, he pushed them through my skin. I didn't feel any sting or pain. Then he tied those skulls on me.

I started praying for the people. The skulls rolled after me. They got tangled and dragged along. Some man was singing for me, and the people cried, "Why do you do this? You already gave your life?" But I guess it was meant to be that way.

Gradually, over the years, I have become like the Chanunpa, with peace always in my heart. I don't know how much longer I will use this body, but I'm not sad for the day it lays down to rest. Sure, I want to live—just like the smallest bird wants to survive the storm to see another day. But my spirit will go on forever. It will go on in peace.

I am not a peacemaker, though. Peacemakers get hurt. In boxing matches, I've seen the referee get knocked out.

Take your spirit and build a cocoon of peace around you, and one day maybe something really good will come from it. Maybe you'll emerge as a butterfly. You'll be red and blue, and people will be attracted to you, and something really good will come from your peace. This is the lesson of the Chanunpa Wakan.

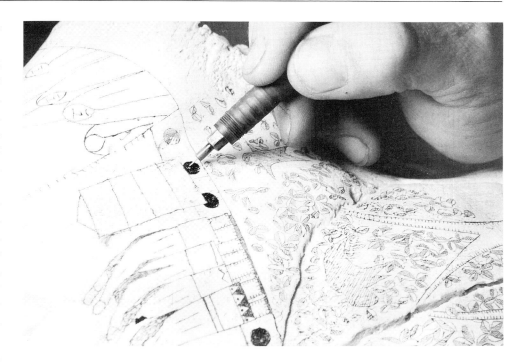

Big Jim inks the coming of the Chanunpa, etching on the skull a tribute to the Sacred Pipe that can last for thousands of years.

WoLakota

WOLAKOTA IS A big word that means peace, but it goes beyond peace in the common sense to a mysterious, holy kind of calm or bliss. The Creator will walk in front of you one day, and you won't even know he passed by. He'll walk in front of you three times during your lifetime, once as a little boy, once as an elder, and another time in a different form. And you'll neglect that spirit walking in front of you. That's how blind we humans can get. WoLakota asks us to take in an orphan, to give him a place where he belongs, not let them send him away to social services. It asks us to honor our elders. In this way, we find peace.

—*Thomas Dubray*

THE CHANUNPA, THE SACRED PIPE

Chapter 5
The End of Time

"Peace is fulfilling your dream and, in the process, redeeming your own identity."
—BIG JIM DURHAM

WHEN BUFFALO CALF WOMAN brought the Chanunpa to the people, she warned them to respect all life—both human life and nature. She warned them that she would return, and that her presence would be a warning to all people that the end of time is near. Old Man Fools Crow saw her walking around in this country in 1974 in the company of another woman. He said this is a bad omen that tells us the end is near.

Ask anyone if they think our world has changed for the better, and the answer you'll get will be no—if you get an answer. If you're trying to stop someone you don't know on a crowded city sidewalk, he'll push past you out of fear of what you might want from him—or want to do to him. You could try your neighbor, but you probably don't know him well enough to ask him. You're nameless and faceless to him, as he is to you. You might as well be a *wanagi*, a spirit crying for its soul.

In the sixties, commentators on the evening news described the soldiers in Vietnam as having "a thousand-yard stare." That's what living with killing does to you, whether you're in a declared war or at war in your life. It steals the light in your eyes and makes them hollow. It robs you of that spark of spirit that makes you human. It strips you of your human identity.

A hopeless loss of humanity caused the Wounded Knee Massacre and Custer's Battle at the Little Bighorn. The Indians and the soldiers had slaughtered each other's people until they were ruled by anger. When your humanity goes, all you have left is anger. Light becomes dark. And in darkness, there are only two emotions—anger and hatred. Aggression is the result. You have to express it somehow, so you kill or you torture without regard. You get farther and farther away from your humanity. Then one

THE END OF TIME

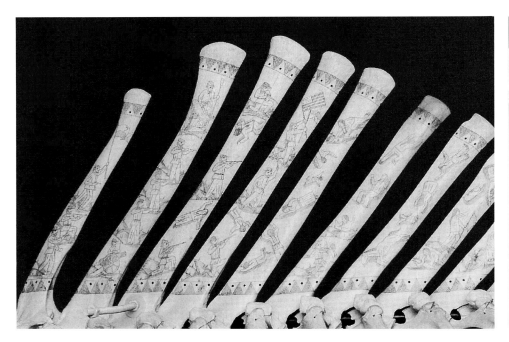

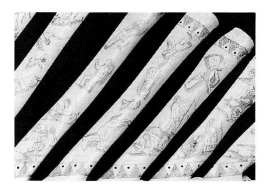

The Wounded Knee Massacre is carved onto the left side of the Sacred Buffalo's hump, showing the senseless slaughter that happens when people disrespect the Chanunpa and Buffalo Calf Woman's warning to walk in peace. On the bitter cold day of December 29, 1890, more than 250 men, women, and children lost their lives at the hands of the Seventh Cavalry. Detail: little girls and babies lay dead in the snow, their tiny bodies shredded by the rounds from the Hotchkiss guns.

day you're standing there—whether you're alone or with a thousand others just like you—and you no longer know who lives inside you. Your hatred feeds on itself, and one day you're lost. You don't know God, you don't know your soul, you don't follow any moral values. You can't explain anymore why you hate. You just do.

Why did those children at Wounded Knee have to die? Do you think the white man who pulled a trigger to kill a baby, or the white man who ran a saber through a little girl, had anything in them but hate and anger? Soldiers claim they're only following orders to kill, but what about the inhuman act of chopping off a child's feet to take its little moccasins? Or chopping off a woman's head to get her beaded bag? What does a man who would do that have inside of him? Nothing. He's without human identity.

At the Battle of the Little Bighorn, Indian men killed 300 white men and then mutilated their bodies so they wouldn't be whole in the Spirit World. What sense is there in combining a spiritual belief with a barbaric act of killing? How can hatred and spirituality—two very strong forces—be shoved into one human being? "I'm going to cut his head off so he doesn't have it on the other side, and we'll never have to fight him again"—to me carving up another human being is a man's darkest act. The Indian people who slit a man's thighs and shoved an arrow in his penis so he couldn't reproduce: what kind of people were they? What kind of man hates so bad that he orders his woman to carve up a soldier? What kind of man would be so confused as to kill Custer and then spare him from being mutilated because he had fathered a child by a Cheyenne woman? These are people without identity. They could stand in a pool of water and look down and not see their own faces.

Both of these massacres bred anger and hatred, which stoked the killing machine. The Indians who killed the soldiers of the Seventh Cavalry at Little Bighorn didn't see

46 SACRED BUFFALO

THE END OF TIME

them as men. They were just whites. Fourteen years later, the soldiers of the Seventh Cavalry killed people at Wounded Knee without regard for whether or not they bore arms. They were just killing Indians. The people on both sides of those battles were faceless. The spiritual identity that controls human life had been replaced by murder—on both sides of the fence.

That hatred and anger is what's pictured on the Sacred Buffalo's hump bones.

Of course, you say, those battles happened long ago. At that time, land and a way of life were at stake. But now people kill over little things. A boy is killed because another kid wants his tennis shoes. An old woman is killed for her two dollars. Did someone accidentally bump your car? Kill them. People are full of hatred and their aggression is boiling over. Now instead of shooting arrows or firing a rifle, we have 30-round clip MAC-10s that destroy dozens of people. I guess I could have put the Los Angeles riots on the hump bones.

But it's not only the physical act of killing someone that destroys our human identity. We have to ask ourselves, do we care enough about our children, our wives or husbands, our parents to do the right thing for them? Because if we don't, on some level we're killing them. We warehouse our old mother or father in a nursing home as soon as we feel inconvenienced by the infirmities of their old age. We turn our heads when our children are sexually abused or slapped around instead of laying our lives on the line for them. We look everywhere but at the poor, down-and-out veteran begging on a street corner for a bowl of soup.

When the Navy stationed Beth in California, I moved out there with her. She had shown me a color brochure with really nice houses by the ocean. So the day Sundance ended in South Dakota, I drove to the West Coast. It was nothing like the colored pictures on the brochure.

We pulled into the area for dependent housing, and it looked like a prison. Concrete block houses stood side-by-side in the compound. There were people everywhere. I just

THE END OF TIME

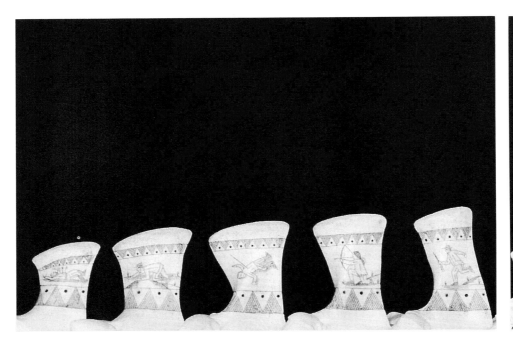 

went, "Oh, what have I done? I can't do this." But Beth told me, "We can try."

I wasn't there two weeks when some little fourteen-year-old boys pulled a gun on me in front of the grocery store. They apparently wanted to go in the grocery store door while I was coming out. They stood in front of me, and one of them said, "What's happening?" He pulled back his jacket and showed me the butt end of a .38 Smith and Wesson with a pearl handle.

I reached into my jacket like I was getting a cigarette and pulled out a .380 Beretta. I said, "Well, whatever, boys."

They melted away pretty quick.

When I got back to the house, I thought, "Those were children! What is this place about?"

Another time, I was just driving down the street when someone pointed the barrel of a double-barrel shotgun at me out the window of a car.

Everywhere you went there were people, people, people. We were living in a compound where people of different races were having a war over the drug business there. Military wives were getting raped in the middle of the afternoon in their houses. I could see death on those people's faces—like they were dead inside. I had no place to build a sweat lodge, no quiet place to pray.

I'm a warrior among my own people and other tribes. I'm a red feather. A wounded Indian veteran. I'm a Vietnam veteran. I've earned fifty-two eagle feathers in my life. For the last 100 years, my family has been involved in every war this country has fought. In the sixteen years this country was in combat in Vietnam, my family served nine-and-a-half years there. Out of that came seven purple hearts, two bronze and two silver stars, and the Cross of Valor. I've earned the right to live free and to live free from fear. My family paid for that right with their blood.

The Navy command decided to start a neighborhood watch in the

---

The End of Time

IF THE PEOPLE don't respect that Chanunpa, it will go back. And that will be the end of time.

—Jimmy Dubray

THE END OF TIME

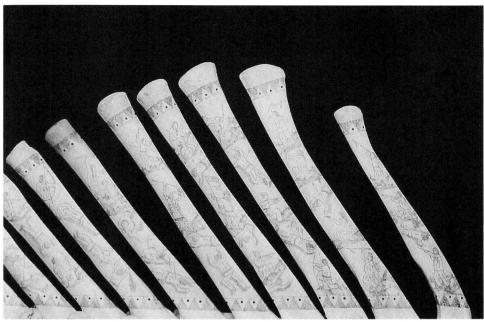

compound with the military wives walking patrol on the streets from 10 P.M. to 6 A.M. when most crimes happened. They held a meeting to lay out this plan. It didn't sound right to me. A captain got up and said he thought the neighborhood watch was great. I finally stood up and told him, "If it's such a good idea for the wives to patrol this area, captain, then you send your wife over tonight."

He just looked at me. I said, "You wouldn't give your wife's life. It's only a good idea when it's someone else's wife's life. But we're talking about dependents here. The word 'dependent' means that they're dependent on you. And I find it absolutely insane that the same people charged with providing security for a nation can't protect its own dependents. I can't have a sweat lodge here because it doesn't seem normal to you. I can't even find a place to pray here. And now—because I'm a dependent—you want me to offer my life up so you can send good reports to Washington, D.C. You want these women to go out and get shot at for something you get paid for providing."

People came up to me later and shook my hand. They said, "What's sad is that you're right. Every day people're shooting guns here, and our dependents have to live here."

It wasn't long after that meeting that I fell asleep in the afternoon and saw all those pictures of the seven sacred rites of the Lakota scrimshawed on the skeleton of that majestic Buffalo.

About four weeks after my dream about the Buffalo, I wrote in my diary:

"Today I start the Buffalo project. I will draw the Wounded Knee first. It's a hard one to do. I feel each person as they die. I know what it feels like to crawl to stay alive and the pain of children who are suffering. I visited my kids about six months ago, and when I said good-bye, I never wept so hard. I've never wept so hard as when I had to leave them. I felt like I was crying from the spine out. My son and daughter were

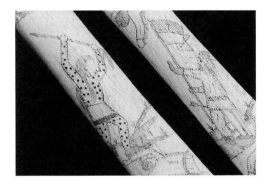

The Battle of the Little Bighorn is shown on the right side of the Sacred Buffalo's hump. In the sweltering heat on June 25, 1876, all of the men of the Seventh Cavalry led by Gen. George Armstrong Custer were killed and mutilated by Native Americans. Detail: Crazy Horse facing Custer.

SACRED BUFFALO 49

THE END OF TIME

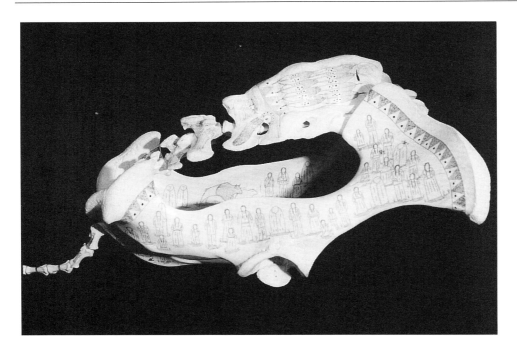

The sides of the pelvis show the result of men's and women's disrespect for life and the sacred ways: faceless, identityless, spiritless people.

Deadly Virus

THE ELDERS SAY that one day a disease is going to come along and wipe out most of the people. Death will be widespread. Who knows when that might happen? Maybe we're in our last days, I don't know. And I don't want to say what I don't know or to add to it or make up an account. I get sick every once in a while listening to people add on to stories. Then, I have to go to the hospital and use that medicine man doctor and that medicine woman nurse.

I will say this: one night I was driving in the Badlands with my brother and I saw a young man running beside the car. He nearly caught up with us, too. I thought,

sobbing. It's a sound I won't soon forget. It's this feeling I get when I draw the children of Wounded Knee.

"In my drawing of Wounded Knee, one man and one boy are alive, and a woman and a girl on a cradle board. They will tell this story for the future of all people. They will carry the burden of memory of crimes against all people—no matter what their race. There's also a horse dead. This shows the lack of respect for all life during this period of what they call 'building a nation.' We must all remember this part of history.

"The Custer battle is not about victory. It, too, is about death and pain. There were no winners in that battle. As I drew it, I felt sick inside my soul. The men are desperate and suffering in the worst way because there is no hope for life here in the Valley of the Little Bighorn. All of the years I've spent living here in South Dakota, I've never been to that place. A friend of mine camped there, and he told me you can hear the horses screaming at night. It scared him so bad that he packed up his camp and left. He talked to an old Crow man, and he told him the soldiers didn't bring their dead out, and the wanagis cry for their souls, and that an Indian man should never go there. I've not drawn any of the horses in this battle. It's not for me to do. I believe that an animal belongs to God and that they are innocent of all the things we humans do. God didn't leave them on earth; they are home with their relatives and the Creator."

Why did these massacres happen? Over dirt. Material things. Possessions. Railroads. Owning rangeland, and running your cattle on it, so you can sell them and make money. It's about money. These weren't spiritual wars. They weren't about, "All right, you Indians, this Christian way is the best and you're going to follow it." Or, "All right, you white men, the Indian spiritual way is the best and you're going to follow it." It was about dirt. Something you can touch—not something you can feel and you can live by.

And since those massacres, millions of people have been slaughtered in Auschwitz and Hiroshima and Siberia and the Congo and Guadalcanal and Iwo Jima.

You, of course, think that you're different than those soldiers and Indians who murdered one another at Wounded Knee and Little Bighorn. But ask yourself, what drives you? People are still driven by

THE END OF TIME

their desire for pleasure, power, and money. They've disconnected from their spirituality.

But inside the Buffalo's pelvis, the four men walking behind the white buffalo calf are just simple. They're following her back toward the Chanunpa on the skull. In my dream for the Buffalo, I saw the destruction of the earth as we know it. The Lakota were warned, according to Fools Crow, that fire will consume the entire earth, and that the earth will shudder. But my friend Jimmy Dubray believes his people can walk into the future if they follow the old, spiritual ways. If you follow the spiritual ways of the Christians, Jews, Buddhists, Muslims, or Hindus, you can walk into the future with a face. If you don't, well, maybe by the time we get down the line five generations to my great-great-great grandkids, this won't matter. Because it won't be about material things.

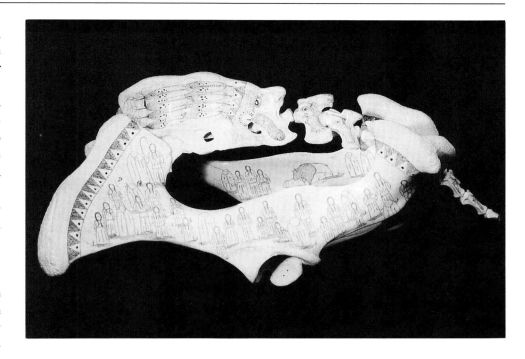

The message on the pelvis is "we're doing all the things Buffalo Calf Woman told us not to do," Big Jim says. He saw the end of time in a dream.

But then, again, it's a big world with lots of people making bad decisions.

Our world's in a bad way. When you were a little child, maybe you lived in a house with your mom and your dad. There was a white picket fence all around your yard, and when you went outside to play, all the rest of the world was beyond the white picket fence. Did you feel safe inside your house? Did you feel safe inside that fence? If your ball went over the fence, would you be safe if you went out to get it if you were careful and looked both ways? In the world we live in now, you don't have that security anymore. The world isn't safe. It has changed. You tell me, are we headed toward the end of time or toward recognizing the spiritualness inherent in all life? Have we lost what we once had as a people? You've lost your freedom to move freely about without fear. Your fear is real. Unsuspecting and innocent people are being killed and maimed in bomb blasts in federal buildings and subways. People are being gunned down in supermarkets and post offices. So you tell me, are we going toward the light or toward the end of time as we know it?

What is peace? Peace is standing in the middle of the Badlands in the middle of the night and hearing nothing but the wind. It's knowing that no one is going to shoot you, and looking up at the sky and seeing the most magnificent array of stars you've ever seen. Peace is getting up

Deadly Virus (Continued)

What? Gee whiz! After awhile, my brother and I stopped and put out some tobacco—my brother was asking for help with a kidney transplant. My brother went on back to the car, but I stood there praying. I picked my first root there in that spot, a root like a stick.

Wherever you look, there's medicine. If you're chosen to know, it will come to you. In that draw west of Boulder, Colorado, there's elk medicine and something else I use. You're in God's garden, and you don't even know it. There's a natural cure for all diseases. Even AIDS.

—*Jimmy Dubray*

THE END OF TIME

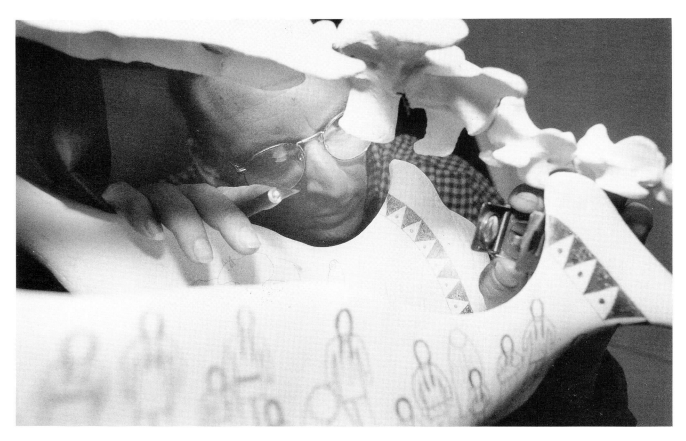

Big Jim checks the pelvis, testing to see if the bone is moist enough to be carved.

every day and not seeing race. Peace is feeding the hungry. Peace is sheltering the homeless with no strings attached. Peace is sticking out your hand to a person sick on drugs and alcohol and saying, "Come on, let me show you something better." Peace is fulfilling your dream. And in the process redeeming your own identity. Peace is the feeling of compassion for a small child who's dying. Peace is sitting down content at the end of the day knowing you've given someone a kindness. Washte. That's peace.

Do you want to know what nonpeace is? At night, when it's dark, take a flashlight and draw the beam of it down so you can examine the figures that raise their weapons in perpetual battle on both sides of the Buffalo's hump. Look at that man crawling to survive. Look at the man shot dead. Look at those little children shot dead. Look at them for a few minutes. That's nonpeace.

We're doing all the things Buffalo Calf Woman told us not to do. Even babies are being born without human identity. This is the most horrible thing.

Chapter 6

Carving the Buffalo

"The Buffalo was brought into the world by a child for the children of the world."

—BIG JIM DURHAM

"HEY, LOOK AT THIS."

Big Jim walks over to the bulletin board above the coffeepot and points to a small, newly printed color photo held by a red pushpin. The people in the photo have small, wistful smiles: Big Jim and Tommy and Beemer stand with a man and a woman and a little boy who looks to be about seven. The man has thick gray hair above a young face. The woman seems thin but resilient looking. Only the child beams with happiness, and his brown eyes sparkle. When you look hard, you see that his head seems unusually large and heavy for his little-boy body.

"That little dying boy is what the Buffalo is about," Jim says. "I'm grateful every day that Tunkashila chose me to do this. I'm grateful every day."

* * *

It was the cabinet-maker Mike Riss who indirectly made the connection between Big Jim and the little boy in the photo. Big Jim and Beemer wanted a buffalo skull carved out of cottonwood for the center of the stand Mike was building for the Buffalo, and Mike recommended his brother, Steve Riss, a Gillette, Wyoming, artist, hairstylist, and city councilman, for the job.

"The first time I went to visit Big Jim in Whitewood," Steve Riss recalls, "I took a few of my wood carvings to show him. My brother had told me they wanted someone to carve a buffalo skull out of cottonwood; he thought I might like to do it. I wanted to impress Big Jim with my ability, so besides my carvings I took along a clay bust I had made of a little boy named Matt Kristensen. Jim barely looked at my carvings; he only wanted to know about Matt. 'Tell me about that boy,' he said.

"I explained to Jim about Matt's genetic defect and its tragic consequences and how Matt has been a big inspiration to me.

"Jim asked me point-blank, 'Are you free from alcohol and drugs?'

"The question caught me off-guard, but I told him, yes I was, because Matt has made me understand I don't need to use alcohol. When I left, I felt that I had made a good connection with Jim and I might get to be a part of the Buffalo project.

"A week later, Jim and I were visiting again.

"'I had a vision this morning,' he told me, and he began describing two people.

"'You know, that boy is already in this circle,' he added.

"I didn't know what he meant, so he took me over to the Buffalo and showed me the right front leg where there's a scene of a man carrying his child away from the Sundance tree.

"'That boy has to come here,' Jim said. 'Can you get him?'

"I remember smiling and wondering what the Kristensens—who are Catholic and have never expressed any interest in Indian spirituality to me—would think about driving

Mark and Roxann Kristensen relax with their son, Matt, on the Sacred Buffalo robe. Big Jim saw the Kristensens in a vision, and later gave Matt the robe to use for as long as he needed it.

all the way to Whitewood from Gillette.

"Jim continued, 'Is that boy's mother short, with dark brown hair cut almost like a man's?'

"I nodded, surprised. That's Roxann.

"'Does his father have real straight hair?' Jim asked.

"I nodded again. As a hairstylist, I cut his hair, and I can attest that it's as straight as a board.

"Jim frowned. 'There's something that confuses me, though. In the vision, the man's hair is white, but his face is young. And he has the bluest eyes.'

"'That's Mark,' I said.

"I went home and phoned Mark and Roxann Kristensen: 'Can you go to Whitewood next Saturday?'"

Mark takes over the story. He and Roxann are sitting in Steve Riss's living room—they look exactly as Big Jim described them from his dream. Their son Matt's nose is pressed against the sliding glass door, beyond which Steve's springer spaniel is begging to come in. Steve lets the dog in and takes Matt and the rowdy pup into the kitchen to serve up some chocolate chip cookies. Matt's voice can be heard—bright and happy

CARVING THE BUFFALO

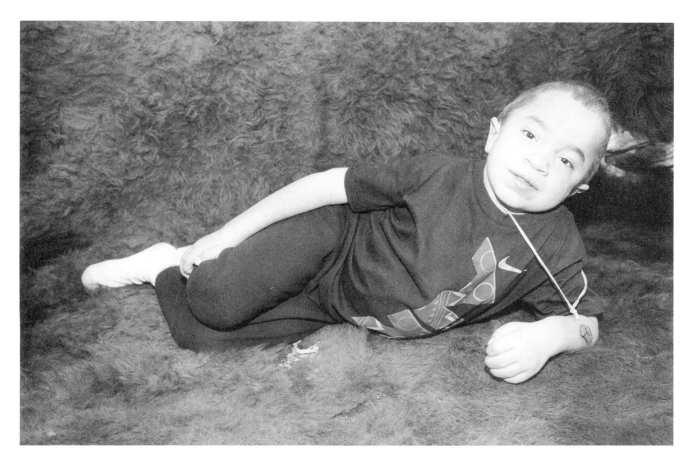

Matt lounges on the Buffalo robe. Matt has been diagnosed with Hunter's Syndrome, a degenerative disease, but Jim says his "man-sized spirit reminds me what it means to truly live."

and full of questions.

"We were scheduled to take our daughters to Spearfish for a swim meet the Saturday Jim wanted to see us," Mark says, "so we decided to drive the extra ten miles or so to Whitewood. Steve wanted to be part of the Buffalo project, and we wanted to help him. Of course, our curiosity about Jim's vision was part of it."

Roxann interrupts. "I was very apprehensive about going, I didn't want to get my hopes up. We've talked to doctors. We know what's going to happen to Matt."

Mark nods. "There's no earthly cure for what Matt has. He has Hunter's Syndrome, a genetic defect where everything in his body is clogging up, his organs are enlarged, and it's in his joints. His clawed hands are what caused us to take him to the doctor when he was four years old. When he was little, his neck muscles weren't developed enough to hold his head up when he fell. So the first four years of his life, everytime he fell, his head would hit and he'd get a big goose egg on his forehead."

"The disease will rob him of his hearing and sight," Roxann says softly. "He'll lose everything."

From the noise coming from the kitchen, Matt seems to be feeding the cookies to the dog over Steve's protests.

"The doctors say that when he starts to go, he'll lose one to two IQ points a month," Mark says. "Already, in an eighteen-month period, he has lost seventeen IQ points. We're on the downhill slide."

"Matt doesn't know," Roxann says. "He's only eight."

No one speaks for a moment.

Mark continues. "When he was diagnosed, we were counseled against getting hooked into trying to find a cure. Of course, we'd accept a miracle—in fact, every year that Matt lives is a miracle—but Roxann was apprehensive about meeting Big Jim."

She nods her agreement. "It seemed bizarre that someone could visualize our appearance. Steve's reaction was wow! But I thought, no, I'm not going to get pulled into this."

The Kristensens recall their first visit to Whitewood, and the long climb up the stairs to the second-floor studio.

"Big Jim looked down the stairwell at us," Mark recalls. "He's a big man, and he's even bigger when you're looking up a flight of stairs at him. His eyes look inside you. I began looking at the ceiling—at anything but him. Later Steve asked if we noticed that Jim's eyes filled with tears when he looked at Matt. But we didn't. Steve asked Jim how we compared to his dream about us. He said Roxann's eyes are lighter than he had seen."

Matt comes in from the kitchen cookie in hand. Steve banishes the dog to the patio.

"Matt, who is never shy, asked Jim, 'Where's the Buffalo?'" Mark continues.

"I wanted to see it," Matt says.

"As soon as I saw it, I felt it to be very spiritual," Roxann says.

She pulls Matt close to her on the sofa.

"Jim walked us around the Buffalo and explained a few of the drawings to us," Mark says. "He showed us the buffalo robe, which was folded up and lying on the floor. Matt flopped down on it and curled up. Later Matt asked Jim what he planning to do with the robe. Jim said he was going to paint pictures on it of how the Sacred Buffalo came to be. Then he asked Roxann and me to leave the circle. We stepped outside and watched as he smudged off the Pipe and put whatever is in his medicine bag on top of the smoldering sage. Then he picked Matt up and went and stood next to the Buffalo's skull.

"Then what happened?" he prompts Matt.

Matt beams. "He told me to put my hand on the Buffalo's head. Then he said an Indian prayer."

"I have no idea how long the prayer was," Mark says. "Before Jim started to pray, he closed the gate on the circle. Roxann and I felt like we were outsiders. It was odd, but once that gate shut, we were spectators. We just cried the whole time."

"And I kept wondering how Jim could hold Matt—at fifty-five pounds—up in one arm for so long with no apparent effort," Roxann says.

"I just closed my eyes," Matt says.

Jim was trembling and crying. Then he put Matt down.

"Jim picked up the buffalo robe," Mark says, "and brought it over to Matt and told him, 'This is yours for as long as you need it—as long as you want it. You do with it whatever you choose.'"

"We were totally shocked," Roxann recalls. "We didn't understand how he could part with something so valuable—especially when he didn't know us at all, or what we might do with it."

Matt smiles. "Then Jim asked me do I want the head. I said, 'Course."

"Jim told him, 'Today you are more of a man that we will ever be,'" Mark says. "Matt hugged him, and Jim just hung onto him."

Steve laughs. "It was so cute to see Matt hugging Jim. Jim's so big, and Matt can't open his arms very far."

Mark is suddenly serious. "The power of the words in there—Jim calls Matt Little Man—the emotion, the gift he gave Matt means so much to us. We're complete strangers, and yet he cares so much."

"Then they gave me a necklace," Matt says.

Roxann hands it to him, and he holds it up. It's a bear with a jagged arrow on it.

"Beemer gave it to him," Mark recalls. "Beemer went and got it and showed it to Jim and Jim nodded. Apparently Jim had given him that necklace."

Even after the Kristensens left Whitewood, they felt the Buffalo continued to change their lives. They began to realize the significance of four in their lives—a special number for the Lakota.

"I'm forty, and Matt's eight," Mark recounts. "It was February fourth when we saw the Buffalo. Matt was four when he was diagnosed in the fourth month of the year.

"And when we went out to get into our Suburban, we noticed that the metal plate on the door says Janesville, Wisconsin. That's where the white buffalo calf was born. Apparently our car was built there. The coincidences are incredible."

Once they took the buffalo robe home, they put it on Matt's bed. Mark would pull it up under Matt's chin when he tucked him in bed, and Roxann would pull it down when she went to bed.

"It weighs at least twenty pounds," Roxann says. "He was sweating."

But then Matt would wake up in the middle of the night and ask Mark to pull it up again.

"After a few nights, we said, 'Matt, isn't that too heavy to sleep under?'" Mark says. "Matt said, 'Dad, it feels like when you hold me.'

"We know its power. We know it's sacred. We took it to Matt's karate club to show the kids—he's in a club for people with special needs—and I've been going to various schools showing the kids the buffalo robe. Several hundred kids have crawled all over it. They love it. He's known at school as 'Buffalo Boy.'"

Mark makes it a point to sit in the hot tub with Matt several times a week; the moist heat seems to limber the boy's frozen joints, and the quiet time gives them a chance to talk. About three weeks after they had seen the Buffalo, Matt told him about a dream he had.

"Matt said, 'Dad, you're God's son.' I said, 'Yeah.'

"He continued, 'I'm your son, but I'm God's son, too.' I nodded.

"He said, 'You're grandpa's son, but grandpa's God's son.'

"This seemed pretty complex to me for a child, so I asked him, '"Are you studying this in catechism?'

"He said, 'No, God told me.'

"I was surprised. 'When?' I asked.

"As near as I can figure, it was the first night he got the buffalo robe. But it might have been later.

"I asked him, 'What does God look like?'

"'A ghost,' he said. 'He wears a dress.'

"'Did he tell you anything else?' I asked.

"'Yes, all of the kids in Wyoming are God's children. And when I go to heaven I'm going to wear hearing aids.'

"'Did God tell you that?'

"'No, but all the ghosts were dressed in white and had hearing aids to match.'

"We visited Salt Lake City shortly after that, and in the Catholic Cathedral downtown, there's a dome with painted angels. When Matt looked up and saw them he said, 'Those are like the ghosts in my dream.'

"It seemed a little incredible. But so many spiritual things have happened since we first saw the Buffalo."

Steve asks Matt to help him clear away the remnants of the cookie feast, and they disappear into the kitchen.

"I guess I've been trying to prepare myself for losing Matt," Roxann says, her voice quiet. "I don't think Mark has done that. That really hit me when we went to see the Buffalo."

"Our priest, Father Thomas Ogg, had already talked to me about accepting God's will," Mark says. "I thought I had already gone through the pain of it when Matt was diagnosed. But after I saw the Buffalo I realized I have a lot of denial. I'm not ready for the idea of his death. All the acceptance and understanding I thought I had, I don't have it. But I'm learning to let things happen and roll with them. Spiritually, I'm a changed man since I saw the Buffalo."

As he speaks, he's rubbing his heart with his left hand.

Roxann says, "I came away from the Buffalo with the realization that I've been very angry for four years—since we first got the diagnosis. But when I walked out of there, I had a serene feeling. I felt different. I wasn't angry."

Matt runs into the living room and crawls up on Mark's lap.

"The reason we met Jim and saw the Buffalo was because I very much wanted to carve the buffalo skull for the stand my brother's making," Steve says, coming in from the kitchen. "Now Matt's involvement in the project has taken precedence in my heart. I will still give all my heart and soul to that wood carving. When I start gouging that wood, it will be with love. But it has taken second place to Matt's spiritual connection with this. Jim told me that first day, 'You're the person we want on this project.' That was the best compliment he could ever pay me. He recognized that I am a good person, and most of my good spirituality at this point has come from Matt.

"Since I've known Matt, I've discovered what it is to know unconditional love. Almost none of us really know or practice unconditional love. Yet, Big Jim loves this little boy unconditionally. I think that's the only time in my life I experienced that feeling."

Steve Riss explains the clay model for the buffalo skull he'll carve out of cottonwood. The skull will be the center of the Medicine Wheel on the Sacred Buffalo's base.

CARVING THE BUFFALO

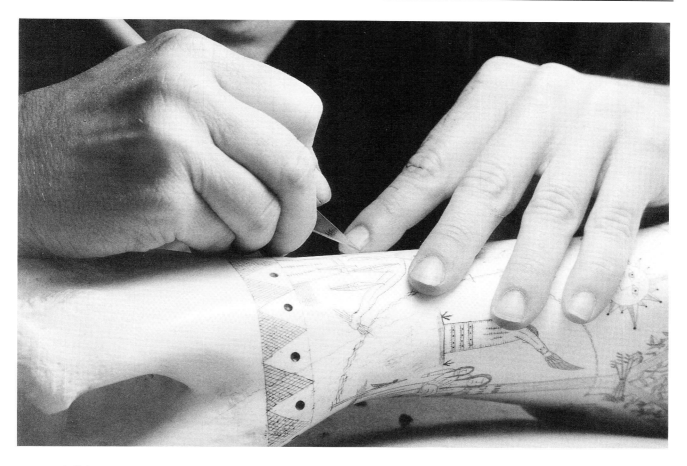

And did Roxann succumb to hoping for a miracle for Matt?

"Yes," she whispers. " I pray every night that God will take him away before the suffering comes."

* * *

Big Jim smiles, remembering the little boy Matt. "When I told Old Man Jimmy Dubray I gave the Buffalo robe away, he just laughed," he says. "He told us that people will come to the Buffalo thinking it has power and healing."

He leans back away from his table, his thumbs hooked in the pockets of his jeans. In the process of making his dream into reality, he's at the stage of carving the figures onto the bones. The big top bone of the right front leg—which the Kristensens saw, and which shows a man carrying a child away from the Sundance tree—lies cradled on protective egg-crate foam rubber on his table. At the front of the room, the Buffalo seems to dance on three legs.

What happened to that little child shown on the bone?

"She died," Jim says. "Jimmy says some people just wait too long, and there's nothing anyone can do. Others—well, Tunkashila takes them early. "

Jim glances out the window. He makes no move to pick up the X-acto knife and get to work. The late-winter sky is the gray of steel wool. The pine trees on a hill behind the schoolhouse look cold. Any glamour that winter might have held for Jim has faded. He

Big Jim carves the "healing" bone, the right front leg bone that shows the third day of Sundance. It is on this day that people come into the circle praying to be healed. Barely visible on the lower side, a man carries his daughter away from the Sundance tree.

Beemer

BEEMER—HARRY LINDSAY to those outside his motorcycle club—is smoothing out a rough spot inside one of the Sacred Buffalo's ribs. He deftly noses the triangular point of a detail sander along the narrow groove.

"On some bones I can't risk taking much material off because the top layer is too thin," he says.

The massive weight-bearing leg bones have a thick, rock-hard layer of calcium, the hump bones tend to be flaky, and the flared ends of the shoulder blades are so thin you can see light through them. Beemer spent 250 hours in the early stages preparing them for carving.

"I worked the bones over with coarse sanding drums on a Dremel first to take off the calcium deposits and smooth over any irregularities," he says.

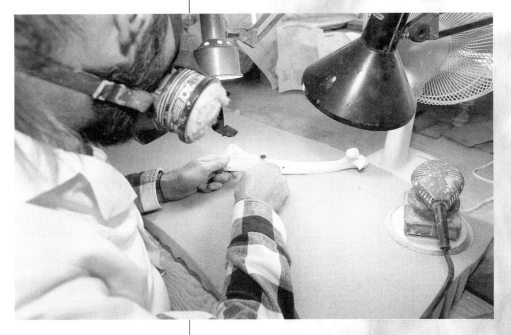

Beemer removes the coarsest calcium deposits from the bones with a grinder. A mask helps him keep from breathing the toxic dust.

A plan to work his way down through six different grits of sandpaper—all by hand—soon fizzled. "By the end of the first week, my fingers were bleeding, and the work was going very slowly," he recalls.

He and Jim were afraid that an orbital sander might remove too much material too fast, making the surfaces uneven, but Beemer's bleeding fingers made them turn to the mechanical solution.

"Actually, I was able to get a much more uniform surface than what I could have done by hand," he says. "Part of what I have to do from time to time is repair damage caused by someone sanding the bones by hand."

Beemer has worked with Jim on the project nearly from the beginning, doing everything from sanding the bones to bookkeeping to disassembling and reassembling the Buffalo eight times. The men met a decade earlier through the Vietnam Vets Motorcycle Club. Beemer is taller than Big Jim and slender to the point of being thin. His eyes are brown behind the round lenses of his glasses. His brown hair is pulled back in a ponytail.

CARVING THE BUFFALO

He speaks slowly in a deep voice worthy of a radio announcer, measuring out his words as though he never wants to have to take one back.

"When Jim first talked to me about this project, we were at bike week in Florida," he recalls. "He told me what he had planned to that point. He didn't ask me for anything. Then I heard someone who sounded like me saying, 'I can do the sanding on the bones.' And here we are."

Since he started the project, he has driven home to Ohio and back nine times in a '87 Chevy S10 that has just turned 243,000 miles. One hill on I-90 between Whitewood and Rapid City reminds him of time spent in Vietnam. It's a toadstool-shaped hill, green on top with a foundation of brick-red soil dissected by erosion. "You spend enough time in Vietnam, everything you have turns red from that dirt—your clothes, your bed, your skin."

Beemer still wears boots from his Vietnam days. He pulls them on one day before he builds the fire for a sweat lodge ceremony. "These boots are twenty-three years old," he says—almost the age he was when he got out of the Army. "Funny, I never expected to live."

The sweat lodge, he says, is where he started on the Sacred Red Road, and the road to the Sacred Buffalo. The Buffalo project isn't something everyone can relate to. He has tried to explain it to friends back home he thought might understand it, "but you just can't put it into words. I feel about it the same way I did the first morning I was at Sundance: the dancers were coming in, the sun was just starting to show over the horizon. My back was to the campgrounds, and all I saw was the Sundance circle and the dancers. You just stand there and feel the drumbeat coming up through your legs. It's the primal heartbeat. It was like I had been transported back three hundred years. Nothing else existed at that moment. And that was just the beginning. I barely recognized the power that was there. It really hooked me."

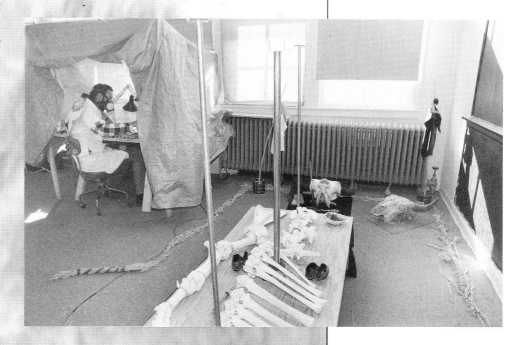

Beemer sands the Buffalo's bones smooth in a makeshift plastic tent that does little to confine the dust, and every surface in the Whitewood studio turns white under the chalky dust.

SACRED BUFFALO

reaches for a squeeze bottle of 4-Way Fasting Acting nasal spray for the sinus headaches he gets when a storm is coming.

"God, I miss my wife," he says suddenly. "It's been over a year now that we've been apart."

He gets up and returns the leg bone to the hochoka.

Then going to the blender, he dumps in a packet of Met-Rx Engineered Foods and adds a banana and some milk. For several weeks, he's been hitting the gym in Sturgis on most mornings and evenings, sculpting the muscles in his body with precision.

Steve brings a bone over to him and points to a penciled figure. "What if we moved her over here?"

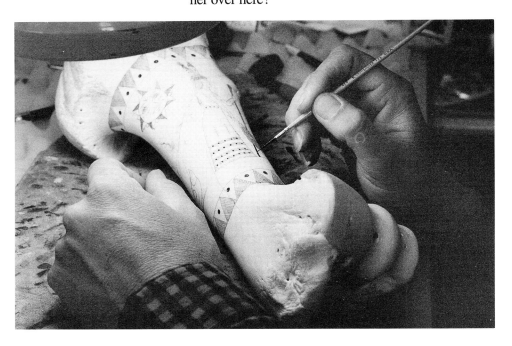

After the scenes have been drawn onto the bones with pencil, Big Jim cuts them in with a knife and then inks them with a pen or brush.

Jim sighs and shakes his head. "That's not part of the dream. We can't change it."

"But wouldn't it look better? I mean, hypothetically? If we could."

"There can't be any ideas added into this, Steve. It all came from a dream. It's gotta be like it's gotta be."

The phone rings. It's the bank saying a check supposed to cover the rent for the studio hasn't arrived from one of the project's financial backers. Jim tosses down the receiver. He strides to the back door and pushing it open takes a deep breath of the frigid air. Any problem that pulls his focus from the Buffalo is unwelcome.

"His mouth is writing checks his ass can't cover," he says to Beemer, closing the door. "People don't realize we listen to every word they say. And we never forget. I guess that's a poor quality in today's world."

Beemer sits at an old electric Smith Corona typewriter making up a time sheet. He types "name" and depresses the underline key—which automatically repeats across the page, then "date" and the underline key, then "work done" and the underline key. The metallic banging echoes off the walls.

"Don't do that, Beemer, " Jim says. "It's driving me crazy. You know veterans—it sounds too much like a machine gun."

The phone rings again.

"Oh, hi, Nick," Jim says and focuses down the phone line on the boy-becoming-a-man. His love for his son fills his voice and becomes so solid and strong that it bridges the long distance like a steel girder. From the conversation, you can gather that the handsome, blonde, brown-eyed teen is between school and supper, and that football camp is going to keep him from traveling to South Dakota to see his dad.

"You know I'd like you to come on out," Jim tells him, "but you do what you need to."

CARVING THE BUFFALO

There's a short discussion about homework and grades.

"I love you, too," he finishes. "And tell Crystal"—Jim's young daughter—"I love her, too."

Jim stands and paws through the clutter of his table for his lighter.

"I've heard that some people don't think I have the right to tell these stories," he says. "But I've lived these ceremonies for seven years. I'm the first breed to carry the skull at Fools Crow's Sundance. See that man"—he points to the right front leg of the Buffalo where the man hangs from the Sundance tree—"I'm one of those men holding that log. I could feel him breathing. I could feel him dangling at the other end—his every move. I could feel his suffering. I've suffered. I've been cut thirty-eight times in ceremony. I've lived without my wife for more than a year. I'm far away from my children. I've lost friends because of this project. I've had people who're afraid of this stick a knife into my back who wouldn't have done it if not for this project."

Jim and Beemer admire the five-year patch from the Vietnam Vets Motorcycle Club on Jim's black denim jacket.

He voice is husky with emotion. Beemer turns to face him, listening.

"Why have I done it?" Jim continues. "Because it was brought by a child for the children of the world. Like for that little boy Matt. I can see him when he goes. He has a smile on his face, and he's thinking of me and the Buffalo.

"I believe that for whatever reason, when the Creator makes us, he gives each of us a great gift. Some people learn to use that gift, and others never do. I told Steve that his great gift is emotion. That really big heart that makes him cry at movies is the magnificent gift God gave him. But he hasn't learned to use it for his art. Do you know the definition of a politician? Someone who can kiss a baby and then steal his candy. There's a disconnection between the heart and the act. Who am I to say Steve hasn't learned to use his gift? I just know. That's the stuff I understand.

"I see things about people. Old Man Fools Crow stared at me a lot. Like something was on me. I figure now, since I see so much stuff in my head, that he knew something about me before I knew it myself.

"For the rest of my life I'll remember that little boy Matt. I've seen and done a lot of things, but I've never seen anyone as big as he is. I'll remember him forever rubbing his little face on the buffalo robe. He was crying. He knows he's dying. I'll never forget that."

* * *

Big Jim and Beemer are getting ready to go to the annual motorcycle rally in Daytona,

The night before Jim and Beemer leave for Florida, work on the skull comes to a stop. A border penciled onto the jaws will later be judged "too heavy" for the delicate lines of Buffalo Calf Woman meeting the two hunters and will be erased.

Florida, and Jim wants his five-year patch from the Vietnam Vets Motorcycle Club sewn on his black denim jacket for the occasion. He rifles through drawers and trunks searching for the patch. Beemer has set up the sewing machine on the coffee table and sits waiting for the elusive patch to appear.

"I've lost my mind," Jim says, coming up patchless after tearing into another trunk.

"Of all the things I've lost, I miss my mind the most," Beemer says.

Jim telephones Beth in Virginia, and though she can rarely get away from her Navy post long enough to visit Whitewood, her long-distance suggestion is that he look in the trunk under the television.

Jim finds the patch there, and he and Beemer progress to trying to decide where to sew it and also a POW/MIA patch onto the jacket.

Jim holds the five-year patch on the right breast pocket. "It looks better here," he says.

"You want it there, you're going to have to sacrifice the use of the pocket or sew it on yourself," Beemer tells him. "I'm not going to sew it on by hand."

"But it's a balance thing," Jim muses.

"It's a personal thing," Beemer tells him.

Finally, the five-year patch is sewn on the bottom right side of the jacket and the POW patch goes prominently on the pocket. The men never forget the 58,044 soldiers—killed in action or unaccounted for—who never came home from Vietnam.

Chapter 7
Inipi, Making Yourself Pure

"The price of spirituality is suffering, and no one can suffer for you."
—BIG JIM DURHAM

IF YOU LOOK AT the natural world, there's no golden-domed cathedral and no million-dollar carving of a man nailed on a piece of wood. You don't need all of that to be able to talk to God. You don't have to put on a big show in order for Tunkashila to hear your prayer. If you're out in the woods with a prayer on your lips and a prayer in your heart, he doesn't look at you and say, "I don't think I'll hear your prayer today because you're not in a big, fancy church." A tree you drive by everyday on your way to work, an eagle wing, a little rock, a bagful of things that means a lot to you—these are magnificent representations of the Creator; learn to use them in your prayers. You can build a tabernacle with about twenty-eight willows and some tarps. Build a fire. Add some rocks and some water and your prayers, and you have a church. A place to pray can be as glorified as the Mormon Tabernacle in Salt Lake City, or it can be as plain as a sweat lodge. Both have the same meaning and the same spiritual value. God doesn't pay any more attention to prayers said in a Baptist Church than he does to the poor, pitiful prayers said in a sweat lodge. A sweat lodge may seem simple, but when you're in it praying and singing from your heart, you're opening the door on the Creator.

Fire seems simple, too—yet *peta owihankeshni*, the fire without end, is the basis of all of the seven sacred rites. You need fire to light sage or sweet grass and smudge yourself. You need fire to heat the rocks for a sweat lodge. You have to go into the sweat lodge before you can go on Hanbleceye, crying for a vision. You can't approach the Sundance tree without going into the sweat lodge first, so you're back to the fire. Everything begins with the fire. You can load the Chanunpa with tobacco and your prayers, but you can't send them up without having the fire to light the Pipe so you can smoke it. The fire is the beginning.

INIPI, MAKING YOURSELF PURE

On the Sacred Buffalo, both the sacred rite of the sweat lodge and the eternal fire are shown on the right rear leg—the North leg. People are inside the sweat lodge praying and playing the drum. On top of the sweat lodge, there's a bear robe with six stars and the sun and a magpie, which knows everything, for healing.

Fire is power. Water is power, too, but a different kind. It's just as strong as fire, but gentler in its lessons. If you stick your hand in water, you can leave it in for a while. But stick your hand in fire, and you'll pull it out real quick. That's power! Fire's a harsh teacher. Watch a fire, and maybe you'll be able to see the spirits rising up out of it. That's how I see fire. Or watch the fire in the sky—lightning—that pops and cracks and makes you jump. All those wachias going across the sky—crack, crack—they're beautiful.

Wind is power, too. Fire and water and wind belong to Tunkashila, and I've seen his power in the cleaning of the land with these forces. I've seen him spin a web of power with these forces that is so strong it can span a whole continent. Fire storms and tornadoes and hurricanes possess relentless power. The power unleashed at Hiroshima is nothing compared to the devastation they can cause. Fifty tornadoes in one storm can reach down like fingers touching the earth, as they did in Tennessee. Fire can consume thousands of acres of homes and trees as it does in California. Water can cover the land without regard for life and property rights as the waters in the Mississippi River did.

Whenever these forces of nature show themselves, stop and consider. If a tornado or fire or accident touches your life, take a look at it and see what it's telling you. Learn from that power what you need to see in your life and what changes you need to make. When something stops your world as you know it, ask yourself: "What am I doing with my life?" Are you loving your children? Are you respecting your aged parents? Are you living the true spirit of the Christian way—if that's your calling—or are you a Christian in name only? Are you teaching your children to have respect for others and all of nature? Learn to read the signs of the natural world for help in living your life.

In the sweat lodge, we learn how to live our lives. We purify ourselves there before we begin anything important—and we pray for guidance. There's a hochoka around the sweat lodge to keep out any negative influences. The Chanunpa is present. There's the drum and the singing of age-old songs. The fire and the water and the rocks and our prayers make the sweat lodge a very powerful force in our lives.

When I was in California before I started on the Buffalo, I built a sweat lodge on the Navy base. It was the first time in history that anyone had built a sweat lodge on a U.S. military base. When the Catholic priest found out I was building a sweat lodge on the base, he had a fit. He told me I couldn't do it, but I cut willow sticks and started digging holes. I told him, "If you can have your church here, I can, too. The Constitution says I have the right to religious freedom." He grumbled a lot. "Just tell me to tear it down," I begged him, but he wouldn't. When the sweat lodge was done, I gathered some rocks and fired it up and took me a sweat. People who had been in the military for twenty years

---

Four Directions Song

Look to the West. Your Grandfather is sitting there looking this way.
Pray to him. Pray to him. He is sitting there looking this way.

Look to the North. Your Grandfather is sitting there looking this way.
Pray to him. Pray to him. He is sitting there looking this way.

Look to the East. Your Grandfather is sitting there looking this way.
Pray to him. Pray to him. He is sitting there looking this way.

Look to the South. Your Grandfather is sitting there looking this way.
Pray to him. Pray to him. He is sitting there looking this way.

Look up above. Wakan Tanka is sitting above us.
Pray to him. Pray to him. He is sitting there looking this way.

Look down at the earth. Your Grandmother is beneath you.
Pray to her. Pray to her. She is sitting there looking this way.

—A Traditional Song

INIPI, MAKING YOURSELF PURE

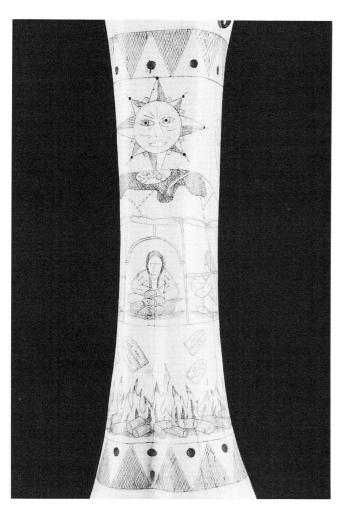
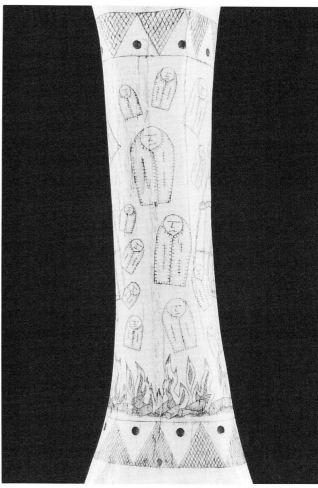

The rite of purification shown on the lowest bone of the back right leg is held inside the sweat lodge. Inside the lodge, the men play the drum and sing, calling in the Grandfathers. The Chanunpa is present. Rocks heated in the fire sit in the rock cradle in the center; water sprinked on them rises as steam. The bear robe on top, with its magpie feather, six stars, and sun, is for healing. At right are the spirits rising from the fire without end.

found out about it and came over wanting to take a sweat. I told them, "Grab a towel, take off your clothes, and let's pray." One day when I came out of the sweat lodge, I found this big submarine parked right behind it.

When you build the fire for a sweat lodge ceremony, you're helping people to pray. Your work at the fire is about helping people who don't have strength or the understanding to build it themselves. They don't have the strength to understand the prayer that goes into the fire. There's a lot of respect in being the fireman. Most people don't see it that way, though. They want to get right up where they think things are happening so they'll feel like they're important. They don't understand that you start at the fire because that's where you learn. I worked the fire for years. I carried the rocks. I got burned. In building the fire, you're building the opportunity for people to purify themselves and pray. People don't realize how important that job of fireman is.

Building the fire seems simple, and most people want to skip it and jump right up to feeling powerful. There's a saying we all follow: "Never teach people everything." I never teach someone anything until he's earned the right to know. You have to realize that if something has true power, it can be very destructive in the wrong hands. And on the other hand, if something doesn't have true power, then why should you bother with it? For example, a sauna feels nice; you go into a little room where fake rocks are heated

INIPI, MAKING YOURSELF PURE

The Spirits in Fire and Water and Rocks Can Make You New Again

AT THE SAME time the beautiful Calf Pipe Woman brought the people the Chanunpa, she told them about the sacred rites that would come to them in visions. These rites, she told them, would help them live good lives filled with many blessings. The rite of purification is one these. It is a ceremony for making your energy or spirit strong and clear so it in turn makes your body healthy and strong. Calf Pipe Woman showed the people how to ask the powers of the universe—the spirit of fire, the spirit of water, the spirit of the rocks from the earth—for help in the presence of the Chanunpa.

It has been said that the people knew about purifying themselves before Calf Pipe Woman came to them. Perhaps this is so. Perhaps not, for she brought the Sacred Pipe to earth long, long, long ago. But this much is true: in bringing the Chanunpa for the people to use in ceremony, the Calf Pipe Woman made the rite of purification holy.

If you were to go to a ceremony for purification, you would come upon a circular, domed lodge that is too short for most adults to stand up in. It is made from the branches of the willow tree and animal hides or blankets. In making the lodge, the men make a tobacco offering then cut an armful of long, slender willow branches, then bend them over and lace them with other branches and tie them together with strips of bark to make a strong frame. They throw animal hides or, more commonly, canvas or blankets over the willow frame and pull them tight to keep moisture from seeping out of the lodge and light from seeping in. In the West, or sometimes the East, but never the North, is a little, curved door so low that you have to get down on your hands and knees to crawl inside the dark lodge.

Today, this ceremony is often called the sweat lodge. People who don't know sometimes think it is like the familiar steam bath or sauna that cleans the skin. But the Inipi, the rite of purification, is a very special ceremony full of prayer and spirit. It is the first step on the path to the vision quest and to Sundance. It is what Calf Pipe Woman told the people they must do to get ready for any really special event in their lives.

The Inipi ceremony has circles within circles and circles. A big, round hochoka encloses the lodge—its prayer ties mark the four quarters. The lodge itself is a circle. Inside the lodge is a circle of sage along the outer edge. And in the center of the lodge is a shallow circle to hold the grandfather rocks.

Outside the lodge door, a few feet beyond the door, there's a circular fire pit where the blazing *peta owihankeshni*, the fire without end, heats the rocks for the ceremony.

When people need to strengthen or heal themselves through the purification ceremony, they go to a leader who understands the ancient ways. It is customary to offer him a Chanunpa to smoke, or at least ordinary tobacco, and to bring a good meal to serve after the ceremony. On the day of the rite, the leader asks a fireman to begin building the fire and gathering the rocks and getting the water. The fireman makes a platform of logs

INIPI, MAKING YOURSELF PURE

in the fire pit to hold the rocks. The first four rocks might be placed on the platform at the four directions, or six rocks might be placed to make the face of Tunkashila. He lights the fire, and it burns for hours as the rocks sizzle in the flames. As he works, he prays.

When the rocks are hot, the leader goes into the lodge. He smudges himself and the Chanunpa, and everything inside the lodge is made sacred in the smoke. He passes the Chanunpa out to be placed on the altar, a little hill of dirt like a mole's mound midway along the sacred path that connects the outside fire pit with the rock cradle inside the lodge.

You crawl into the lodge and go sun-wise, from left to right. In crawling, you remember how small and humble you are in the face of real power.

With everyone in place around the rock circle, the leader asks for the first rocks to be brought in. The fireman passes them in, and the helper beside the door uses two deer antlers to arrange them on the circle. The first rock goes into the center for Wakan Tanka, the One Who Is Everything. The next four go in the West, North, East, and South of the circle to honor the grandfathers in those directions, and the sixth one goes in the center for Grandmother Earth. All the rocks from the fire pit come into the lodge, none are left out.

The leader puts a pinch of *pejuta*, medicine, on the first six rocks, and the fragrant, green smell fills the close, little space of the lodge. When all the rocks are in, he asks that the bucket of water be handed in. The door is closed tight, and the lodge becomes dark and quiet.

The rocks glow red in the rock circle, and they seem to throb like a glowing heart as they radiate their heat. The heat pushes against you and past you and bounces back on you from the wall behind until you become the heat.

The leader lifts his voice in song and prayer and his words fill the soft space. He sprinkles the water on the rocks. The living water dances on the hot rocks, and the steam created from the union rises up and wraps around you until you become it. It is the hot breath of the rocks, and you feel its power.

It is said that stones—being very, very old—possess knowledge, and in the dark heat of the lodge filled with prayer, they speak. You as a person know what has been done, the spirits know what has been done and what will be done. Sometimes the messages are for someone present in the lodge, and sometimes they're for someone outside. Outside the lodge, even a small rock, held in your hand, can help you find the answers you seek. For the stone people are the grandfathers.

Prayers are said and songs are sung. The door is opened briefly four times during the ceremony with the words Mitakuye Oyasin. For in this ceremony, you share your blessings from the spirits with all of mankind and all the animals and the birds and all of nature down to the smallest worm. In the lodge, all are one.

At the end, when the leader has closed the ceremony, you crawl out of the lodge to stand in the light reborn. Your energy surges clear and strong, and it strengthens your body to use as you will.

Mitakuye Oyasin.

INIPI, MAKING YOURSELF PURE

> ### Four Grandfathers
>
> I TURN TO the four directions when I pray. Each direction has a grandfather sitting there.
>
> —Jimmy Dubray

by electricity, you throw some water on them and sweat and you come away refreshed. But a sauna is not the same as a sweat lodge, where you go to purify and strengthen your spirit through your prayers.

Watch, sometime, what actually happens at the fire in front of the sweat lodge. Someone who knows its power will stand beside it and drop something in and stare into the flames. He'll be asking Tunkashila for some special quality for that particular fire. Maybe he'll go over to the fire four different times and put in something different each time. Or maybe he'll go to one of the four directions, or to the prayer ties, and offer a prayer or some medicine. You'd never notice him if you weren't watching.

There's another old saying, "It's not for sale." I wish that were true of religion. People without any real spiritual knowledge try to run a sweat lodge—or a vision quest—for a fee. They learn to sing a couple of songs and to go through the motions and then they offer to run sweats for people who will pay the price. The people who pay have no idea how much preparation and prayer goes into running a real sweat lodge ceremony, or that the advisor for a vision quest must be spiritually responsible for them. At best, the people who pay to go to a sweat lodge just waste their time and money; at worst, they can be hurt bad.

Unlike religion, true spirituality isn't for sale. The price of spirituality is suffering, and no one can suffer for you. The sweat lodge is a truly sacred rite.

* * *

> ### Sweat Lodge Rocks
>
> ROCKS ARE VERY old—like grandfathers. They're sacred, and in the sweat lodge, they hear your prayers. You must collect rocks for the sweat lodge that haven't been used before. We go into the sweat lodge to purify ourselves, to become one with nature. We might have been thinking wrong about a person we met, or we might have thoughts about doing something wrong, or we might have harmed a person or an animal. We have to pray for things to be set right again, so we go into the sweat lodge to pray. We never start something important without going into the sweat lodge. We go to get spiritually and mentally fit for whatever is ahead. Going through a sweat lodge ceremony is tough, but after you accomplish it, you feel good.
>
> —Thomas Dubray

Big Jim: The Lakota Way is about suffering. You went into the sweat lodge yesterday for the first time. Did you suffer?

Reporter: Yep.

Jim: I heard Verdell Red Cloud tell you people, "We're in here suffering." We Indians give the Creator our suffering. We give him ourselves.

A long time ago, they tell me, Christian people gave flesh. Jesus gave the ultimate gift—his life. We Indians are still giving our flesh. We're still piercing at Sundance. We're still suffering. We do it because we realize our emotional attachment to our bodies and our comfort, and we want to give the Creator our best. This whole Sacred Buffalo is about suffering—the suffering and the belief of a people. Just look at it: those poor men pierced to the tree at Sundance, the drummers playing for hours on end, the people suffering in the sweat lodge. Now, when you look at that Sacred Buffalo and you see the Chanunpa and the hochoka and the sweat lodge, you know what those are about. You suffered for that knowledge. You paid for it. You earned the right to talk about it to some degree. You didn't get it for free. You didn't go to K-Mart and take out your wallet and say, "Wow, this really hurts my pocketbook." You paid for it with your suffering.

Verdell asked me last night, "'Can't you get one of those little electric engravers to carve the Buffalo bones?" I told him, no, that I have to use a knife.

INIPI, MAKING YOURSELF PURE

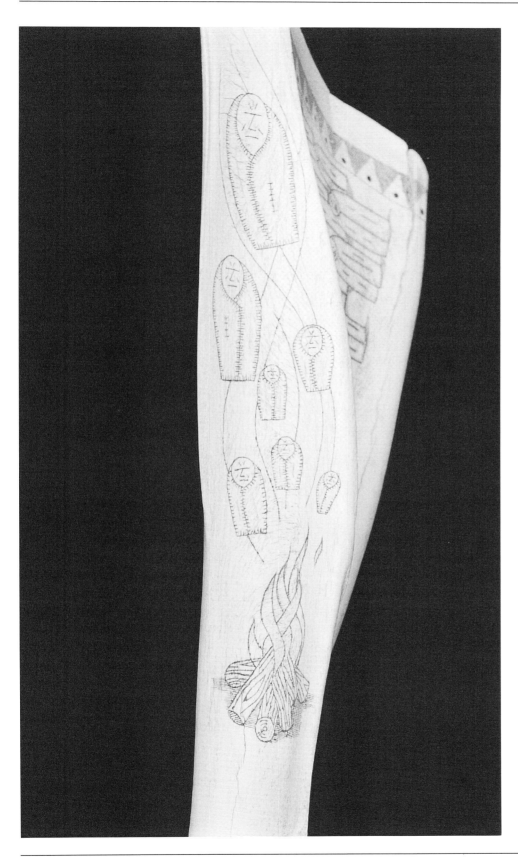

The seven spirits that rise from this fire on the left scapula represent the sacred rites. Fire is at the beginning of all the sacred seven.

Sweat Lodge

IN THE SWEAT lodge, we pray to Grandmother Earth, and we know she hears us as we stand on her surface—on her *chante*, her heart. We plead, and we pray that she gives us understanding first. We pray to the four directions. We give some of the water back to her that she gave us, some of the blood. When we come into this world, there's a little blood and a little water involved in our birth. When you go into the sweat lodge, you say, "Mother, I'm back." Gee, it's been hard for the young ones to learn to say that.

You have to have a good reason to go to the sweat lodge and pray. You have to look inside yourself and find the reason. You don't go lightly into these holy things where that Chanunpa is involved. You have to have a good reason to go up the hill to seek a vision. You have to have a good reason to go to Sundance. You need to walk a whole year giving thanks to the sun. Sometimes it takes three or four years before a person can get out and do these things. It's not an overnight thing.

When you go into the sweat lodge, remember what you pray. The Chanunpa is there, so don't lie! Make sure you remember every word you say. Sometimes you get nervous and you go blah, blah, blah, especially in a sweat lodge. You get so hot in there that you promise everything. A million words come out of your mouth. You promise that you're going to buy everyone a Cadillac. You come out, and whew! you're so glad to be out in the air. The next time you go in you forgot you promised a Cadillac, and you promise to buy a pickup truck for everybody.

—*Jimmy Dubray*

"Why not?" he asked. Because there has to be suffering, I told him. He understood. 'Washte, good," he said. "You do it your way."

We have to suffer to create the Sacred Buffalo. We get cut, but it doesn't matter. When we're building a sweat lodge up at Bear Butte and someone accidentally cuts a big chunk of flesh off their hand, someone else yells, "*Wopila*. Thanks." Because a flesh offering has been given. Some people say that's masochistic, but it's not. Nothing gets serious until we start talking about taking your hide. I can take your coat and you might complain, but when I say, "I think we'll get seven fleshes from you." Whoa, that's different! It's about pain and belief.

Reporter: How did you learn to go through the pain to the prayer?

Jim: Once when I was a boy, my twin brother and I were playing baseball. I was catching and he was pitching. On one crazy pitch, I got hit in the side of the head with the baseball. I had been a .350 hitter before then, but after that I got scared. I'd step back out of the batter's box every time I swung. I was afraid of getting hit again because it hurt.

One day my dad came out of the house, and said, "Go to the barn and get that bucket of baseballs." He told my twin, "Go get that catcher's mitt. I'm going to teach Jim not to be afraid of that ball."

My dad put me up to bat. He pitched the first ball, and I swung and stepped out. I did the same thing on the second, third, and fourth ones. Each time, he'd holler, "Don't be a coward, it doesn't hurt all that long."

The next time I stepped back, he threw the ball at me and it hit me in the back. I dropped the bat and grabbed my back. He threw another ball and hit me again. He hit me with about ten baseballs. I dropped to the ground. Then he just walked into the house.

I never stepped out of the box again. Sometimes I'd step in front of the ball just to get on base. The reason was, I could deal with the pain. It's like being scared when you go into a dark room; once you get in, it's okay because there's nothing there. Baseballs can only hurt you a certain way. Once you feel it, it's old pain—not new pain. You can learn to deal with it.

Reporter: Most people's reaction would be, "This hurts, I want to get away from this." How do you stay there and go into prayer?

Jim: When you're going to be pierced, you've prayed your prayers, and you've come to give a gift back to the Creator. You go to the Sundance tree and you touch it, and you feel warm and good, and then you lay down to be pierced. Of course, you always feel a little fear. But when you look up at the tree, your mind goes away. You lose yourself in the beat of the drum. You take comfort from something in your mind—to me the drum is my mother's heartbeat. Like when you're just little and you lay on your mom's chest and listen to her heart beating. All you hear is thum, thum, thum, thum. You remember all your prayers from the beginning to the end, and they're all you can think about.

Reporter: When Indian and non-Indian people get hung up on pain, what is the failing?

Jim: Their fear of pain. They think about the pain.

Reporter: Is the problem not the pain then, but the fear?

Jim: Oh no, it hurts. It really hurts. It's the pain that causes the fear. They think, "If it hurts this bad now, how bad is it going to hurt if I start pulling harder?"

You watch them. They're all proud at first, then once that pain hits them, they say, "Oh, God!" and when they hunch over, they're in trouble. Their shoulders come forward to try to keep it from hurting. They've lost the prayer. If they'd stay in their prayer and quit thinking about the pain—just use it or make it their friend or whatever—they could handle it. It's like life pain: the pain of being an alcoholic, pain of regret, pain of loss, pain of being with Vietnam veterans who have problems. It's the same thing. Learn to use it instead of fighting it.

There was a young piercer at Sundance a year or so ago who starting crying. He was hunched over like a hawk protecting his prey. He was scared. It hurts, and the hurt is real—people who come out there just for the status symbol of the scars are generally the ones who can't make it. They want some scars so when they take their shirt off, people will say, "Ah, a Sundancer." But they get scared of the pain. They think it's going to hurt worse and worse. To me, it's like the baseball pain. It can only go so far.

Reporter: They told me at the sweat last night that the third round would be the worst. It was so hot right in the beginning I didn't think I could stand anymore. I thought my hair was going to combust. But moment by moment, you manage it.

Jim: Nobody has caught on fire yet. I've been in the sweat lodge when it's so hot you can't even open your eyes. Your skin starts to blister. You hear people hitting the ground. Bam, and they're down. There's the shock of being confined in a place where you have to do one of two things—you make it or you don't. You have fear, you have pain—but think, in only two hours, you were given so many gifts. Where did the strength come from to stay there? Each person in there had a little something to offer. You thought, "I want to run. No, I don't want to weaken these other people with my weakness." So you stayed. I told you before you went in that you'd fall flat on your face. You thought, "No, I won't."

Reporter: After awhile, I knew I wasn't going to pass out.

Jim: I never expected you to hit the ground. The only reason I said that was so you'd fight me. You asked me for help. Well, that's the way it comes.

Reporter: I decided that being involved was my choice, so I just quit whining.

Jim: Some people think that Indianness is highly overrated, but it depends on who's administering it. I already knew what was going to happen: I knew there'd be fifty rocks and two five-gallon buckets of water. Verdell's is the hottest place on the planet to sweat.

Reporter: I kept thinking, I helped gather these rocks and now look!

The Four Directions

WE SING THE four direction song to acknowledge the four winds. And we acknowledge the spirits of the animals associated with these directions as our brothers.

West is the home of the Thunder-Beings and, with them, the horses. The thunders have tremendous influence over our lives. They bring the rain.

The buffalo is in the North. The buffaloes live among the pine there, so when you want to get the fire hot, you use a little pitch pine. It burns fast.

In the East, there's the black-tailed deer. It used to take a real good warrior to run one down on foot because these deer are faster than white tails. If we're up early in the morning, like we should be to greet the morning sun, we know they're up chewing on the soft grass. The black-tailed deer is life, it's healthy food, it's good medicine.

The South are the winged ones. When the winged ones come back in the spring, you don't need a calendar. When the ducks or geese fly over, you know the warmth is coming again and life will be good.

All these four directions are interlocked into our everyday lives. So every day we sing the four directions song. People may say the Lakota way is pagan, but that's not so. We don't pray to that animal, instead we're saying that we're all together in the universe as one. We honor the four winds and the animal spirits in a way that respects them, that says "you help me survive, and I'll help you survive, and we'll go through life like that." That's what that four directions prayer means. We praying as brother to brother.

—*Thomas Dubray*

> ### Prayers Beside the Fire
>
> I STARTED AT the fire. The head fireman told me a lot, but he always left something out. That gave me space to think about it, and then later on, we'd talk. I recognized that even though I'd turned my back a long time ago on everything spiritual, I was standing at the edge of something powerful.
>
> When I start a fire, the first thing I do is scout for material. I pray on it and give a tobacco offering to the Grandmother Earth for the gifts we're about to use—for the wood and the rocks and the water. I do this to show proper respect so that everything is done right and our prayers in the sweat lodge are heard.
>
> The first two logs that go into the fire pit are the thickest—about six inches in diameter and four feet long. They are placed lengthwise West to East. Next, twelve smaller logs, about the thickness of a man's arm, are cut and laid across the others like a platform. Rocks gathered from the river are placed on these.
>
> I enjoy preparing the fire. Some people think it's a lowly job because it's hard work. It is hard work, plus your face gets seared from the heat of the flames and hurts doubly when you go into the heat of the sweat lodge. But I really enjoy the fire because everything of importance starts with the fire. I've learned to look for the spirits in the fire, to watch the sparks, to watch the way the flames move. Attitude is really important when I'm working the fire because it affects everything I touch.
>
> —*Beemer*

Jim: I did little special tricks with the fire to help you guys out so the rocks would be good and hot. But I didn't get in there with all you people, did I? There were women in there, and I don't sweat with women I'm not related to, and I don't sweat where it seems to be a contest. The sweat lodge is about prayer. It's about life. You've got to experience it to learn from it.

Beemer used to ask a lot of questions. He wanted to learn everything right away. But if his lessons were going to be good ones, he needed to earn them one at a time. Over the years he's learned that patience is the only true friend we have. Like for a sniper. Time is a sniper's only true friend. Patience is our only true teacher. Learn to use time like pain, and it becomes your friend.

When you try to mesh the non-Indian world with the Indian world, the hardest thing to understand is that it is time that will teach you what you need to know. It's when you get eager and try to make things happen faster that you make mistakes. Maybe your mistake will hurt you or someone else. I knew you were going to fight me and that, no matter what, you weren't coming out of that sweat. So now you know about strength and a little more about lessons and about help—Indian help. Non-Indian help is about "give me your hand and I'll help you up out of that hole" while Indian help is about "I'll help you learn how to pray to get yourself out of that hole."

Reporter: Everything I needed to get through that moment was there.

Jim: Learn to pray. I tell people who want to go into the sweat lodge, "You better learn to pray now." I saw one last week who didn't. He came flying out of that sweat lodge. Then all he did all night was make excuses for himself. In shame. Well, really, there isn't any shame involved in coming out. You didn't know that, did you? You could've come out of that sweat lodge anytime, and nobody would have thought anything about it. It's between you and the Creator. That's all. You had the key. All you had to do was to say "Mitakuye Oyasin," and then leave.

Chapter 8
Hunkapi, Making of Relatives

"I base my decision to make a man my brother on whether I'd be willing to die for him. It has to be thought about."
—BIG JIM DURHAM

IN TAKING A MAN as my brother, I bring my father a new son to honor him.
Taking a friend as *hunka*, a relative, is a happy time filled with the richness of joy. It's a time of putting on a good feed and giving gifts, it's a time of realizing that your family has grown in direct proportion to the number of kids he has and brothers. You don't just gain a brother, you get new sisters, nieces, and nephews. You're all one, big happy family then. That's what the Hunkapi means to me: "We're all in this together."

The Hunkapi ceremony is shown on the right back leg of the Sacred Buffalo. Before the sacred rite is performed, the little boy looks different from the people he's standing with. But afterward, he's the same as they are—he's family—and he has a *wiyaka*, an eagle feather, to show his new status. They have honored him during the ceremony by giving him an eagle feather.

One of the saddest things I ever hear a person say is, "I'm an only child." That's too bad. A man who has a large family is a rich man. There's richness in life when different people come together. If one has a tragedy, another can help. When a father passes on, his children aren't fatherless because another father can take over and be responsible for them. When the veteran Bill died, his three children gained many fathers. Through the making of relatives, there's never a gap.

Your responsibilities to your new brother are the same as to your own family. Financially, emotionally, whatever—you must be there for each other. If he wants to borrow your truck and you know he's responsible, you lend him your truck. If he has a history of bad driving and he's been denied insurance, you don't. You treat him exactly as you would your family, because he is family. And all the people related to your

HUNKAPI, MAKING OF RELATIVES

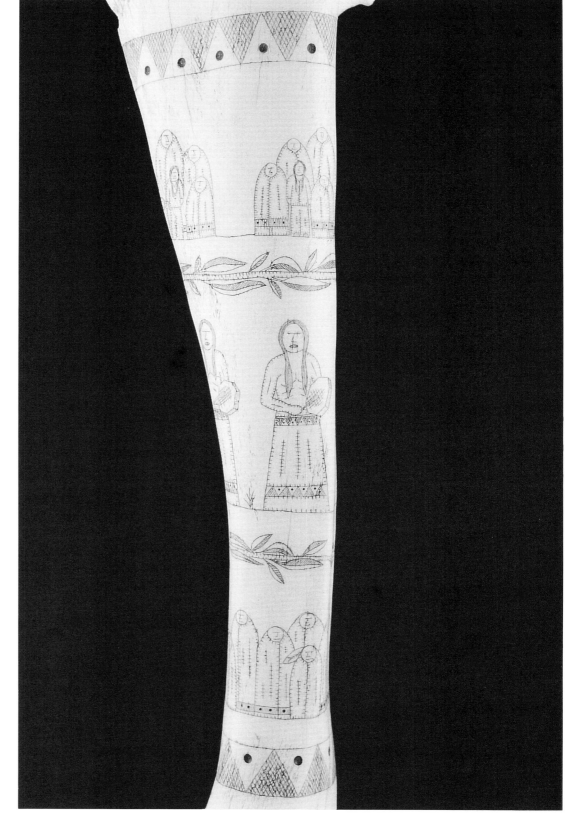

The rite of making new relatives is shown on the middle bone of the back right leg. At the top, the little boy looks different than the family around him. But then the Hunkapi ceremony is held—drums are played and songs are sung and a great feast is eaten, and the little boy becomes just like his new family—except that he has been honored with the gift of an eagle feather.

relations are related to you—whether hunka or natural. For this reason, it must be a family decision to take a person as a relative. Recently, when I took Dr. Keith in Oklahoma as my brother, I took his three daughters as my nieces and his wife as my sister-in-law. Later, when I drove Nick down there to visit them, I told him, "These are your sisters."

Some people view the responsibility involved in the making of relatives as being a real negative. Today, many people don't exercise their God-given right and ability to have children because they don't want to support them. "I can't afford kids," they say, or, "I've got one kid, and I can't afford another." It's a sick society that creates the climate where people think that giving life to a child costs too much money and where people aren't willing to share.

I see the richness in getting a new uncle, a new grandpa. In a big family, you're never without a relative to help you. There's always someone there for you. And you're always there to help someone else. Having family is the most beautiful thing in the world.

For me, choosing a man to become my brother is based on respect. I respect and care very much for all my brothers. I base my decision to make a man my brother on whether I'd be willing to die for him. It has to be thought about. You have to watch a person for a long time before you decide to make him your hunka. Because once he's family, you do whatever you can to help him.

* * *

ONE OF MY SONS is a spirit. This is James Dubray speaking. I took a spirit for a son. He scared me when I first saw him because he didn't look like anything I'd ever seen, but later I adopted him, and now he's one of my boys.

I decided to get my sons Chanunpas. Their uncle was a Yuwipi man, and he told them how they must earn them by obeying all rules he gave them. When the time came for him to bless their Chanunpas, he said, "You boys are going up on the mountain where Tunkashila will see you standing there with your Chanunpas. But I will do the praying here." Those boys didn't sleep at all that night on the mountain. All they could do was pray—or a man was there standing with them. He was a man with all sorts of animals in him. From his waist down he was shaped as a buffalo, and his head was a buffalo. I saw him, and he scared me, but I adopted him as my son. I always count him now as one of my boys.

Walking the Sacred Red Road

CALF PIPE WOMAN brought us seven sacred rites that would keep us on the Sacred Red Road if we followed them. Many people have come to me wanting to know about the sweat lodge, Hanbleceya, Sundance. They don't much ask about the others. Sometimes the word "traditional" is used to describe the sacred ceremonies as a way of putting them in the past. Like they just exist in history. I've heard people call them "myths" or "legends." They don't realize that spiritual people still believe in and perform these seven sacred rites. The making of relatives, the keeping and releasing of a soul, the making of a woman—all of these are done year round. All them are done at Sundance, although almost no one notices. They are done by special invitation. The wise ones are invited. And the sickly and the misfortunate and the orphans. It's not like Christmas where I give you something and you give something to me. Or a party where someone wants to be seen so he'll invite a huge crowd. The real ceremonies are done quietly. The Chanunpa taps a power that is very real for those of us who pray with it and respect it.

—Jimmy Dubray

The Holy Grandfather

JESUS SAID, MY Father and his Father and I are one.

—Jimmy Dubray

Making Relatives, Making Peace

THE HUNKAPI IS one of the sacred rites made holy by the Chanunpa. It is the rite of taking someone as your brother or father or child—making him exactly as close to you as if he were born into the relationship.

No one now can remember who first used this ceremony to take new relatives. It has been said that the ceremony first came in a vision to Bear Boy, a Lakota holy man, to establish a lasting peace with a tribe that was at war with the Lakota. He dreamed of an ear of corn—which the Lakota didn't grow then—and when in his travels he came upon a patch of corn, he knew that he should make relatives of the people who grew it. Through this ceremony, he made a bond with them that will endure until the end of time.

Another story is told of a chief who had four very brave warrior sons. Each of his sons was killed in the line of duty to the people, and the chief was inconsolable. He mourned his young sons so very much that he gave away all of his possessions and all of his wife's possessions and went up on a hill to sit with his grief.

The chief sat on the hill for a long time until he had a vision. The whirlwind spirit came to him and spoke to him. "Go north into the pines," it said, "until you come upon a tipi standing alone." It told the chief to bring back whatever he found in the tipi.

The chief traveled far north into the land of the pines, and the fourth day he came upon a lone tipi. He went inside and discovered a little baby boy and a little baby girl. The chief brought them back with him and adopted them as his own son and daughter. The people were so happy for him that they held a big feast. The boy grew up strong and brave and girl grew up industrious, and both were a great credit to the chief.

Through this sacred rite, the people could take a stranger as family. It is said that when you take a person as a *hunka*, a relative, you forge a bond with him or her that lasts forever. You honor a man—and do him a great favor—when you choose him as a father or a brother. You honor an older woman by taking her as your mother. You honor a little child in taking him as your own child. When you become kin in this way, you are true kin just as though you were the same blood.

In the old ways, the chosen hunka was bound to help his new brother in every way—even going into war with him. If his new brother became ill, he'd help pay the medicine men. If his new brother took children, he'd help care for them. If his new brother grew poor and hungry, he'd give him food and clothes. This is still true today. Deciding to honor a person by adopting him as your father, brother,

HUNKAPI, MAKING OF RELATIVES

or son is a grave decision, and once you do so, you are expected to follow the old, honorable ways of taking responsibility for all your relatives.

Traditionally, when a man wanted to make another man his brother, he would first discuss it with three trusted friends. Today, a man should discuss his plan with his brothers and father for the person he will make his brother becomes his brothers' brother and his father's son. He then asks the man he wishes to honor—or in the case of a little child, someone who can speak for him or her—for permission to make him a relative. If the honor is accepted, then a big feast is planned.

In the traditional rite of making relatives, two wands with hair from a horse's tail are waved over the two people becoming relatives to represent the sacredness of the Calf Pipe Woman. An ear of corn represents survival of the two. Sometimes the two new relatives are painted with a red stripe to seal their relationship in the spirit world.

In preparation for the Hunkapi ceremony, the men who will become brothers invite many people to come join them. It is a happy time of giving many gifts. Sage is burned, and then sweet grass. Songs are sung. The drum is played. The man who has asked to honor the other by taking him as a brother presents him with an eagle feather. If it is a woman who is being made sister or mother, she is given an eagle plume. For no bird is more revered than the eagle since he is a messenger of the spirits. The Chanunpa makes the rite holy, and the men smoke the Sacred Pipe together as brothers.

Taking a person to be your relative forges very special bonds of peace. There is the bond of peace between two people who honor each other and accept each other as brother or father, sister or mother. In this way, neither will ever be lost and alone and uncared for.

There is a bond forged between families and communities and the people of the men and women who choose to become relatives.

And there is the peace that comes from knowing that we are all one—no matter what our race or background. It is said that Wakan Tanka is everything and is in everything, and in the making of relatives, we understand that we all are one with the universe.

Mitakuye Oyasin

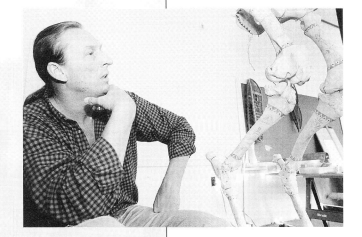

Big Jim explains the details of the Hunkapi, where the bone shows the little boy wearing the eagle feather his new relatives have given him.

Prayer Ties

PEOPLE DIDN'T ALWAYS have cloth to use in making a *wopahta*, a prayer tie. Maybe our ancestors used buckskin or a leaf to wrap their tobacco offering. Or maybe they just offered the tobacco itself. Nowadays, some people use the colors of the Sundance grounds in their prayer ties—black, red, yellow, and white. Some say they represent the races. That's their version of it. Here's mine:

Black is the night that comes and takes away your cares of the day. What you did yesterday is gone with the new morning.

Red reminds us of the Sacred Red Road. Red tells us that if we think of and do only good things, we can stay on the path that brings us and our families many blessings.

Yellow is the morning sun and the dawn that brings us new life. Everyday we are new again. Yellow asks, what are you going to make of today?

White is a reminder that some day you'll be standing in front of the Creator, pure—without guilt—because someone has taken your sins away for you. You're set free. White is for asking for forgiveness and forgiving others.

All of these colors come down from the sun. Blue and green and violet and all the colors of the rainbow come down to us from the sun. Each color is like a prayer tie. Full of hope.

Some people are actually selling tobacco ties at so many dollars a yard. Those three-dollar medicine men aren't medicine men at all—all they see are dollar signs. They say that if the Catholics can sell the rosary, they can sell those. But how can you know what kind of prayers have been put into those ties?

You have to make your own prayer ties and put your own prayers into them. But the prayers you make—are they just words, or are they meaningful? Are they heartfelt? Or are you making them because you see someone else doing it? If you pray with your heart and then walk everyday with your prayers, you become them. Your life becomes a prayer. The Creator is with you all the time.

After you've made your prayer ties, take them somewhere where there's no one around and hang them in a tree. Or if you keep them with you, burn them once you've received the answer to your prayers.

We talk about using cloth to make prayer ties, but actually your skin is your cloth. Before we started this book, we smoked tobacco in my Chanunpa—which once was Grandpa Fools Crow's. The smoke went inside you, and it came out. You said a prayer. You are the tie. Your skin is the cloth. This is good.

In Christianity, when they talk about communion, they say that Jesus gave his body to us, which is the bread of life. He gave his blood, which is the blood of life. In the Lakota Way, we give of ourselves to the Creator in return for his blessings. Look around your house; you might view all your possessions as being yours, but they don't really belong to you. The only thing that's 100 percent yours is your flesh and blood. We Lakota give our flesh back to the Creator, and we give him our blood. A flesh offering is a little piece of skin that's wrapped in a prayer cloth for a very special prayer.

—*Jimmy Dubray*

Chapter 9
Carving the Buffalo

"Every line is a prayer. Every day is a prayer."
—BIG JIM DURHAM

A SMALL DESK HAS been shoehorned into a space near the windows beside Beemer's plywood table. A woman sits there intent on one of the Buffalo's ribs. She's working at carving the thousands of lines that make the shading on the rib's wiyakas, the feathers. A weak spring sun lights the red in her long brown hair. Big Jim towers over her, watching her work.

"Lay the knife down on that cut. It'll give you a smoother cut. Don't be afraid to cut with that blade. That's just your fear coming up."

She makes the adjustment to his satisfaction.

"You know how to get your work as perfect as it can be?" Jim asks. "You live the story in your head as you're carving it. Visualize what you're carving and you'll do a good job. Play it over and over for as long as it takes you to finish."

Teri nods.

"Do you know what these wiyakas are?" Jim asks.

"No. But they're beautiful."

"They're all about spirit. The wiyakas on the outside of the ribs represent spirits. Each of them represents a person, 163 people. As I look at each one, I think about a different person I've known. The wiyakas each have individuality; they're fat or thin, crooked, each is unique. Like people are. They are *Wanbli gleska wiyakas*—spotted eagle feathers."

Teri goes back to work. Jim opens the back door that opens onto a fire escape and surveys the coming spring. The wind is still cold, but the hill behind the schoolhouse shows signs of greening. Days like this turn a man's mind toward motorcycle riding.

Teri comes from a part of Jim's dream about the Sacred Buffalo.

Teri Krukowski came from Florida to help scrimshaw the feathers and spirits on the Sacred Buffalo's ribs.

"We were in Florida at a friend's house," he recalls. "Teri was there engraving a silver bell. I knew her a little; she had prayed with us once at the Vietnam Veterans Wall with the Chanunpa. I was sitting there when she came over and held a little scrimshawed bone under the light so I could see it. I remember noticing her hair. I had been wondering when the brown-haired woman would show up. I asked her, 'What color are your eyes?'

"'Brown,' she said.

"'Let me look in your eyes,' I told her. I saw a light spot in one of them just as I had in the dream.

"I considered her work, and I considered the help she needed to go on through the rest of her life. It was all there. So I explained the project to her, and I said, 'If you're the one, you'll be ready to leave for South Dakota on Monday.' It was Friday.

"I called Beth in Virginia and told her.

"'You mean the brown-haired woman you've been waiting for?' she asked.

"'Yeah, I'm taking her back to South Dakota.'

"Beth said, 'Hmmm, sounds like another person has found their way there.'

"It's like Jimmy told us: we all need healing. That's who the Buffalo draws to it. People with a need for peace. I told Beemer, 'She's not a whole human being. I saw a vision of her in the sweat lodge, and she didn't have a face'—meaning she had no identity of her own. Her identity came from someone or somewhere other than that beautiful place inside her. So maybe the Buffalo brought her to it to give her back her life," he finishes.

Teri nods. "It didn't take me long to decide to come up here," she says. Her words twang with some hybrid Southern-style accent. "Jim Bear told me, 'Don't take a whole lot of time thinking about this.' So I just said yes, and here I am."

Her eyes settle on the Buffalo, which stands without the ribs that are being carved and inked.

"It's like Jim Bear said"—the name comes from his motorcycle club name Running Bear—"part of me is blank. I've known that for a long time, but I didn't know how to get rid of that shield inside of me that keeps me from really living my life. It's spooky how it's all come about. Everyday I feel better. When Jim and Beemer found me, me and the whiskey bottle got along real good. But the Buffalo's bones have a lot of power. I know they do, because now I feel like I never drank a day in my life. I feel clean inside. I feel good. I even have my memory, which I lost a long time ago. I thought I was incurable."

"You can be a drunk or a gold-digger. You can be anything you want to be until Tunkashila calls you to go to work." Jim says. "Then you're his."

Beemer nods. "We're going to make a T-shirt that reads 'Amongst the Wretched Ones,'" he says. "It's an understanding among warriors."

CARVING THE BUFFALO

"Or like Old Man Fools Crow said, 'Don't look at me, look in me,'" Jim adds. "That's my favorite saying."

Footsteps sound on the wooden stairs.

"Lucy, I'm home." Joe, Jim's youngest brother, yells up the steps where he's coming from the shower down in an unheated basement. Up from Florida, he has been Jim's sounding board for the project since its beginning. He's a comfort to Jim. And he turns out solid meals for the group using only the most basic tools, giving relief from Healthy Choice frozen dinners and Subway turkey sandwiches.

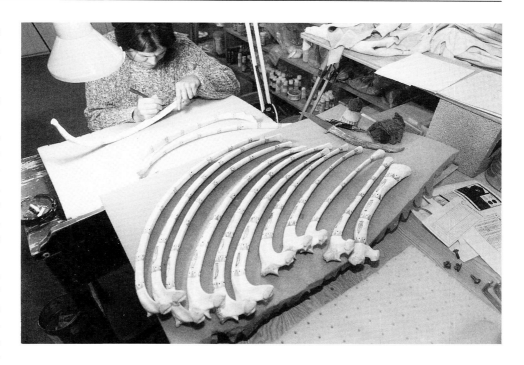

"He's the Betty Crocker of Whitewood," Beemer says.

"He's the king," Jim says. "Elvis has entered the building."

Joe puts his stuff on the table that Tommy Dubray once occupied. He's tan and lean from working on his boat. There's an easy understanding between the brothers.

"I want to end my life as I began it," Jim says, "with my brothers—and my sister, fishing and wading in the creek. I dream of a time when our whole lives rotate around each other as they did when we were young. We'd have 10,000 acres and each of us would live on it with our families and finish life like we began—simple and together. In that equation are good men like Beemer and Irish. They fit into the family. So we don't have to say good-bye anymore.

"And you know how I want to be remembered?" he adds. "That I tried. I never gave up."

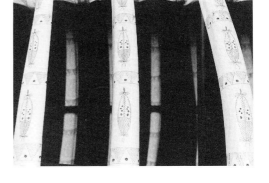

Teri works at carving and inking the 163 feathers on the outsides of the ribs and the 163 spirits on the insides.

* * *

Beemer's birthday is celebrated in the schoolhouse, as is Jim's. Birthdays and holidays spent without family take a toll on the men.

Beemer gets a balloon that says, "Too Bad You're Old." He's forty-six. He gets a candle that chimes Happy Birthday, and Jim gives him a fishing pole.

"So now you're somewhere between forty and death," Joe says.

"Okay, make a wish," Steve says.

They light the singing candle, and Beemer blows it out.

"Ah, too bad, you're still here," Joe says.

"Your wish didn't come true," Steve says.

Beemer shakes everyone's hand. "It's been the best ever," he says.

* * *

It's a Thursday when everyone gathers in the living room for a meeting. The room is somewhat smaller than the studio but with the same high ceilings and tall windows that give it a pleasant spaciousness. Comfortable, man-sized furniture in a southwestern print has been oriented toward a television where videos are viewed nightly to break the monotony of small-town living. Favorites are played and replayed so many times that they become part of the fabric of daily life. From the *Wizard of Oz*, "If I only had a brain," song in a lion's tremolo. From *Monty Python*, "He's not quite dead yet," delivered with a British accent. From *Tombstone*, viewed fourteen times, "I'm your huckleberry," in the slow drawl of Doc Holliday.

At an early morning celebration of Beemer's forty-sixth birthday, Big Jim gives him a fishing pole. Jim's wife, Beth, (left) and Teri wait for him to blow out the singing candle.

Pen-and-ink portraits of Native Americans—Chief Joseph of the Nez Perce, Geronimo, and Sitting Bull among them—solemnly survey the goings-on from the gallery on the wall. There are Jim's prized possessions: a stuffed hawk, an elkhide on which he painted the Wounded Knee Massacre, his tall *sagye* (staff), his medicine bundles.

Behind a wall, the men have partitioned off cubbyholes no bigger than closets for their beds. Jim's cubicle is unadorned, Beemer's holds family mementos, and Steve's is what the men call a "shrine" to his girlfriend—a collage of photos of her face and figure. Since Joe and Teri came, quarters are even more cramped: Joe sleeps on the sofa, and Teri sleeps on an air mattress behind a smaller couch.

Life in the military helped prepare Big Jim and Beemer for the close-quarters living in the schoolhouse. "The way we set up our cubicles for sleeping and personalized them is similar to what we did in Vietnam," Beemer says, "but there's one big difference: in Vietnam, your area of operation was a place you went to create another world. Here, we don't use our beds as a refuge or place to get away from each other."

Meetings are called when there's a need to talk about stuff to do and gripes. This one starts with the flak that results from barracks-style living: keep the downstairs door locked, who forgot to take out the trash, and who hasn't yet coughed up the money for their long-distance phone calls? Someone dipped a tuna-coated knife into the mayonnaise jar, and Beemer got food poisoning.

"Lucy, you've got some 'splaining to do," Joe says.

Jim reminds everyone that they need to sign the contract stating that they won't take away drawings or photos of the Buffalo. Photos already taken will be bought back.

CARVING THE BUFFALO

"We just can't let these original drawings get out yet," he says. "Not till we're done. Okay? Everyone understand?"

Beemer reports that the wood for the shipping crates cost $150 more than was planned. "We need a total of nine crates," he says.

"It'll take a week to build them—not counting adding the foam inside," Joe says.

Jim taps his thigh with a pencil. "What are you going to use for handles?"

Beemer answers. "Rope would make a durable, inexpensive handle."

"That's a good, practical solution," Jim says, "but it creates a hole in the crate. The problem with a hole is that it's an open invitation to varmints."

Beemer agrees to look into another alternative.

"How's Mike Riss doing on the stand?" Jim asks.

Beemer visits the woodshop nearly every week. "He's got the wormy maple for the base, and he's about to laminate the wood for the medicine wheel. He's right on schedule."

"How far are we along on the ribs?" Jim asks.

Steve answers, "We're almost done with the feathers."

Jim nods. "Teri can do some of the finish work on those."

Steve mentions hearing some talk against portraying the seven sacred rites of the Lakota on the bones. "I'm wondering what protesters could do in opposition to it," he says.

"If it comes to that, we'd station a twenty-four-hour guard up here and then we'd move it to the East Coast just like that," Jim says, and slaps his thigh.

Space is tight during the process of carving the Buffalo. Beemer reads a letter from home in his tiny cubicle, the walls of which are from the Buffalo's packing crate. Teri beds down each night behind the couch.

SACRED BUFFALO 85

Beemer nods. "Once the crates are done, we're mobile."

"But I don't anticipate that happening," Jim says.

"I was just asking," Steve says.

Jim turns toward Teri. "Teri, you need to concentrate so you're consistent in your lines. That's not saying anything bad. You're doing a good job, but that kind of repetition is hard on you. Overall, though, we're doing great."

Beemer consults his notes. "During the final stage, we need to make a specific checklist for each separate bone so we know everything's perfect. We need a system—such as using different color stickers—so we know when a job has been completed."

"I've gone over the whole thing," Jim says. "Everything. I've marked everything that needs to be reinked."

"You may know how that's going to work, but we need to know, too," Beemer tells him.

"Well, simplify it then," Jim says.

Steve has a suggestion: "Maybe each bone ought to be finished as we go."

Jim shakes his head. "No, I have to do the major things so that if something goes sour—if I get rubbed out—the work can be finished. Now, are there any personal issues?"

"We're coming down to the end," Beemer says. "We've been through a lot, so we know how to clear out the personal stuff. Let's not let anything fester."

"When's David going to be done taking photos?" Steve asks.

"What kind of inconvenience have I put in your life?" Jim says.

David says he'll be taking photos until the moment the Buffalo leaves Whitewood.

"Another thing," Beemer says, "you three who are handling the bones have to be more careful with them. You need to keep the foam rubber over the edge of your work tables."

Jim agrees. "We've got to stay spiritually focused. It's hard to do that when we curse. Every time you say something ugly with that bone in your hands, it bothers me."

"I'll stop," Teri says. "Why didn't you tell me before?"

"Because I had to think about it," Jim says. "I wouldn't ask you to do anything I wouldn't do. But we've got to make a habit to watch it. Joe, you're the king because you cook for us. Steve, you need to quit picking on Teri. Basically, though, I'm happy with everything. We've done a beautiful job on this."

The meeting over, Jim makes a shot of espresso—a taste he developed in California—heating milk for it and stirring in Nestle's Quik. He drinks it from what he

An early morning shaft of sunlight illuminates the Sacred Buffalo. The Buffalo wears a rain tarp to keep moisture in the bones and protect them from the dry South Dakota winter.

calls his "sacred fly fishing" cup—a big, blue mug decorated with tied flies. He loves fly fishing. "I'm a hell of an angler," he says.

Voices sound from the living room.

"Hey, Beemer," Joe says. "I asked Teri to get me Twinkies and milk—and she did it!"

"I only did it because I was getting up anyway," Teri counters.

"Yeah, well, you lost all the respect you earned so far," Joe tells her.

"Aw, heck, I only did it because you remind me of my little brother."

Jim smiles. "When we were in the military, we worked in small teams," he says. "We were the biggest clowns in the outfit—until it was time to work. Then we were the best. That's what this situation reminds me of. These people here—they joke around, but they're the best. We're under pressure now. Every cut with the knife, every minute, counts now."

* * *

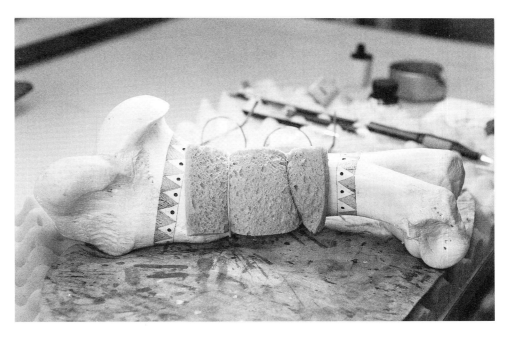

Each bone is wrapped in a barely damp sponge to give it some extra moisture before it is carved.

Jim sits on the floor inside the hochoka, the Sacred Buffalo towering over him. He spots a brown rock the size of a pea. He picks it up and turns it over and over in his fingers.

"How did this get in here?" he asks.

He looks around him on the floor for another pebble or some clue as to how it entered the hochoka.

"You know what this is?" he asks.

It looks like a small piece of gravel.

"It's a gift. It's very special when something comes to you instead of your going to look for it. I'm going to put this in my medicine bundle."

He examines it again. One pointed side looks to him like a wolf's face.

"It really wanted to get in here," he says.

He places it on the plywood under the midsection of the Buffalo.

"Let it stay in here awhile and soak up some of this atmosphere."

* * *

Jimmy Dubray predicted at the blessing ceremony for the Sacred Buffalo that the figures on it would come alive and that it would reveal the presence of other animals. Nine months later there are horses on its legs. Bears make up its tail. An owl and four eagles fly on its vertebrae, and the knob at the top of each rib looks like an elk's face.

As work on the Buffalo progresses, the unusual becomes commonplace. One night Teri has trouble getting to sleep. "It was right after my prayers, and I was just dozing

Teri

TERI KRUKOWSKI HUNCHES over a bone at her desk, wielding an X-acto knife with precision as she cuts the details into one of the 163 feathers on the ribs. She's the "brown-haired woman with a light fleck in one eye" that Big Jim predicted would come to help with the Sacred Buffalo.

She's also an expert craftsperson. For ten years, she has engraved knives, guns, and motorcycles using only a hammer and chisel.

"It took me two years to get the art down," she says. "I practiced on my bike, and it took me 1,800 hours to finish the engraving."

She had been scrimshawing deer antlers, horns for black powder, and antique ivory—when she could get it—for two years before she came to South Dakota. Now, she's working sometimes ten hours a day carving and inking the ribs of the Sacred Buffalo, a long time for precise work where every cut has to be highly controlled. "But it doesn't feel like it," she says. "You get involved in it, and it seems like three hours."

Mid-thirty, she has long, lush brown hair that she sometimes marcels into a mass of waves. Her body's lithe from twenty years of professional dancing.

"But God didn't put me on earth to be a dancer," she says. "I love metal engraving. I take a course in it every year."

But she says it's her work on the Sacred Buffalo that has given her a new way of looking at life. There's power in those bones, she says, and whatever you give to them of yourself, you get back tenfold in things that count—peace and understanding. "I'm finding myself here," she says. "It's bringing a lot of peace inside of me, and I believe you have to have that in order to give it to others. I'm thinking now about things I've done—like aw, I shouldn't have done that, so I apologize, and now I can go on. There's no future in the past.

"I hadn't talked to my sister in fifteen years. I'm real strong about bloodties, but I wasn't getting along with her. I held a grudge for many years. But after I came here, for some reason, I picked up the phone and started calling her like I talk to her every day. What made me decide to call? You tell me! We laughed and told each other we loved each other. I think it's because I found peace inside myself."

Teri's unique slant on a Southern accent gives Big Jim and Beemer and Joe a lot to pick on, and the mood in the studio has picked up since she arrived. She looks for a "thang," she's going to take a "bubba bath," she stares out the "windder," she sleeps in a "holler" behind the couch, and she likes "maders." (Translation:

CARVING THE BUFFALO

thing, bubble bath, window, hollow, and tomatoes.) But accent aside, she's well able to hold up her end of the banter.

Every week she works on the Buffalo, she finds more of herself. "I've learned a lot from Jim Bear. I made some mistakes," she says, "but he taught me how to correct them. It took me some time to learn to focus. He explained it over and over to me. The word, focus. It finally got into my head what it means to focus: not just paying attention, but reaching in there, and nothing else is around you. Now I don't see or hear the music and everyone walking around doing what they have to do. This here Buffalo is Jim Bear's work, and I have to get as close as I can to what he's thinking and what's in his work."

Teri reinks a line on the leg showing Hanbleceya.

She's well suited to carving on the feathers, she says. "I've always loved feathers. They're soft. They flow. They're stimulating. Did you ever see a feather fall? It looks like they don't have a problem in the world."

When she gets ready to leave the Buffalo for Florida, she gets a cold sore. It's nerves: your friends and family always want to keep you from changing too much so they don't feel out of step with you. But with her new perspective, she knows she'll be fine.

"This Buffalo really got into my heart," she says. "If I was to go back to a poor way of life, I'd feel I was disrespecting the Buffalo. I never thought I could change overnight. But I got closer to the spirit, which I was really missing in my life. I learned that reality can be great."

Joe Durham, Jim's younger brother, becomes the "Betty Crocker" of the Whitewood studio. He whips up homemade meals using two electric frying pans, a crockpot, and a portable convection oven set up in the hall.

between wake and sleep. It had been a tense week. There was a lot of pressure, and I had been praying strong to relieve that tension," she says.

"A man came to the bottom of my sleeping bag. I saw him plain as day. He had dark, long hair and wore a top hat. He held a fan of feathers. He waved the fan over me once, and I went right to sleep.

"When I woke up, I asked Jim Bear, 'Who has a fan of feathers?'

"He told me a holy man carries an eagle wing.

"'Did you ever see one wear a top hat?'

"'Yeah,' he said.

"I think it was a holy man who put me to sleep. I think it was his way of telling me not to worry."

Beemer has heard the faint laughter of children in the halls. "It doesn't bother me," he says. "After all, this is a school."

Joe says he's normally not superstitious, "but things have happened here to make me feel this is my destiny—just like it's everyone else's destiny for one reason or another. When I saw Peder—one of the financial backers of the project—for the first time, I had a really weird, strong feeling. It shot through me like a bolt of lightning. I saw his long eyebrows, and I immediately thought of Nick's vision where he saw Jim with long eyebrows. We could never make sense of that. But when I saw Peder, a big shot of understanding hit me—Nick had seen those two men as one. Both are involved in this project for a reason. That really spooked me.

"Another time, I was lying on the couch. I wasn't asleep; I was just lying there resting. Suddenly, I felt a hand on my back. It patted me twice. Distinctly twice. I sat up and looked around. No one was there. It was real scary."

Steve remembers one night when he was alone in the schoolhouse. "I was sleeping when a really loud noise woke me," he says. "I heard something land really hard in the next room. It was so loud that it brought me straight up to sitting. It sounded like a heavy chair had fallen over hard. I got up and looked around, but I wasn't able to find anything that might have made a noise like that. I looked at my watch, and it was 5:30 A.M. I still can't figure out what caused the noise.

"I used to get scared staying here all by myself. Then I thought, Heck, I'm not all by myself. There's a ton of stuff here."

* * *

CARVING THE BUFFALO

Jim shows Teri how he wants the inked lines to look on the ribs.

It's spring when Jim starts the daily ritual of loading the Chanunpa every morning and smoking it every night after prayers. Every morning after the first cup of coffee, Beemer moistens a few sage leaves with saliva and lights them, and each person ducks into the smoke to cleanse him or herself. They file barefoot into the hochoka, and with the dusky smell of sage in their nostrils and the sound of Jim's drum in their hearts, they honor the Creator and the Pipe. Jim beats the eight-sided drum that Jimmy Dubray gave him—an old drum Jimmy says is more than 100 years old—and sings in a high voice full of feeling.

He sings the Four Directions song, and each person honors the Grandfathers, turning to the West, North, East, South. The Creator and the Grandmother are honored. Each person serves for a four-day period of being responsible for loading the Chanunpa each morning and gathering everyone together to pray and smoke before going to bed.

"We started smoking the Chanunpa each day because it seemed people were starting to treat their work here like a job," Jim says. "They needed to become spiritually responsible for what they do each day. For example, no one ever seemed to notice that the Chanunpa is on every one of the Buffalo's legs and that one of the ceremonies is the Pipe ceremony. Do you know which leg it's on? And so we sing in the morning, 'You are first, you always have been, you always will be—Tunkashila.'

"But to understand the Chanunpa, you have to walk with it. You can't talk about what you've never walked. In order for every person to have the spirituality this Buffalo requires, they need to take their shoes off and pray to each of the four directions. They need to be responsible for the spiritual well-being of everyone here.

"Today Beemer's responsible for taking care of us spiritually. You have to know what it feels like to be responsible for people. This Buffalo is really about people. When you're spiritually responsible for them, you get the full feeling of everything you're supposed to do for them. You pray for good food for them. You pray for Tunkashila to guide them. If something bad happens during the day, you go into the hochoka, pick up the Chanunpa, and pray for their spirit. You ask to be given the understanding and guidance to help them. When you start feeling other people, you start understanding them.

"Your walk in this world is not free. If it's a burden for you to take your shoes off and pray, then good. There are many people suffering more than we are. Every day I tell you to remember the old men and the old women and the children in your prayers. We're standing in a schoolhouse that thousands of children have passed through on

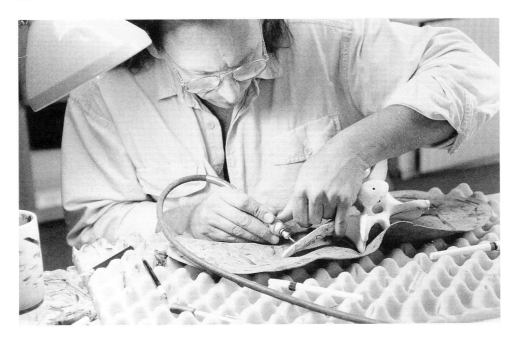

Jim Durham drills little round indentions in the bone to be inked later.

their way to life. The spirits of those children are here; we have heard them laughing. Be responsible for them. Walk that Sacred Red Road. Don't just talk about it. Learn the songs. Learn to pray for people so it makes them feel good."

He exhorts them to pray each morning that what they need to live the day will be available to them: the food, the feelings, the ability to make right decisions. He tells them to place their trust in Tunkashila.

The circle of people changes daily. Beth comes to South Dakota for the funeral of a friend, Bat. Friends and strangers drop by. Travelers come to join in. The Chanunpa is passed to each person in the circle. You receive it with gratitude and pray with it in your hands. It is warm from the heat of those who have held it before you and hard as a rock—as durable as all time. The stone and the wood: you lift the stem to your lips and cradle the bowl in your palms. The person beside you lights the tobacco for you, and you inhale the cloud of smoke deep into your body and release it into the circle.

"With visible breath, I am walking . . . walking,"—this is the song the Buffalo Calf Woman sang. Through her, the ancient people learned to pray to the Creator.

In praying and smoking together, you all are one.

"Mitakuye Oyasin," you finish—which includes all of nature everywhere.

"Everyone here wanted to pray silently," Jim says. "They didn't want to talk out loud with that Chanunpa in their hand. But I asked them to pray out loud. They're praying to Tunkashila, but when they speak out loud, they're helping others with their prayers. If you get a little something from someone's prayer, that's how it's supposed to be. Prayers are for both you and to help others."

"I ask myself, what is my responsibility for the Buffalo? Have I borne the responsibility for that dream? Have I had to pay for other people's mistakes? Yeah, I'd say so. But if you believe in this way, you do what you're told. You might as well just tell the Creator, 'Whatever you say, Bub.' Even if it galls you. Even if you've fought it before. I've tried fighting, and I got spiritually slapped around until I gave up."

And with the smoke thick within the circle, people shake hands all around—people who seem so different from one another yet who are so very much the same, praying together in peace.

Chapter 10

Keeping and Releasing of a Soul

*"I'd probably keep a relative's spirit and walk with it.
It would depend on how badly it wanted to go on."*

—BIG JIM DURHAM

DURING THE TIME WE were carving this Sacred Buffalo, a man died—a Yuwipi man by the name of Bat. He came once to see the Buffalo. "It's beautiful," is what he said.

Bat was in the hospital when his brother Jimmy Dubray came to sit with him. Bat was only in his fifties, but his heart was giving out. I guess the medical people wanted to hook him to this machine and that one, but Bat knew better.

"What's the temperature outside, brother?" Bat asked.
It was a nice day in March—finally warm after a spell of cold, cold winter weather. Jimmy told him it was about 65 degrees.
"It's a good day to die," Bat said.
He passed away on that day.
That's peace—knowing when your time's up and accepting it.

Sometimes, though, people don't want to let go of a loved one just yet. The spirit can be kept at this earth level for four days, or even as long as a year, to keep the loved one close to the family. During that time, the family benefits from the help of that spirit, but walking with the soul is a serious responsibility.

The keeper of the soul—the one who walks with it for however long it's kept—must be a good person who is willing to separate from the demands of daily life for that period. He can't be involved in any argument or anything not peaceful. He can't even use a knife during that time.

When Bat passed on, I helped to set up the tipi on the reservation for the keeping of the soul ceremony. And because Bat had been here to the studio to see the Sacred

KEEPING AND RELEASING OF A SOUL

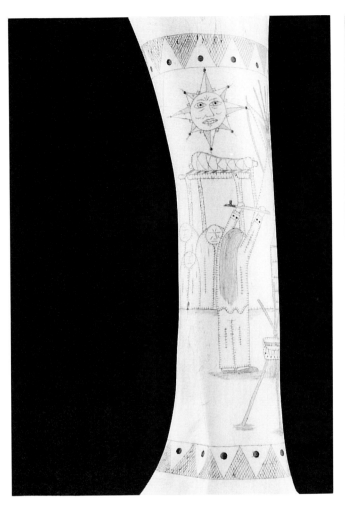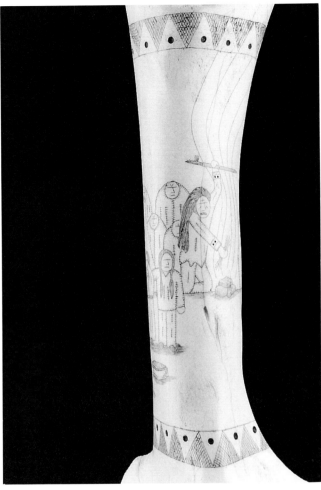

In the rite of keeping and releasing of a soul, shown on the highest bone of the back right leg, a spiritual man raises his Chanunpa high as he prays. A child has died—and the body placed on a scaffold—but to help comfort the parents, the spiritual man promises to walk with the soul for a year. He puts the child's spirit in the bundle on the tripod (front right), honoring it and living with it in a tipi. At right, the spiritual man, his hair unbraided as a sign of mourning, purifies a lock of the child's hair in the smoke of sage.

Buffalo, I felt there was a special connection there so I left the gate of the hochoka open for four days and four nights. I could picture the Buffalo going down to the reservation and sticking his head into the tipi and sitting there with Bat.

This sacred rite is on the highest bone of the right rear leg. In that carving, a little boy has died, and his parents are crying. You'll see the tipi for the ceremony behind them. Before the boy's body is placed on a scaffold burial mound, a spiritual man takes a lock of hair from the boy's head and purifies it in the smoke of sage. The spiritual man's hair is long in that picture because he's mourning.

To keep the boy's spirit, the spiritual man puts the lock of hair in a spirit bundle and puts the bundle on a tripod. He prays with the Chanunpa.

He gives the spirit bundle to the person who has agreed to walk with the spirit. He will live in the tipi with the spirit of the child for as long as it is kept on Earth. He will feed the child's spirit and honor it and put it outside on nice days. He might keep it for four days or even a year. Tunkashila or the spirit itself will tell him when to release it.

I'd probably keep a relative's spirit and walk with it. It would depend on how badly it wanted to go on. When my dad goes, well, he really misses his mom. He talks about her a lot, so my brothers and sister and I will have to decide: will we walk with him four days and let him go to grandma? Or will we keep him because we love him too much to

KEEPING AND RELEASING OF A SOUL

let him go? We'd have to pray on it. But we know now that he'll always be with us, no matter what. He'll always have the power to come back to us in our dreams and help us with life's problems.

I started to tell you all at lunch today to look at the old man who walked in. He looked into my eyes. I started to tell you, "I'm going to show you the face of death. Remember it. Look into its eyes."

But then I thought that this isn't for everyone at this table. If it was, everyone would have heard it.

That old man is suffering. He's alone. He doesn't realize that the only thing that will fill him now is the Creator himself. He needs to let God in; he needs to walk with God.

You can learn to see these things. It's a gift from the Creator that will help you understand that the reality of life is death. And no, it's not as bad as you think.

To understand life, you have to know death. You can't live if you're afraid to die.

* * *

Yuwipi Ceremony

The Yuwipi is not one of the sacred rites, but it's a very special ceremony for calling the spirits to help sick people get well or help people find something lost or stolen. It's shown on the left scapula of the Sacred Buffalo.

In a Yuwipi ceremony, a Yuwipi priest is wrapped up in a blanket and then tied up with rope. He's laid down on the floor, and then the lights are turned off, and he calls the spirits to help those who have asked for the ceremony. He dreams of the Rock, and what he sees about healing or a stolen horse is what the Rock told him.

Bat did one once for a woman with a tumor the size of a grapefruit in her stomach. First we took a sweat, and then I helped him set up the hochoka and black out all the windows. This is one ceremony done in the dark. When Bat was ready and the lights had been turned off, the power of the songs caused the spirits to come. The spirit hit me with a fan like an eagle's wing. I could hear the eagle flying, flap, flap, flap. It hit me in the head and around the shoulders. It told me something about piercing. When the lights came back on, Bat asked me, "What did the spirits tell you?"

"The spirits told me to seek the truth," I said. They had told me something else, but I didn't want to say.

"Washte," he said. "But they told you something else. What was it?"

"I'd rather not say," I told him.

"What was it?" he insisted.

"They told me to seek the truth, then tell it."

During a Yuwipi ceremony, you can hear the spirits come in. You can smell them. It's a real weird smell, like nothing you've smelled before. Musty, except that's a weak word for it. Not bad, but indescrib-

---

Never Say Good-Bye

THERE'S NOT A word for good-bye in Lakota. Good-bye hurts too much. It's too final. The word we use is *doksha*. It means later.

—Jimmy Dubray

Giveaway

WHEN MY NEPHEW died, my sister gave away all of his things—his bedroom set, his bicycle, his clothes and shoes, his baseball stuff—everything. The reason? To mourn him. And she wanted people to remember him. The people who got his things will always remember him.

—A Lakota Woman from the Rosebud Reservation

Dog

SHUNKA HAS A lot of power, and it's used during certain ceremonies for its power to heal. A dog is boiled, and then everyone gets a little piece of the meat to eat. So when people call us dog-eaters, it doesn't bother me. Only one time did I take a dog. I was told to feed the thunder people. The dog offers a simple gift, but a good one.

—Jimmy Dubray

Walking with the Sacred

KEEPING AND RELEASING of the Soul is said to be the oldest of the sacred rites that Calf Pipe Woman brought to the people. It is said that it was done the first time for a little boy who died. The boy's parents were very sad and asked a spiritual man what they could do to keep his soul, as the Calf Pipe Woman had promised them they would be able to do. They took the spiritual man to where the child's body lay.

"This child appears to be dead," he said, "but he is not dead. We will keep his spirit among us, and our generations will be blessed."

The spiritual man asked that a special tipi be set up for the Keeping of the Soul. When that had been done, he loaded his Chanunpa with tobacco offered to the four directions and the One Who Is Everything and the Mother Earth.

Then the spiritual man cut a lock of the child's hair. He smudged it with sage to drive away the negative influences and with sweet grass to make it pleasing to all the universe. Then he spoke to the spirit within the hair. "Stay among the people and help them," he said.

He carefully wrapped the lock of the child's hair into a bundle and put it into a bag. The bag was placed on a stand with three legs.

The people wrapped the child's body and put it up on a scaffold, as was the custom, to return it to the Earth.

Then the spiritual man smoked the Sacred Pipe.

The father walked with the soul of his child for a year. During that time, he lived apart from his family in the tipi with his son. He tried to look only at beautiful things because his eyes had become the eyes of the spirit. He never listened to arguments or angry words because his ears had become the ears of the spirit. He thought only positive thoughts. The father fed his son's spirit as though it still lived in the body. When the weather was warm, he took the spirit bundle out of the tipi and set it on its tripod facing South. In this way, the three legs were the West, North, and East, and the missing one was in the South. For it is to the South that one finds the Spirit Trail.

The Keeper of the Soul prayed often for the good of the people, that they might live in peace and have plenty of food to keep them. In return for the bounty they received, the people gave meat and hides for the boy's spirit. The boy's mother tanned the hides and pounded the meat with chokecherries and fat for the day when her son's spirit would be released. In this way, the people rejoiced in the boy's life, and many blessings came upon them.

When the day came to release the boy's spirit, the people were happy because they knew it would be a day of blessings. On that day, the spiritual man loaded his Chanunpa. He asked that a "soul post" of wood be set into the ground in a lodge big

KEEPING AND RELEASING OF A SOUL

enough to hold many people. The soul post represents the soul, and all of the child's possessions were placed around it. Women brought gifts of food and placed them at the foot of the post. They put bits of food into a wooden bowl.

When the ceremony began, the spiritual man made sure that the food from the wooden bowl was put into a hole beside the soul post. A little chokecherry juice was poured on top of it to represent life.

He called four young virgin girls into the lodge. They were happy because by taking part, they and their future children and all generations to come after them would receive the gifts of the boy's spirit. The spiritual man picked up the spirit bundle and talked to it, telling it that it would soon be going on a journey. He asked the child's father to honor the boy's spirit by touching the bundle, and then the spiritual man touched each of the young girls with the bundle.

Finally, he walked toward the door of the lodge, pausing four times. Each time he stopped, he said to the spirit, "Look back on your people so that they may walk the straight path without fail."

The moment he passed out of the door, the spirit was released to travel the Milky Way to the spirit world.

Today, as then, after the ceremony for releasing of the spirit, a great giveaway takes place. All of the dead person's possessions are given to orphans and the poor. A great feast is eaten, and food is given to those who need it. Everyone comes to touch the four young girls who took part in the ceremony so that they, too, will be blessed. There's much rejoicing for the one who has gone on the spirit trail.

The family of the released spirit may decide to keep the bundle containing the lock of hair as a remembrance of their loved one, but the spirit no longer lives in it. That happy spirit has left the Earth.

This sacred rite helps both the spirit of the one who has died and the loved ones who remain on Earth. Through the ceremony, the soul is purified so that it and the Great Spirit become one. In this way, it is able to return along the Spirit Trail to the place it came from. And in keeping their loved one's spirit, the family members learn that all spirit—and especially the Creator—is eternal.

It is hard for some people to understand the idea of the Keeping and Releasing of the Spirit. They wonder whether it is possible. Apparently the United States government believed in the power of the ceremony. In 1890, the government prohibited the Keeping of the Soul, and in fact, it was required that on a certain date, all souls kept by the Lakota should be released.

Mitakuye Oyasin.

KEEPING AND RELEASING OF A SOUL

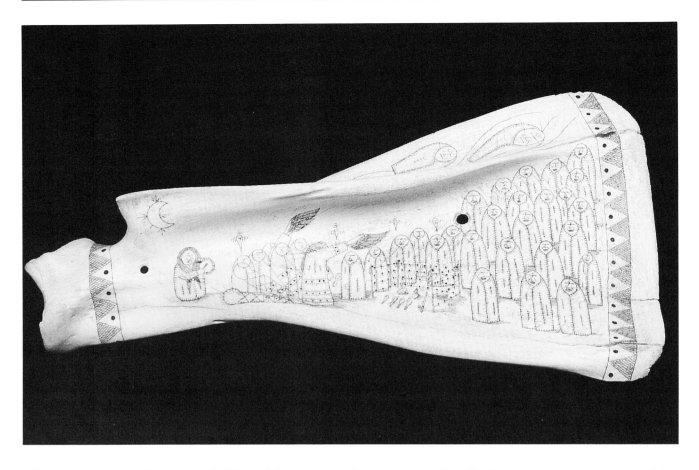

The Yuwipi ceremony, shown on the left scapula, is performed for healing or to find lost or stolen items. The Yuwipi priest is wrapped in a blanket and tied, and when the room becomes dark, he is freed from his bonds. He stands holding the eagle-wing fan and calling upon the spirits, represented as gourds. On his altar are gourds, a wopila bowl, a smudge shell, a medicine bundle, and a Chanunpa. The people at the ceremony sing to the sound of the drum. Four spirits stand behind the Yuwipi priest.

able. Then little gourds go flying around—literally flying. You can hear them shaking and moving through the air. The priest is speaking, the little gourds are flying, and then there's a big stomping sound—or a sound like a heavy ball rolling but it's really a huge gourd. It lights up like the moon. It's really pretty. I've held children during Yuwipi ceremony's because they get scared.

It takes a person close to the spirit world to be a Yuwipi priest. It's a hard life. Bat held the ceremony five nights a week sometimes. His living room just had chairs on the perimeter, to make room. They tell stories about a man playing around with it, and the spirits tied his hair in little knots.

On the scapula, people are singing, except for four men. They are the spirits from the four directions who have come to help in the ceremony. They are standing behind the Yuwipi priest. They walk through life with him and help him get untied. Four *wagmus*, gourds, are flying around, and on the Yuwipi altar is a wopila bowl, a smudge bowl, a medicine bag, and a Chanunpa.

The Yuwipi ceremony kind of spooks me. There's a lot of power there. I remember when Bat asked me to take his gourds out to the van after a ceremony. I was getting ready to put the gourds in his briefcase, when Dutch, from lower Brule, came up and touched me and I jumped in the air. I thought the gourds had me! Now people tell about how Dutch caught me shaking those gourds all around and under my arms. It's a big joke now.

Bat's dead now, but he did a lot of good as a Yuwipi priest. For one thing, the woman's tumor went away.

KEEPING AND RELEASING OF A SOUL

Jimmy Dubray, Spiritual Leader of the Oglalas

WHEN I WAS SIXTEEN, I fell asleep one afternoon and had a dream. My mother told us never to sleep in the afternoon, but guess I did anyway. In my dream, I had on an apron and little thin moccasins that came up just below my ankles, and somebody was hollering at me to look West. I looked up and saw a big thundercloud. It showed me men riding horses, and every time their horses moved, the thunder sounded. The horses snorted and lightning came out of their nostrils.

One of the men told me, "Boy, look over yonder. See that city? Those people are ignorant. They don't listen, so they need to be destroyed, or they'll go on and destroy everything." He threw a cane, a staff, at me, and when it hit the ground, it shook like it was alive. I was afraid. I knew that whatever the men told me to do, I had to do it. So I hit the city with the staff. It turned out to be an anthill filled with flying red ants. So nowadays, when I see a city, I know that there are people there who can spiritually or physically hurt others.

Another man on the lightning-breathing horses came up to me. "Look over there," he said. "That thing is always moving; he's restless. Destroy him before he destroys others." I took after it. It was a jackrabbit. From that I learned that restless, gossiping people infect others with their lack of peace. My resolution is to try and mind my own business.

A third man on a thundering horse came to me. He pointed at a woman lying on the ground asleep. She had a baby on her arm, and she was pregnant again. I guess people're supposed to space out their babies or think about creating a generation or a family, but without thinking, pleasure gets in the way. That woman didn't know how to control that pleasure so she was in trouble. And she was sleeping on the job: she was married to her husband and her house, and she was forgetting her housework. The man told me to destroy her, but I couldn't. She looked like one of my aunts. So I threw the staff down, and it became a corral post, with horses in the corral.

I woke up. I was sweating and cold. I hollered to my mother and told her what had happened. My grandpa George Poor Thunder was a Yuwipi man. She told him, and he said, "You kids were told not to sleep in the afternoon. The spirits move around then. Many are called, but few will be chosen." He marked me with sage.

My dad had gone out, and when he came back in the evening, he told us there had been a strong thunderstorm. His sister had fallen asleep outside near the corral. Lightning struck the corral, but it didn't hurt any of the horses, and it just kind of moved my aunt. My mother pointed at me, so I told my dad what had happened.

For awhile after that, if I was around during a thunderstorm, my mother had to cover the mirrors to keep them them from getting cracked and to cover tin or iron or metal to keep it from attracting lightning. I couldn't sit in a vehicle during a thunderstorm or the mirror or the windshield would crack.

I was eighteen when Uncle Sam called. My brother-in-law and I and another fellow were outside drinking firewater. We figured if we

The Sacred Buffalo

THE PEOPLE HAVE always used everything on the buffalo to survive, and now we've taken one and made it into a skeleton to show the world the history of the Lakota's seven sacred rites. The spirit of the buffalo is in that carcass, and it will stay with it. It's alive. The buffalo prays for the people, and so those who have worked with the Sacred Buffalo skeleton must pray for the people. The buffalo gives itself to the people, and those who have worked with the Buffalo skeleton must give themselves to the people. They will have to say, "I did this, and I never asked for anything in return." Because freely you get, and freely you give.

Anyone who appreciates this Buffalo skeleton will be freely blessed. This is the gift of the buffalo.

—Jimmy Dubray

were going to be Uncle Sam's boys we'd better learn to drink firewater. It was raining, and lightning hit the tree near where we were standing and knocked us all down. My brother-in-law was on his back, I was on my hands and knees, and the other was lying sideways. Years later, I became an evangelist, my brother-in-law became an Episcopal minister, and the other taught catechism. We got knocked off the mule, I guess, to make us believe.

But still we didn't believe enough. Later, I became an advisor, and my brother-in-law became a Yuwipi man. He was lying there all wrapped up. Lightning was shining, sparks were flying, and I laughed. He said, "I know why you laugh. You remember the time lightning knocked us down." I told him, "Remember, brother-in-law, you called them, 'Come back, you sonofabitch, you bastards, and I'll whip you.' We're here now. You whip them. I give up."

I ended up with grandpa Fools Crow. He's related to us on my dad's side, so he's an uncle, but he called me, "my son." It was an honor to work with him for a number of years.

The first time I was called to do some spiritual work, someone called me twice. "Jim," said a voice, "Jim."

The third time, it said, "Oh, Jim."

I said, "What?" without turning my head around to look.

My wife thought I was crazy. But that was the beginning of when someone called me to work.

In 1957, during the Asiatic flu epidemic, I nearly died. I was so far gone that they took me to the undertaker. He was gong to embalm me, but when he discovered I was alive, he took me back to the hospital. I weighed seventy-seven pounds. Both of my lungs had collapsed, and the tissue in the left one was gone. I gave myself up, you know. I had thought I knew how to pray, but I didn't. I prayed the Indian way, and I prayed the Christian way. But when it came down to it, I didn't know how to pray.

One day something with great big eyes stood above me. Its eyes were so huge, and it said, "Son, this is how you pray." He told me I'd be leaving there shortly. It was an ant! An ant taught me how to pray. I prayed like he told me, and the next day I was sitting up. The voice asked me, "Do you believe in God?" I closed my eyes, and there was nothing there. I opened my eyes, and the world we live in was there. I had no choice. I said, "I believe."

They were going to cut out my lung, but then I had an X-ray. The doctor came in with tears in his eyes, and I was really scared. He said, "Something happened. Something's wrong here." I asked him, "What is it?" He went on, "Your lung is whole. There's nothing wrong with it."

I learned from that experience that there's a God and there's a place of darkness. God didn't create the darkness. You create it yourself. I think I had a glimpse of a few angels, too, but in all these years, no one has ever believed it. They pretend to, though.

Feeding the Spirit

Jimmy Dubray: Did you put food out for the old guy?

Reporter: You mean the dog?

Jimmy: No.

Reporter: Oh, you mean the spirit. No, I didn't. Is it too late?

Jimmy: It's never too late.

I take a bit of meat from my plate and a slice of fried potatoes turning cold and go out into the chill March air. Night has fallen. I walk out onto the prairie, the dry grass whispering at my ankles. On a little bald patch in the grass, I set down the food. The next morning it is gone. Of course. Food is scarce on the prairie in early spring. What ate it? Does it matter? The point was the offering.

Chapter 11

Tapa Wanka Yap,
Throwing of
the Ball

"Everyone wants to catch the ball because it's a great honor to receive those blessings of life for the people."

—BIG JIM DURHAM

THROWING OF THE BALL is often celebrated during the time of Sundance because that's when families all come together. It's fitting that everyone be there for it because it represents the gift of life.

Throwing of the Ball is pictured on the Sacred Buffalo's right scapula. There's a little girl with a ball standing inside a big circle of people. Her grandmother is with her, and men stand at the four directions of the circle waiting for her to throw the ball. Everyone wants to catch it because it's a great honor to receive those blessings of life for the people.

You'll see a tipi and a sweat lodge on the Throwing of the Ball bone and seven buffalo skulls. The women use the tipi and the sweat lodge to prepare for the ceremony, and the skulls represent the seven sacred rites.

I have taken part in the Throwing of the Ball ceremony along with Nick. We both tried real hard to catch the ball. I won't tell you who finally got it. I will tell you that it's a happy time.

Most people don't understand what this sacred rite represents, and as a man I'm not allowed to talk about it, but as a spiritual leader, my friend Jimmy Dubray can explain it.

* * *

I HAVE A LITTLE joke to tell before I talk about the Throwing of the Ball. You know, we Lakota people often have nice, round faces, and this joke has to do with that face.

One time I called my wife honey but she didn't like that.

SACRED BUFFALO **101**

TAPA WANKA YAP, THROWING OF THE BALL

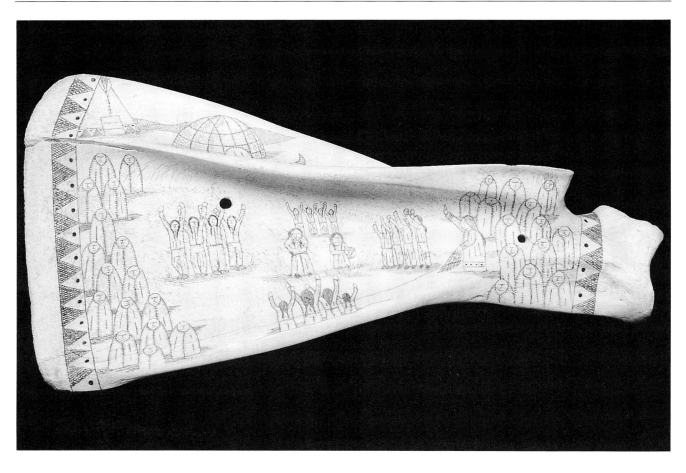

The Throwing of the Ball rite, which brings blessings to the people, is on the right scapula. A young girl stands holding a ball that represents life. Her grandmother stands with her. When the spiritual man gives the sign, the little girl tosses the ball to men at each of the four quarters. The one who catches it receives the blessings of the life for all the people.

Woman

THIS GOD, THIS Creator, this Spirit must have a woman. I have not seen her, but perhaps someday I will.

—Jimmy Dubray

"I stay away from bees," she said.

So the next time I called her dear, but she didn't like that, either.

"I can't run very fast, and I certainly can't jump fences," she said.

You see, we're both old grayheads, now.

So the next time I called her pumpkin, and I really got into trouble.

"With this wide face I have, I certainly don't like that," she said.

So now I call her love.

There's a great deal of ceremony connected with the Throwing of the Ball, and a lot of very deep meaning. We try to keep it sacred as much as we can—you don't just go and buy up a ball and throw it up in the air. Last year, this rite was done during the days we were at the Sundance ground, but most people didn't know it. They should have sat and watched. But we said to keep it hush because someone would want to take the ceremony and put a price tag on it and say that they could make some old lady not a virgin for thirty years become a woman.

A ball must be made—traditionally out of buffalo hide—so the people whose daughter and granddaughter is going to throw the ball prepare it for the ceremony. They lay out the buffalo hide and cut a circle, then sew the skin and stuff it with hair from the buffalo. They don't just go out and buy a ball.

The girl's people arrange for a spiritual man to come and conduct

TAPA WANKA YAP, THROWING OF THE BALL

the ceremony, and he brings his Chanunpa because this is a very special day. They invite lots of people to come and celebrate and feast. They invite the orphans and the elders especially.

During the Throwing of the Ball, a *winicala*, a little girl, stands in the center of a circle of people facing her. A girl can be part of this ceremony until she starts claiming the moon. After she's about twelve years old, she can no longer throw the ball.

A grandma stands with her and sometimes a grandpa, and a few people stand just inside the circle at the four quarters.

When the spiritual man starts the ceremony, he gives the girl the ball he has blessed. The ball represents all the gifts of the world. I think it was Mahalia Jackson who sang, "He's got the whole world in his hands." Well, in this case, the girl has got the whole world in her hands and she's about to bestow all its blessings and bounty on the people. When the spiritual man tells the girl to throw the ball, she throws it toward each of the four quarters. Each time she throws it, the people there return it to her. Finally, she throws it high up into the air, and then one of the orphans or elders catches it and gets the gift—a blessing. The person who gets the blessing accepts it for the sake of all the people everywhere because what the throwing of the ball brings us all are understanding and health.

You see, the seven sacred rites bless us all. We Lakota perform

The sweat lodge and seven buffalo skulls are carved on the top of the right scapula. The skulls represent the seven sacred rites that are observed throughout the year and at Sundance.

Goodness

EVERYTHING GOOD COMES through a woman. Virgin Mary brought the man called Jesus. The Star brought the Chanunpa. She has the power to bring life and to destroy it.

—*Jimmy Dubray*

TAPA WANKA YAP, THROWING OF THE BALL

> ### A Horse of a Different Color
>
> A YOUNG WOMAN WAS being courted by two young warriors who wanted to marry her. One day she told one of the young warriors: "You have to bring two horses so Grandpa can approve our marriage. If he says, good, and accepts the two horses, we can get married. If he rejects them, well, we don't get married." The other young warrior heard about this arrangement and rushed over to the girl's house. "Why did you ask for just two horses?" he said. "You're worth more than two horses." The young man grabbed her grandpa and took him outside. "Here's 360 horses," the young man told him as he opened the hood of his new red truck.
>
> —Jimmy Dubray

them on behalf of all the people of the world. We say, "All my relations," and all the people on earth receive the blessing, no matter if they don't even know about us at all, or about the Throwing of the Ball. It's as simple and as complex as that.

Making of a Woman

This is Jimmy Dubray speaking again. You know, men aren't really supposed to talk about what is a woman's business, but as spiritual leader of the Oglala people, I get many questions from people who have heard so much misinformation that I feel I have to talk about everything.

The Throwing of the Ball is related to the Making of a Woman. When a girl comes to the point in her life when she is ready to become a woman, her family rejoices. She has reached a new stage in her life, and some time in the future, when the time is right, she'll be given the great gift of motherhood. This is very special.

When a girl gets her first moon and begins claiming the moon each month, it's called "my daughter or granddaughter starts sitting outside once a month." In times past, a woman on her moon left the family home to dwell for four days or so in a separate tipi that was reserved for just that purpose. Today, most women don't really leave the home, but one thing is still very important: a woman on her moon should never come around a spiritual man who is carrying medicine with him. She should never come into the presence of the Chanunpa during that time. And she should never take part in any of the sacred ceremonies. At Sundance, the women establish a moon camp away from the Sundance grounds. All of these things they should do out of respect.

What that time alone gives the woman on her moon is four days to do needlework or beadwork. It gives her four days away from working in the kitchen—the other women cook food for her. She can tan hides to make moccasins, and she can go into the field to collect the moss and cherries and roots to dye them. She just can't do anything connected to spiritual work.

When a girl first claims the moon, many preparations have to be made for the ceremony that makes her a woman. A tipi has to be set up. Her grandma or the elderly ladies—that over-the-hill gang—must teach her what do during the ceremony. A spiritual man is called to do the blessing, and he stays up on the top of a hill and prays while the old women take the girl into the sweat lodge and help her purify herself and prepare herself for the ceremony. The next day, before the sun comes up, the women put her in a tipi facing the East, the lodge facing the West.

There's a lot of teaching that goes on during that time when a girl becomes a woman. At least there was in the old days. People spent time with each other then. Nowadays, they're hyper. The young people are always on the go, and even the elders' minds are scattered. People have to do this, they have to do that. Grandma has moved. This affects her

> ### Eagle Plume
>
> A WOMAN GETS AN eagle plume when she gets her name—not an eagle feather like a man gets. The plume means a thought. We tie a plume on a woman because women think much quicker than men do.
>
> —Tommy Dubray

TAPA WANKA YAP, THROWING OF THE BALL

Making the Circle of Life Eternal

THE THROWING OF the Ball represents the eternal nature of the circle of life.

In the old times, when the rite first came and the spiritual man taught the people how to perform the ceremony, he described to them the four ages of the buffalo people. In the first age, the little buffalo calf stood in the center of the Buffalo People. Suddenly, the little calf became a young girl, and as a girl, it tossed a ball to the West, where the sun goes down. The Buffalo People in the circle all changed into two-leggeds, too, and one of them caught the ball and returned it to her. The little girl tossed the ball to the North, up the straight path. Again the ball came back to her. She tossed the ball to the East, where daybreak and wisdom come from. Again she got the ball back. She tossed the ball to the South, where the generations come from and go. The ball was returned to her once more.

Finally, the little girl tossed the ball straight up into the air. As she did this, she turned back into a buffalo calf, and all the people standing around her turned back into the Buffalo People. The ball fell to the ground in the center of the circle. The buffalo couldn't catch the ball because they didn't have hands. When the ball stopped rolling, the little buffalo calf pushed it with her nose until it rested at the feet of the leader of the Buffalo People.

"We four-leggeds can't catch the ball," the leader said. "The universe truly belongs to the two-leggeds."

This is because, according to the wise men, only men and women—of all of God's creations—are able to purify themselves through the sacred rite of the sweat lodge and knowingly humble themselves to him in sacrifice.

So, today, before the sacred rite of the Throwing of the Ball begins, the spiritual man gathers what he will need: a ball, which in the old days was made of buffalo hair and covered with buffalo skin, sage and sweet grass, and as always, the sacred Chanunpa. Traditionally, the ball is painted red, a sacred color that represents the world, and blue to represent the heavens. It has four dots to represent the four quarters, and two lines that go all the way around the ball. In this way, the ball becomes the heaven and earth and is very sacred.

When all is ready, the spiritual man waves his eagle-wing fan to signal that the game of life should start. The little girl who has been chosen stands in the center of a circle of people holding the ball. Her grandmother stands beside her, and singers start their songs. At that moment, the little girl represents the Creator in his eternal youth, for the ball is the universe and the Creator is the One Who Is Everything in the universe. At that moment, she can look forward into the future and see the generations that will come after her.

The girl tosses the ball to the West, and someone standing there catches the ball and offers it to the four directions and the Above and the Earth. The ball is returned to her, and she tosses the ball to the North, to the East, and to the South. Each time the six directions are honored, and the ball is returned to her. Finally, the little girl throws the ball straight up, and the people scramble to catch the great gift of the universe. Some people try hard to catch the ball, and some don't care much at all. In life—as in the rite of Throwing of the Ball—some people try very hard to catch the Creator's blessings—living their lives in a good way full of honesty and spiritualness—while others never keep their eyes on the ball.

And because people are trying for the ball—not the Buffalo People who have no hands—one person catches it and returns it to the center one final time. The Creator's blessings have been caught and returned to him. That is the meaning of the Throwing of the Ball.

Mitakuye Oyasin.

> ## Wisdom for a Woman
>
> ONCE A MONTH or so, when you look up and see the Morning Star, when you see the Sun break over the horizon, take a little water and put it outside. And maybe he will call you sister or mother. Perhaps you are the Mother of God.
>
> When you get up in the morning, take a little sip of water first thing. Water is life. Calm yourself and put a smile on your face.
>
> For what you see is a reflection of how you feel. If you think I am cranky, it's because you are. If you think I am agreeable, it's because you got up in a good mood. How you see the world is how you see yourself. This is under your control.
>
> Traditionally, Lakota women always serve the men their dinner first, then the children, and they eat later. It isn't that anyone is "better" or "more important" than anyone else, as some people claim. It's a matter of respect for their men, who are prepared to defend them with their lives. At my grandma's table, the women served the men, and then later, one man would stand ready to serve the women while they ate.
>
> To the Lakota people, eye contact is improper. In the English culture, you're taught to look at people when they talk, but we respect people by keeping our eyes down.
>
> Just as a man must respect a woman, a woman must respect herself. The body is sacred, so respect yourself and keep yourself covered. Out of respect for yourself, don't bend over from the waist. Learn to stoop by bending your knees and keeping them together. In days past, mothers and grandmas used to teach their daughters these things.
>
> Woman must watch the circle and keep the fire going. She must keep the living water.
>
> —*Jimmy Dubray*

children, and her daughters move. Years ago, there was an elders' club where the elderly ladies got together and played hand games. They talked to the young girls, and in a few months, the girls got a degree—all the teaching of the earth was put into their hands. They learned how to handle the products from their bodies and how to purify themselves afterward. They learned the cycle of life. A girl has her monthly time, but she's a virgin. Next, she knows a man, and a man knows her. She has children and learns to deal with the things life brings. At she gets older, she passes on what she has learned to the next group of girls. Generation to generation, the teaching goes on.

We have to have respect for our young ones. A young girl is a holy thing. The Christian religion talks about the Reverend Mother, and people get the impression it's only one person. But every family has its Reverend Mother. There's a virgin among us, and through ceremony, she becomes a woman. She doesn't know man. A man isn't supposed to touch her. He may comfort and protect her, but he shouldn't look at her, he should put his head down out of respect. If he wants her as his own, he might bring horses. But when a man and a woman get together, that's forever. There's no throwaway. That union is a beginning with no end. Because one day, from that virgin, a child will be born. And future generations will be born. This is the teaching of the buffalo.

In the ceremony that takes place in the tipi, the spiritual man gives the girl a name that belongs to her alone, and a song that is hers alone. No one else sings that song. The buffalo comes into the ceremony, too, because it was the Buffalo Woman who taught us the ceremony. The spiritual man is part of that buffalo, and when he makes a motion toward the girl, her mother gives her sage to protect her. In this way, the girl learns to keep herself modest and pure until the right man comes along. The occasion of becoming a woman is a happy time, and many people are invited to share in it if the family can feed them. In this way, a girl becomes a woman, and much later, when her moons stop and she becomes a grandma, she might become a wise woman.

Just as the women teach the girl about the ceremony, the same is true of how the men teach a boy. When a boy is ten or twelve years old, he's going to have to go out there and hunt his first animal. His first kill will probably be a rabbit or a little bird. When he brings it back, his father and uncles will tell him to give it to an elder. His first kill will go to a person who is not able to go out and hunt on his own, so to him the tiniest animal is huge. This gives the boy more blessing. By this time, he's already started going into the sweat lodge to purify himself—many times when we men are praying in the sweat lodge, children come and stick their heads in and we don't mind at all because the children are innocent and sacred. Later, the boy goes out alone to seek the vision that will help guide him into manhood. And then, he'll begin the journey toward Sundance.

What do we elders teach our young ones today? Do we teach them the ways to take care of themselves physically and spiritually? If we

TAPA WANKA YAP, THROWING OF THE BALL

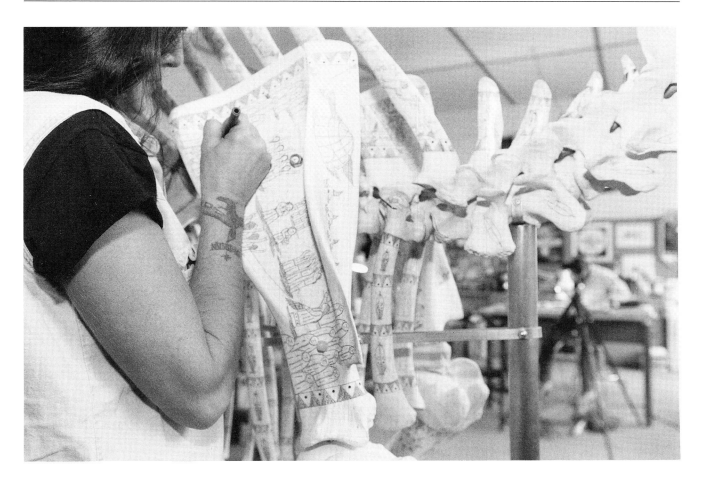

Teri reinks the Throwing of the Ball on the right scapula. In the center of the bone stands a little girl ready to toss a ball that represents life and the blessings of the world.

send them to the grocery store with some money and a shopping list, do they bring home the right food? If we leave them in the company of those who tempt them, do they know the difference between right and wrong? Have we given them the strength to resist the bad things? In this century, we've lost so much of our respect for our young and our elders. We don't really trust our young ones, and in return, they don't trust us. That trust and teaching have to come back into the family, or we're doomed. I, too, am guilty of this mistrust.

This is a shame, because as I have told you, the young girl holds the whole world in her hands.

A Mother's Love

I HAVE SHED many, many tears because my sons are out there pierced to the Sundance tree. It hurts me everytime they pierce, even though I know I must let them go. I weep, but I always try to be strong for what they're doing. My brother told me, "Don't say no to them. They do not belong to you." I always keep that in my mind.

—*Florine Dubray*

TAPA WANKA YAP, THROWING OF THE BALL

Chapter 12
Carving the Buffalo

"My dad told me you can never leave footprints on this planet other than the footprints of your children. My dream has been to leave more."
—BIG JIM DURHAM

"I SAVED CARVING THE skull 'til last," Big Jim is saying, "even though it's the biggest and most difficult piece."

He leans against his drawing table surveying the Sacred Buffalo. The strong spring sun shines into the room through old, yellowed window shades giving the skeleton the richness of old ivory. The animal stands with its jaws wide open—not wired shut as usual—and it looks as though it's speaking. Head held high, the massive beast seems to send its voice into the silence.

Visible on the inside of the Buffalo's jawbone, four grown buffalo follow the little white buffalo baby out of its mouth. It's a message of hope and renewal for humankind through right living.

On the altar in front of the Buffalo, the Chanunpa stands loaded from the morning ceremony. There's a pink stone sculpture of the little boy Matt, and a new addition—a piece of the Berlin Wall contributed by an East German who stopped by to see the Buffalo. A chunk of Milky Way, two pieces of meat, and a Whopper malted milk ball have been added to the wopila bowl. The bowl of cigarettes is overflowing.

"People ask me, 'Why didn't you carve it first? The Pipe came before the ceremonies,'" Jim muses. "But I saved it 'til last to keep the edge. And because the Chanunpa came to help people. That's what we need now—help. In about four weeks, we'll face the greatest emotional pressure of all—the pressure from the outside. People will shoot at us with their words. Are we doing something magnificent? Or are we fools?"

Beemer is at the sink behind Jim's table scrubbing one of the Buffalo's hump bones with a toothbrush. He's taking off dirt accumulated during the scrimshawing process. Dishes that had littered the sink dry in the drainer.

CARVING THE BUFFALO

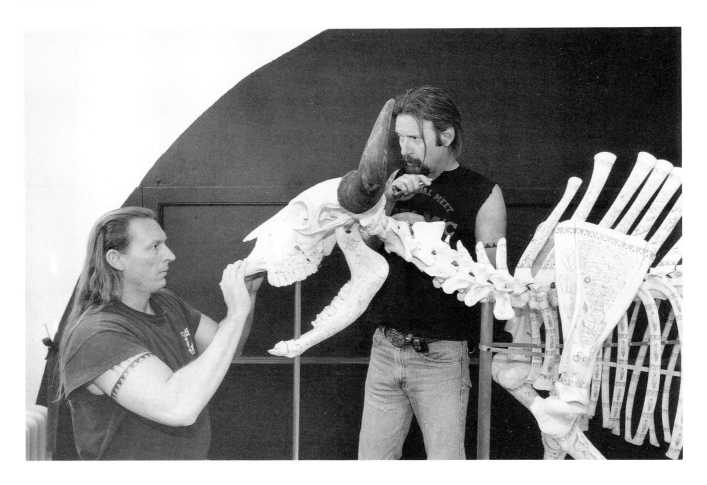

Jim and Beemer prepare to remove the Buffalo's skull so Jim can scrimshaw it.

"Let's take the skull off," Jim tells him "And the neck bones. I need them, too."

Penciled onto the neck bones are the four wise men from the inside of the pelvis. These men have faces. They have made it back from the end of time.

Beemer removes the Buffalo's skull and places it on the foam rubber on Jim's desk.

Jim puts on gold-rimmed magnifying glasses, which—a friend teases—seem to add at least twenty points to his IQ. He considers the pencil-drawn figures for a time, then holds a mirror behind one side of the skull and compares the figures drawn on both halves. The skull shows Buffalo Calf Woman presenting the Chanunpa to four leaders of the people. The men honor the Pipe, and in their ancient tradition, they also honor the sacred buffalo people, raising the Pipe and a buffalo skull high. In the center of the skull, the Sundance tree stands ready to help the people give thanks to the Creator; its branches support figures of a man and a buffalo and the prayers of the people.

Jim makes fine, but decisive cuts into the bone. Some of the skeleton's bones are hard; some are as soft as chalk. It takes precision and confidence to carve the thousands of lines that detail the scenes on each bone. More than 6,550 lines have been carved onto the left rear tibia to show Hanbleceya. And that figure doesn't include the lines that make up the shading.

"I can't believe we carved this whole skeleton," Jim says.

The knife slips and the blade punctures his thumb, drawing blood.

CARVING THE BUFFALO

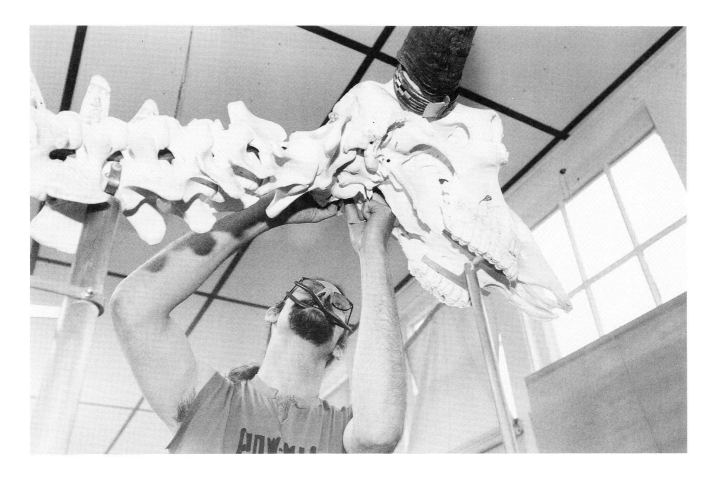

Beemer loosens the screws at the back of the Buffalo's skull to remove it.

"Yeow! Wopila!" he says. "Thanks."

He lays down the knife, and takes off the magnifying glasses. The mishap reminds him of the suffering and sacrifice the Sacred Buffalo project has demanded.

"If you want to accomplish your dream, you've got to pay for it," he says. "You've got to get beyond your resistance to the personal cost—no matter how high it is—and do it. That's the only way you can turn your dream into a reality you can see and touch.

"You have to be willing to give everything you have to make your dream come true. When you can do that, you're a believer."

Jim gingerly pokes at the cut on his finger and goes to the sink to run cold water on it. His fly fishing mug is upside down in the drainer.

"Beemer, you took the character out of my cup," he says.

"There was two weeks worth of chocolate on the rim," Beemer replies.

"Now it has no past, only a future," Jim says. "And in the immortal words of JFK, you must know where you've been to go forward."

Jim seems restless. He opens the door to the fire escape and steps outside. The buds on the trees have burst into tender leaves. Cows on the hill graze on the newly green grass.

"We'd better ride now," Jim says about their motorcycles. "The clouds are coming in."

Teri jumps up and looks out the window. "I heard it's going to rain from now 'til Monday," she says.

Jim takes a deep breath. "Boy, it's nice out, and we're locked inside."

"We need a good blast of cycle therapy," Beemer says.

"Let's ride 'em and weep," Jim says.

Jim sets the Buffalo's skull inside the hochoka. Beemer and Teri close up shop, and within minutes the three of them are ready to ride. Jim looks in the mirror over the sink while he runs a plastic brush through his long, sun-lightened hair. He hits a tangle. "Look at this one," he exclaims.

"Nice weave, Bro," Beemer says.

"It's a Whitewood thing," Jim says. He sprays Nexus Maximum on his hair and pulls it back into a pony tail.

Joe decides to go to the grocery store and the bank while they're gone.

"What are you doing for lunch, Steve?" Jim asks on his way out the door.

Steve from Ohio is sketching some possible logos for the studio. "I'll be here for a while, and then I've got some errands to run," he says.

"Well, we'll be back in a couple of hours," Jim says, and closes the door.

Jim's mounts his red-and-black Harley Davidson custom soft-tail low-rider. Beemer's Harley is a black FXE Superglide, and Teri rides a '85 Low-Rider FXRS Harley that she calls "White Feather." The throb of the bikes' engines rattles the window panes until they roar away.

Jim draws the Coming of the Chanunpa on the skull, the last piece to be scrimshawed.

* * *

Midafternoon, after Jim comes back from the motorcycle ride, a man and woman drop by the studio. They own a local photo shop where a roll of film taken of the Sacred Buffalo has been dropped to be developed. They stay for less than five minutes, apparently just wanting to see in person the skeleton they recognize from photos they have previously developed for Jim.

"That's it," the man says.

After they leave, Jim turns to David, the photographer. "Is there any chance this film is yours?" he asks.

"Not a chance," David says. "I take all my film back to Colorado to be developed by a professional lab."

"Well, it's not ours, either," Jim says.

When Steve comes back from his errands, Jim confronts him.

CARVING THE BUFFALO

"Did you take these photos?" Jim's eyes blaze with anger.

Steve admits that he did.

Jim and Beemer are angry—and feel betrayed. Their trust—and the contract prohibiting taking photos of the Buffalo—has been broken.

That night, when the Chanunpa is smoked, each person in the circle speaks about the wrong thinking that has occurred. Every word must be carefully weighed when the Pipe serves as the balance. Jim warns again that a person must not lie with the Pipe in his hands, nor make promises he can't live up to.

Beemer scrubs the fingerprints from the bones before they are reinked for a final time.

"Your every act—your every word—is magnified when you live with the Chanunpa," he says. "I want you all to know what a big responsibility it is to walk with it."

Steve apologizes and agrees not to touch the Sacred Buffalo until he and the other men can go into the sweat lodge together. He agrees to prepare a ritual giveaway and to place dried beef and chokecherries on the sweat lodge altar. He promises seven pieces of flesh to atone.

That done, the sins are forgiven.

"But not forgotten," Jim says. "My dad taught me always to forgive but never to forget."

Several days later, shortly before Steve is to leave for home, more photos from another roll of film are discovered in his possession—these a grave dishonor to the Chanunpa itself. Steve leaves before the project is complete, but the photos stay within the hochoka. That which is sacred has been preserved—by the power in the prayer ties on the door, the protector spirit Big Nose, and the Sacred Buffalo itself.

"I credit the Buffalo with giving me those visions (about Steve)," Jim says.

Within the group, there's anger over the betrayal, but also sadness over Steve's missed opportunity.

"The Buffalo has so much to give us," Teri says. "I don't see how anyone could go about lying and stealing around here. I feel the goodness and power. I only hope that when it goes on tour people can tune in to that."

"The Buffalo brings out the best and the worst of what people have in their hearts," Jim says. "Like Jimmy Dubray said at the blessing ceremony, only the true of heart will be able to stand here with it."

* * *

It's a quiet spring afternoon. The sky is mostly gray. The phone is strangely idle. Jim sits at his table playing a harmonica—a shiny Hohner. He remembers being a kid and

The Buffalo

THE BUFFALO WHOSE skeleton became the Sacred Buffalo grazed for seven years on a ranch near Wind Cave in South Dakota. In a park near there, old male buffaloes—the grandfathers—munch on prairie grass alongside the road. A breeze ruffles the long, dark, coarse hair on their massive shoulders as they move slowly forward, heads down, pinching blue-stem grass between their bottom front teeth and upper lip to rip it free. Snorts punctuate the rhythm of their breathing, and their flashing eyes follow your every move.

Bull buffaloes past the age of five tend to be ornery and unpredictable. Males weighing as much as 2,000 pounds and standing taller at their humps than most men trample fences and battle over females. The hole in the Sacred Buffalo's forehead is from a fracture probably sustained during a fight.

The Sacred Buffalo comes from the species Bison bison. The common term "buffalo" stems from the French word for oxen, *les boeufs*. Scientists speculate that the bison's ancestors developed in central Asia and crossed the Bering Strait Land Bridge during the Ice Age to spread south into North America. Today, two other species of bison exist: a Wisent bison with a small head and hump in Poland and Russia, and the Wood bison in Canada.

Just 200 years ago, the Great Plains were the domain of magnificent herds of buffalo and the Native Americans who depended on the animals' meat and hide for food and shelter. But after white soldiers and settlers flocked West, the number of buffalo dropped from an estimated 30 million in 1800 to just a few hundred by 1890. In trying to force the Indians onto reservations, the U.S. Army was losing as many as two dozen soldiers for every brave killed. Realizing the Indians' reliance on the buffalo, the military encouraged the slaughter of the buffalo as a means to win the Indian wars. The buffalo nearly disappeared within 25 years. By 1905, 700 of the surviving 800 animals were on private preserves. Now 200,000 bison range on private and public land.

The buffalo that became the Sacred Buffalo was headed for slaughter when Jim Durham identified him as the animal from the dream and arranged to buy him. The buffalo was blessed before he was killed. "I was there," recalls taxidermist Les Lutz. "He didn't suffer."

The buffalo's bones went to Ohio State University's Department of Veterinary Biosciences where research associate William (Bill) Richeimer had agreed to prepare them to be carved. "Jim had told us the buffalo was going to bear the history of the Lakota, which was why I decided to tackle it," Bill recalls.

In the lab, research assistant Barb Shardy and students Jacque Shepherd and Shane Donley boiled the bones to remove the flesh, degreased them in trichloroethylene, and whitened them in hydrogen peroxide. The process took several months with Barb, Jacque, and Shane sometimes putting in thirteen-hour days in order to accomplish the extra work along with their regular duties.

The final step was wiring the 180 or so bones together. "When we put it together, we were awestruck at the size of the skull and the thoracic processes (the hump)," Barb says.

Bill estimates the department put more than 800 hours into the project, yet he didn't charge for time or materials. Barb, Jacque, and Shane donated all their overtime.

"It was an honor for us to be able to work on it," Barb says. "We'd do it again in a second."

CARVING THE BUFFALO

sucking air through a harmonica as he mowed acres of grass for the man he called Muskrat.

"I'm perplexed," he says. Pain dulls his eyes.

He stares at the Buffalo, then plays along with Neil Young's "Helpless" when it comes on the radio: ". . . Big birds flying across the skies, throwing shadows on our eyes, leaves us helpless. Helpless."

His wound from the seeing his Chanunpa desecrated in the photos is too fresh to heal.

"When I was a kid, the mouth harp was as close as I could get to my dad," he says mostly to himself. "A while back, my dad's dog died. He really loved that dog. Rayette was her name—named for Ray Charles and the Rayettes. I happened to go visit my dad shortly after that, and I found him sitting in the shade of the house. He started talking about the things he used to do with that dog. He cried when that dog died. I had never seen him cry before.

"'I just can't hardly take it,' he said.

"I listened to his sniffling. 'I saw your dog,' I said.

"He looked up at me. 'Where at?'

"'On the other side. She was with her mom. They were running together. In a field.'

"'Does she suffer anymore?' he asked me.

"'No, her hair is shiny, like she's been eating a dozen eggs a day.'

"I realized then that my dad and I weren't the same as we'd been when I was a kid. I had become much stronger.

"My dad stuck his hand out toward me. 'Thank you for telling me.'

"'Yeah, I gotta go now.'

"'I really miss that dog,' he repeated.

"'She's with her mom. She doesn't miss you anymore.'

"'Hmm, that's good,' he said.

"I drove sixteen hours that day, and it dawned on me that whatever had ever been between us, I had made my peace with him."

Jim puts the harmonica back in its blue-lined box and puts the box in a drawer.

"I see things so clear in my head, it's like they're movies," he said. "I can be talking to someone, and they just start rolling."

He looks at Teri where she sits at her little desk reinking the wiyakas carved on the ribs.

"Teri asked me the other day if I have any clay," he says. "I told her no. But I was looking at her and laughing. She is the clay."

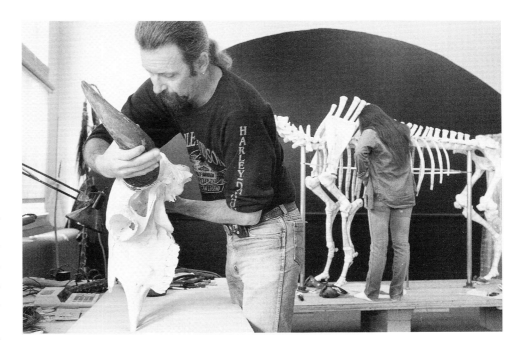

When the skull has been completely carved, Beemer prepares to reattach it to the body. He treats it with the utmost respect.

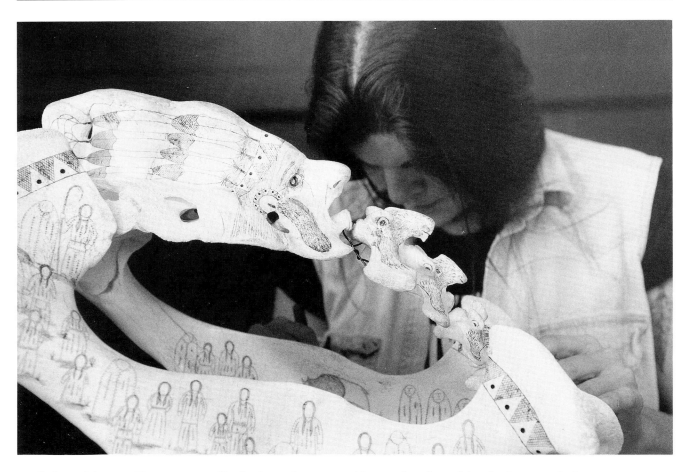

Teri spent dozens of hours reinking the lines Jim carved. Here she works on the facesless figures on the pelvis. Tunkashila, the Grandfather, is over all life. Three of the seven bears on the tail are visible in this photo.

Jim had seen her once without a face in a vision in the sweat lodge.

Teri lays down her pen. "He's right about my face being white or blank," she says. "Three years ago in West Virginia, we had a memorial for a veteran. Fifteen of us were in a group picture. When the photo came back, everyone's face was there but mine. My face was white. We couldn't figure it out. I asked everyone what that meant, but hearing Jim Bear, it all makes sense. I'm not a whole person."

Jim smiles faintly. "When she asked me for clay, I was thinking 'Yeah, I have clay. It's you.' But I wouldn't have ever said anything unless this had come up. Because you can't mold clay with words. You can only do it with action."

"There's a lot of power in this Buffalo," Teri says. "A lot. I'm learning so much."

Jim continues. "So why do I see things like that? Who knows? It's a knowing. I've already experienced our last day here. I know it. That's what makes me different. I can live it in my head long before it happens and know exactly how it's going to happen.

"I can see that little boy Matt's face when he goes, and he's smiling.

"I saw the way the earth would end, but it was so horrible that I didn't want to be responsible for it, nor for my children to be responsible. I talked to Tunkashila about it and asked that he bring me another one.

"I've seen good times ahead for the Buffalo.

"I saw my own death. I saw my grandkids. I was sitting outside in a place with aspen trees painting hides. I was really wrinkled. Nick was wearing an oxford cloth shirt and fancy pants and he brought the grandkids over to see me. He was still proud of

Teri reinks the figures on the hump bones. She's working on the figures portraying the Wounded Knee Massacre, while the spirits representing Custer's Battle of the Little Bighorn are visible.

me. I started talking to him, telling him a story and he was grinning.

"A young man came here asking me for power to get his woman back. I didn't give it to him, but I did give him a warning. I saw his woman with her head spinning around like she's crazy. I saw a massive amount of horribleness in her. I remember saying to Tunkashila, 'What do you want me to do?' The next thing I know a warning is coming out of my mouth: Be careful what you ask for because you might get it. That man and his woman don't go together. They're of the same species, but they clash because they're different. They fight. They're not the same. They're two people separated by a wall. There's a door, but it's Tunkashila's door. I told him, 'You come here and ask me for help to open the door, but you may be very sorry.'

"Maybe my vision is a tool. People ask me things, and when they hear the answer, they sometimes want to get up in my face and say, 'That's bullshit.' Maybe that's why Tunkashila built me so big. So they don't.

"But I told that young man the advice I was told. Maybe we saved a tragedy from happening. Maybe we saved a child from being born into hardship from that union and saved that life gift for someone else. The chemicals on earth today are so different from what God put in us; we've been altered so badly from what we eat and drink that we don't have the same genetic body we grew from so long ago. Maybe the chemistry between those two would have created a very sick human being, with potential for bad. So maybe those words I said saved something bad from happening twenty-five years from now. I wonder about these things. I don't know. The words just come out.

"Another day a boy came by, and the first second I saw him I saw a movie of him hanging himself in his room. A bottle was on the night stand. Maybe he was planning it, maybe he was going to get drunk and do it by accident. I told him what I saw, and it scared him. Then Tunkashila took over. The boy quit drinking.

"But I can't change things. Only Tunkashila can change things. I'm only a guidepost. People come here with a problem, and I just tell them, 'This is what I think.' It's no more than a guy swatting a ball. God does it all. He puts the light in your heart. He gives you the power to live. He gives you the desire to become what you need to be."

Jim pauses to watch Teri. She lays down her pen and lights a cigarette. She stubs out the cigarette and rummages in her desk drawer. She stands up, she sits down.

"What's wrong?" Jim asks.

"I don't know," she says. "I think I'm getting a headache."

Jim gets his medicine bundle and pulls out several little plastic bags of dried herbs. Into a glass of hot water he puts a pinch of this, a stick of that. He won't say what they are.

When Joe gets a fever from the flu, Jim provides him with relief from a different combination of herbs.

The door is open onto the afternoon. White clouds bloom like shining mountains in the spring sky. A bee flies into the studio through the open door. Jim gets up and makes himself a cup of espresso—this time from a blend called Marrakech.

Sitting again at his table, he ponders the matter of how much a person should attempt to change the events of people's lives.

"You become a player in the movie, but you don't know until you see the movie which part you'll play," he says. "Inevitably, God takes you and shoves you into a role. I sometimes listen to myself talk, and I find out that there're two of us. When I say something I never thought of before, I ask, 'Where the hell did that come from?' It makes you realize just how small you are. You are controlled by something else. You joke, you visit with people, and then all of a sudden someone will ask a question, and out of your mouth flies a statement you have absolutely no knowledge of. Where does it come from?

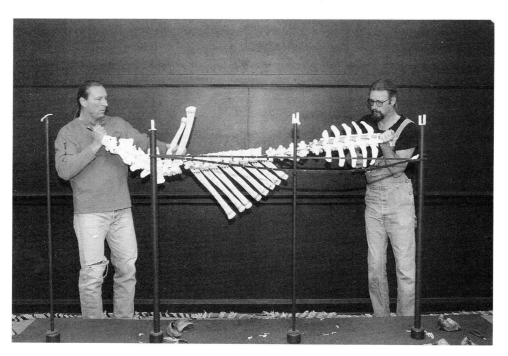

Jim and Beemer work at disassembling the Sacred Buffalo. It is the last time it will ever stand in the Whitewood studio where it was carved.

"One time I was singing a song to honor someone who'd died: Bill, the guy in Ohio whose kids are my kids now. I wrote a song, but then I forgot the words. I went into the sweat lodge with Bill's kids—they took the urn with his ashes in there—and I starting singing in this beautiful voice I've never heard. Beemer was in there, and I heard him weeping. He told me later that it was the most beautiful thing he'd ever heard. I said, 'Yeah, me

CARVING THE BUFFALO

too.' It was Spirit singing. So you become a tool, a player.

"During the sweat, I saw Bill running, chubby and healthy, and he looked back and smiled at me and then kept on going because on the other side was his mother. He met up with her, and they just started laughing. I remember him whistling a song. I repeated it to his family, and they said, 'How did you know that?' It was because I heard him whistling. His little boy said, 'That was my dad's favorite song.'"

He pauses for a long time. When he speaks again, his voice is husky.

"I think my gift was given to me for a reason. I am who I am. I have asked myself, 'Gee, all I ever see is disaster. Am I destined to spend the rest of my life watching people die?' Try walking in my shoes once. Try looking at people and seeing what's in store for them. Try knowing what people are going to do to themselves. You'd shoot yourself.

"I've talked a lot about it to Tunkashila. Maybe I'm supposed to help people if I can. Like giving them that one little thing—like a little inyan that's with them all the time. The Buffalo is a gift I've brought to the world, and it will reach out so far.

My dad told me that the only footsteps a man can leave on this Earth are his children. But I wanted to leave more. My driving dream is to do my art so Nick and Crystal will know me from the inside. I have this fantasy that I'll put my work in a secret room, under lock and key. Then someday, my children will go inside, and they'll know me from my work."

Beemer dismounts the pelvis.

A cut from the *Division Bells* album by Pink Floyd has come on the radio, and bells sound in the studio. The sun has broken through the gray and light streams in shafts. Visible through the open door, an eagle appears, soaring in the light. It's joined by another eagle, and they spiral higher and higher.

"Why did Tunkashila bring that man [Steve] here?" Jim asks. "He betrayed people on a piece so sacred. But I knew. I knew. It's my error. I should have let him go, but we were well into the project when I saw what would happen—it was February—and I didn't think I could find someone else and train him or her and still stay on the schedule.

"But because of this Sacred Buffalo, I've learned that there are things more important than my own will. I've learned that there has to be something more than your need to satisfy your own desires. I've learned I had to take second place, that the Buffalo was first, and that I had to take a backseat in order to bring it out in a time frame to satisfy the dream.

"I learned that not everything is black and white. Tunkashila taught me that—using Steve as the tool. I used to be horrible about acting first and thinking later. Sometimes I get a horrible feeling of guilt for things I've done. As Joe would say, 'Lucy, you've got Hail Marys to do.' It's bewildering to me to think that inside each person lives many people. How can one person be capable of doing great good and also bad?

"But Tunkashila has taught me there's not only black and white, there's gray—gray achieved through spiritual belief. Gray achieved by putting your own desires behind what you know is the greater good."

* * *

The Sacred Buffalo is disassembled for the last time in the studio. Beemer removes the bones and puts them on shelves covered with foam rubber. The animal looks small, lying there in pieces.

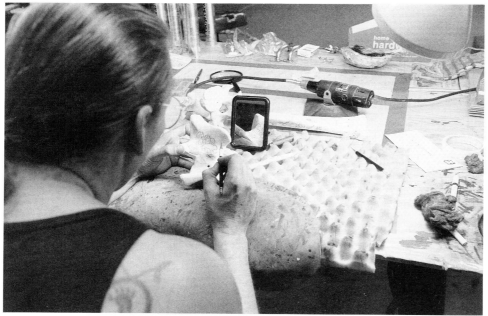

Jim finishes carving the white buffalo calf, her mother, and four wise men on a vertebra in the neck. He uses a mirror to make certain both halves are perfectly matched.

"The greatest painting in the world—the Sistine Chapel—can probably be reduced to twenty gallons of paint," Jim says.

He lingers over the bones.

Beemer disassembles the plywood platform, too. The stand Mike Riss is making is nearly done.

"We're at the end of the line," Jim says. "I'll never stand here again and look at this Buffalo. The next time we see it all together, it'll be ready for the world."

A date—June 19—has been set for the Sacred Buffalo to be reassembled in the first-floor gym; there it will be honored in a private ceremony one last time before it begins its journey among the people of the world. The last scene from Jim's dream needs to be completed there.

Jim has set Teri to work packing up the studio and the living room. Boxes stuffed with art supplies, dishes, and appliances make their way down the steps to join with a flow of stored boxes marked Moyer-Durham that were never unpacked from Jim's and Beth's last cross-country move. The boxes collect next to the downstairs door where they will be loaded into a rental truck bound for the East Coast. Skis, a weed-whacker, fishing waders, a child's dollbuggy loaded with teddybears and dolls, living room furniture, a table and chairs, even the refrigerator: everything must go. Teri and Joe are going East, too.

"I think about all the time we've spent here," Jim says, "all of the good things and the arguments. We can never live this time again.

"I remember the day Beemer and I brought the Buffalo up here—how excited we

CARVING THE BUFFALO

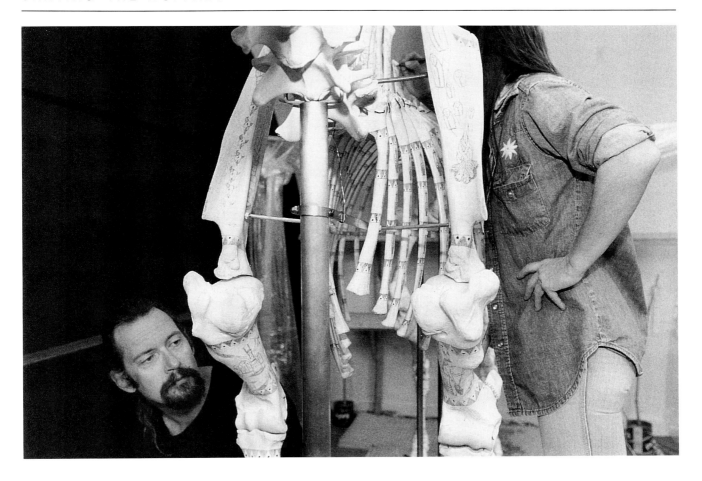

Beemer scrutinizes each line on every bone, making a detailed list of any that need to be reinked. Teri is working at reinking the bones on the hump.

were. We just sat there and looked at it, and we were scared. But today is the beginning of another phase of the dream."

With the space inside the circle empty, Jim puts his sagye in the center, rigging some cinder blocks to hold it straight. He covers the blocks with black cloth and places a red cloth down on the floor to receive the skull.

"This way if someone comes, and I'm not here, the boys will take care of it."

He's referring to the seventeen eagle feathers on the staff, each a representative of a veteran. A red feather and a yellow feather fly from the top.

"There's an old veterans' song," he says, "'They are charging from afar, they are charging from afar, they are charging from afar, the bad mouths are coming.' Now we have a sentinel."

But even though the bones are crated, the power and the spirit of the Sacred Buffalo still fill the circle.

"Churches are built big and ornate to look powerful, but the power doesn't lie in the building," Jim says. "The power is in the innocence of a child, the power is in suffering, the power is in your faith. That's power. That's what we call good medicine."

Chapter 13

Hanbleceya, Crying for a Vision

"People come to Hanbleceya wanting to be put up on the mountain. No one tells them the true price of the experience: four days without food or water. Does it sound easy? Go out in the woods and try it for just one day."

—BIG JIM DURHAM

I WENT ON MY first vision quest a long time ago when I was a teenager. I went through one period of doing what they call lycanthropy. It's a dreamer's fast: you find the spirit of an animal in your dreams and become that animal. The experience is so real that if you become an eagle, you can look down and see the land below as an eagle does when he's flying high overhead. If you become a bear, you can feel the dew of a morning when he walks through the cold woods. You can look down at your paws and see the wet fur. You can see breath coming out of your nostrils and forming clouds in the cold air. It takes a tremendous amount of dedication and belief to change yourself into an animal, but you can do it through your suffering.

Once I asked my brother to watch over me while I went on this dreamer's quest. He didn't want to. I told him, "Well, at least take a pair of binoculars and check on me everyday." He said he would, but he never did. I lost two whole days on one vision quest. I thought I was gone just a couple of hours, but I guess I was out there two days. My ex-wife hollered at me about where I'd been, but I couldn't understand her concern. I didn't realize I had been sitting on a cliff for two days.

People sometimes come to South Dakota hoping to experience the Lakota Way. They come with a little knowledge and a lot of ignorance. Some are sincere in their motives to become more spiritual; others come hoping to get power. What they all need to know is that no matter what you come for, you're going to have to pay to get it. You have to pay for it through your suffering. People come to Hanbleceya, crying for a vision, wanting to be put up on the mountain. No one tells them the true price of the experience: four days without food or water. Does it sound easy? Go out in the woods and try it for just one day.

Unlike other people, I was afraid of getting sucked in at Bear Butte in South Dakota, and I kept my distance for a while. Then, one time, I went there with another guy and we were walking up the mountain in the middle of the night. I looked up and there was a big Indian wrapped in a blanket. He was about twelve feet tall and was standing on a bush. My first thought was, "Damn, he's big. He's almost too big to fight." Then I looked into his eyes, and I knew it was the Old Man of the Mountain.

The guy I was with saw him, too. I told him, "Don't you say a word about this to anyone."

"We have to tell someone," he said. "We can't just keep this."

"You just keep quiet about it," I warned.

Actually, I saw the big Indian twice. The second time, I was standing on the side of a cliff as I was going up to get a man I had pierced two days earlier and hung in a tree. The same guy was with me the second time, too. I looked up and saw that big Indian on the left-hand side of the cliff above us. My mouth dropped open. He was standing there solid and real just like a human being.

"Grab a tree and hug it and start praying real hard," I told the guy.

I put my arms around a tree and began to pray. I realized then that Hanbleceya on Bear Butte is not a game. It's the real stuff.

Eventually, the guy who also saw the Indian told someone who told Jimmy Dubray. One day, I was sitting at the dinner table with Jimmy and he asked me, "Did you see him?"

"No," I said, knowing full well that he knows when you're lying to him.

"Hmmm," he said. "He's big, isn't he?"

"Yeah, sure is."

I haven't been afraid of much since then.

On the Sacred Buffalo's left rear leg—the East leg—is the story of Hanbleceya, crying for a vision. The vision quest starts with the Chanunpa, which on the lowest bone is held by eagle claws. There's a wopila bowl of food offering to spirit and a wopahta. Hanbleceya begins in the sweat lodge pictured there, at the fire.

Once the vision questers have purified themselves, they're taken up on Bear Butte by the holy man as shown on the middle bone of that leg. The holy man leads four men higher and higher, with their relatives following behind them. The men carry their prayer ties and blanket and four chokecherry branches. When they reach the place where they'll pray, they each set up a hochoka using the chokecherry branches to mark the four directions and a string of 405 tobacco offerings for the good spirits.

Each man has his blanket, his Chanunpa, and his cansasa—that's all. They pray for days for a vision to guide their lives. On the top bone of that leg you see them suffering as they cry out to the Creator. One man is staked out, pierced to the Earth at his hands and ankles until he has the vision he seeks. Another man on that bone is dancing with his Sacred Pipe, a buffalo skull pierced on his back. I pierced a man like that once. I hung a buffalo skull on him and left him there to dance with

---

Hanbleceya Song

Grandfather in the West,
I am standing here. See me.
The wind is blowing in my face.
I am standing.

Grandfather in the North,
I am standing here. See me.
The wind is blowing in my face.
I am standing.

Grandfather in the East,
I am standing here. See me.
The wind is blowing in my face.
I am standing.

Grandfather in the South,
I am standing here. See me.
The wind is blowing in my face.
I am standing.

—*A Traditional Song*

HANBLECEYA, CRYING FOR A VISION

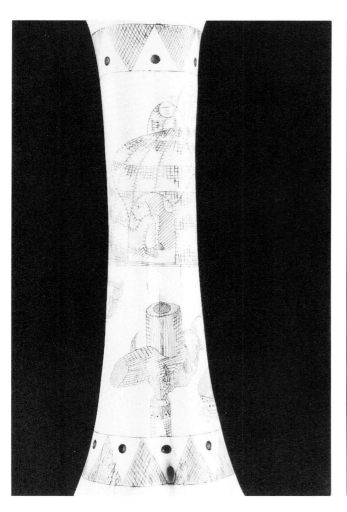
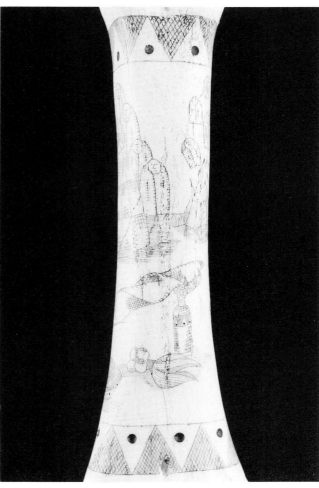

it for four days. It really upset me because I had to pierce him really deep so the skull would hang on him for the whole time. He cried, but that's part of it. His suffering helped him learn to pray.

That bone also shows a buffalo and a woman. A man came to Hanbleceya one year dressed like a buffalo and his face painted half black to pray for his dead mother. During his fast, he saw the buffalo spirit come for his mother. I saw it, too. She was a spirit, and you could see Bear Butte through her. She came to tell her son doksha, that she was going on to the other side to wait for him. It was sad, really sad.

At Hanbleceya, each man has to carry his own cherry branches and Chanunpa and prayer bundle up Bear Butte. No one else is allowed to carry them. And if a man drops anything, he's supposed to be brought down. Frank Fools Crow taught us that. One year, a man came saying that he truly wanted to suffer.

"I want to go to the hardest place on the mountain," he said.

I was asked if I knew of a place for him on the North side. I know the mountain like the back of my hand, so I was asked to put him up.

Crying for a vision starts with the Chanunpa and the sweat lodge.

Guidance

■ ASK GOD TO help me make decisions.
■ If you think about it, you know you make your own turnarounds. I used to go to grandpa Fools Crow when he was alive, and he'd always tell me, "Hey, you tried that and you say it's no good, so let's try this way and maybe it'll work." I had great spiritual teachers.

—*Jimmy Dubray*

HANBLECEYA, CRYING FOR A VISION

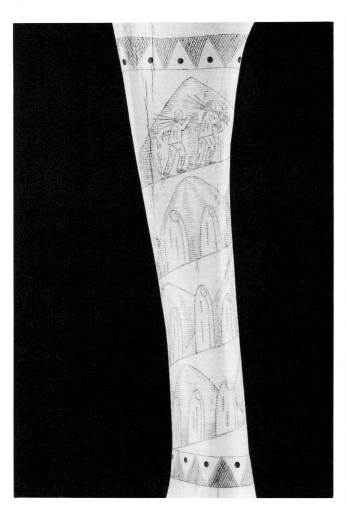 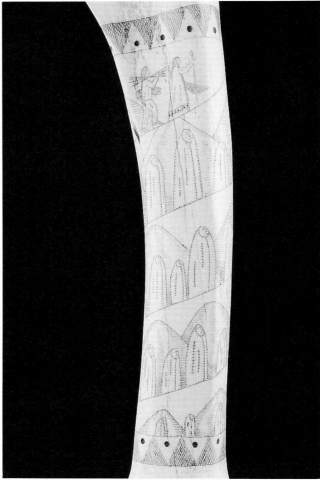

Hanbleceya, crying for a vision, is shown on the entire back right leg. On the middle bone, four men (three are visible in the photos) follow the spiritual man, with the eagle wing fan, to the top of the hill. They carry their Chanunpas, chokecherry branches, and blankets to where they will fast and pray four days. The men's families follow behind for support, although they will stay in camp during the four-day vision quest.

The man said he wanted to truly suffer so someone told him to take his shoes off for the trip up. You see, he was asking for really strong prayers for his dad, who was dying.

On the way up, the man walked behind several others I was putting up to pray. On account of his prayers, I took them straight up the mountain, then on the path a little ways, then straight up, then on the path again, heading toward a cliff that's a perch really—only wide enough to stand on. I've fasted on it myself.

I stopped four times and prayed to the four directions. After the fourth time of stopping to pray, I could feel the man being mad. His feet were bleeding from the rocks, but it was what he asked for, and although he was whining and mumbling, I kept on going. The climb really got hard, and he was behind me steadying himself with one hand and carrying his things with the other. Suddenly, I didn't hear him behind me. I turned to look. A tree had grabbed his prayer ties, all 405 of them, and they were dangling from a branch. He laid down his Chanunpa and cherry branches and started down the mountain after them. I stopped him.

"Pick up your Chanunpa," I told him. "You're done."

"You can't do this," he protested.

"Enough," I said. "Don't say another word. You're finished."

HANBLECEYA, CRYING FOR A VISION

I took him all the way back down the mountain and told him to sit by the sweat lodge. "Just pray about what happened," I said.

Then I went and told the rest of the men what I'd done.

"You brought him down?" they asked. They couldn't believe it. "That's the right way, but . . ." they began.

I interrupted. "Old Man Fool's Crow said that's what you should do when someone drops his bundle."

But they argued with me, and finally, I took him up to a different spot on the mountain and put him up to pray for twenty-four hours. When he came back down, I learned he had prayed for my death. He had prayed for Tunkashila to hurl me to my death on the rocks for being so mean.

I confronted him "Do you have a problem with me?"

He wouldn't look at me.

Months later, that same man came up to me with a war club.

"I've had this for ten years," he said. "My dad told me that someday I'd meet the man who deserves it. And you're that man."

He handed me the war club four times in the Lakota tradition. On the fourth time, I accepted it. Washte.

He told me that he had come to Hanbleceya that year to pray for his dad's life. His dad died, but he passed on without too much suffering. He believed I had helped him. But I had just done what was right. It wasn't mean, really, just strict.

The thing is, at Hanbleceya—and in the sweat lodge and at Sundance—you're responsible for men's lives. Crying for a vision isn't a glorified, mystical game. People suffer. They cry to the Creator. They get too cold, they get too hot, they get wet and shiver. They see things and get spooked. They're alone, and they're afraid. A man could die up there on the mountain, and you have to take care that doesn't happen. When Hanbleceya is done without the proper ceremony, it can affect the way the vision comes. You have to tell a man you're responsible for, "Do exactly this." Bear Butte isn't a playground. When the thunderstorms start up in the spring and all those spirits come back, there're a lot of things roaming around. My friend Jimmy Dubray can agree to that.

* * *

LET ME TELL YOU a little story before I talk about Hanbleceya. It'll make you think.

A bunch of us were over at Grandpa Poor Thunder's once when one fellow said he saw a white owl sitting on a wire.

Grandpa Poor Thunder told him, "Well, then, why don't you throw a knife at it, and maybe you'll be able to knock some of its tail feathers off so you can use them?"

With that, the whole group of men started throwing knives at the owl.

"Don't you think that's kind of silly?" I asked them.

The Eagle

WHEN YOU SEE an eagle flying, you know that Grandfather is there to accept your prayer. For this reason, a wise person always has a prayer in mind when he's in eagle country. It's sad to think some people don't acknowledge the wisdom of nature. Look at the superior strength of a golden eagle, or a shining (bald) eagle. Look at how high they can fly. To get into the Creator's thoughts, we have channels—or mentors. We have the *wanbli*, eagle, and the Chanunpa, and through them our prayers are boosted up to the Creator. Consider this: you can pray alone, or you can go to a church and pray where there's the cross and a priest, and maybe your prayers are heard extrafast there. The eagle takes our prayers up and passes them on to the higher eagle.

The most powerful feather on a wanbli is the center tail feather. To the old Lakota people, the tail feather of the Wanbli gleska is really sacred. You have to be straight in action and purpose in order to use it—you have to be powerful like the eagle. You can use that center tail feather to doctor people, or pray for them, or smudge them off. You can use it to talk to the Great Spirit. The tail feather is meant for both men and women.

Our reliance on the eagle connects back to the circle of life. Everything is related. We need everything to survive.

—*Thomas Dubray*

HANBLECEYA, CRYING FOR A VISION

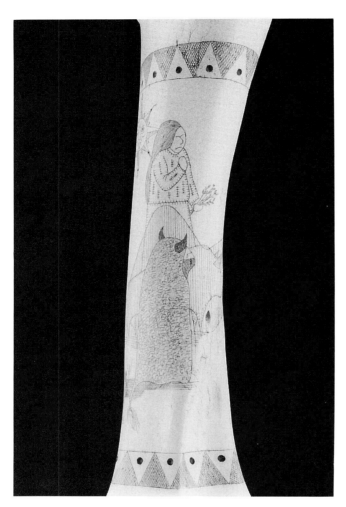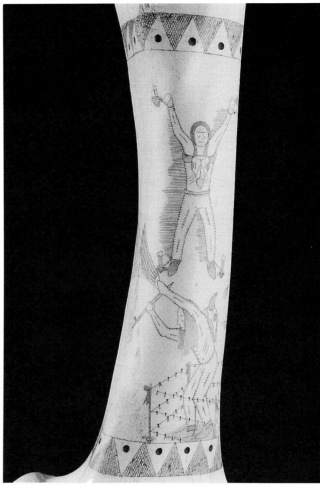

During Hanbleceya, spirits and visions come to those who fast and pray. At left, a man, his face painted half black, wears a buffalo robe to pray for his dead mother. He sees the buffalo spirit come for her. Bear Butte is visible through her rising form. A man who is staked out prays with a buffalo skull pierced to his chest, while another man dances with his Chanunpa inside his hochoka.

"Why?" they asked.

"Because you're just imagining that owl being there," I said.

You know, sometimes you imagine things—your mind puts them there. So you have to be alert every moment of every day or you don't see things as they are and understand them.

On the other hand, sometimes you believe things *aren't* there—when, in fact, they really are.

The point is, every moment presents you with a Y in the road, and you have to decide which way to go. There's good and evil with us all of the time. If you choose wrong, you may waste a lot of time going down a dead-end road, and then you have to come back to where you started. But, in fact, you can never come back because things have changed. So every moment you have to see things right and make right decisions.

The first time I went to fast in the wilderness, a buffalo skull was my altar. The first night I was there, there were four cigarettes near it. The second night, I heard a woman singing about love. I had believed the buffalo skull was from a bull, but I guess it was a female's skull. During the night, the female buffalo became a woman and sang the song of the four directions. She sang about how I would meet peace, and if I would hang onto peace and share it wisely, I would go a long way with it. But if I misused it, my

128 SACRED BUFFALO

HANBLECEYA, CRYING FOR A VISION

life would be short, and I would have to give an account of why I used it unwisely.

The next morning, I saw a hawk come to me. It dove to the ground and came out in the East. It dove again to the ground and came out in the West. It repeated this to the North and to the South. In the South, it looked at me and said, "Look at me, I am *kila*."

That word means awesome. Yet it was only a little hawk, not an eagle.

Two meadowlarks were sitting there talking. One of them said to the hawk, "Don't be telling him that."

The meadowlark looked at me and said, "He likes to lie."

The hawk said to me, "It's going to rain; a thunderstorm is coming."

The meadowlark said to him, "Don't tell him that. It's not going to rain."

And it didn't.

When you finally get interested in the natural ways, you don't go to sweat lodge and Hanbleceya and Sundance without a reason. If it's meant to be and the force of the Lakota spirit wants you, the opportunities will come to you. But the process takes years. When you do go on a vision quest, you can't lie about what you see. You can't say, "I had a dream that I'm going to pierce at Sundance," and then just try to go and do it. It might sound easy to you, but if you haven't really seen the vision of what you're supposed to do, you won't have the energy to carry it through. You'll just slide down to the ground. You have to be careful and truthful about your motives. You have to have an advisor to help you get prepared. But most important, you have to have a reason.

Me, I had a reason to go up the hill at Bear Butte. I had a reason to give thanks at Sundance. My young son Stephen had life-threatening allergies, and the doctors told us that the only way he'd be able to live was in a bubble. He was in Fitzsimmons Army Hospital in Denver and then National Jewish Hospital, and we didn't have the cash to stay with him. We only had enough money for a motel for a couple of nights, so my son told me he wanted to come home to die. I told him, "Okay, you come home. It won't cost us very much to take care of the body." He and I were happy, but my wife Florine and the nurses called after us, telling us he wouldn't live long if he left.

I was a Christian at that point. I knew about the man called Jesus Christ who heals all things through belief, and yet I wondered why this tragedy was happening to our family. Once we were home, we took Stephen to Rosebud Reservation where Grandpa Fools Crow was the chief of Leonard Crow Dog's Sundance. Stephen was supposed to stay away from dust, sage, trees, and so forth, but there we were camping! He was the size of a twig and yet he was hauling water. And on top of that, Uncle Leonard and Uncle Dennis wanted him and my son Tommy to go into the sweat lodge with them.

I stayed outside the sweat lodge while my sons went in. Afterward, Uncle Dennis gave them a Sundance shawl, and the two boys and their

Morning Star

IF YOU'RE going on a journey, you want to start out on the right foot, don't you? That's why we get up each morning and look at the morning star. It's the first sign that the new day is starting. It's the bringer of wisdom. Get up early and see if the Morning Star looks shiny. If it does, that's how your day is going to go. What counts is how you first look at the day—and how you look at yourself.

Talk to the Creator then. You don't have to talk out loud or make a big thing of it. Doing something just to be noticed is not too good. I've been told by the old people that talking silently is good enough. The Creator gets the message. Even in a sweat lodge, you can just pray silently. The Creator listens to you.

That Morning Star waits for the faithful, but then it starts to fade.

—*Thomas Dubray*

Vision Quest

IN THE SWEAT lodge, you can get a vision of when to go to Hanbleceya or Sundance. Some people use seven rocks for the four different rounds—twenty-eight in all. That's twenty-eight for the days of the month. Multiply that by the thirteen moons in a year, and it equals the longest day of the year. That day in June is the most powerful day of all.

—*Thomas Dubray*

Searching for the Way to Live Your Life

HANBLECEYA, OR CRYING for a vision, is the sacred rite undertaken by a person who stands at a crossroads in life. The time for "lamenting" may come when a youth begins to mature and seeks direction for his life, or when a man wants to do something very special—such as pierce at Sundance, or when a woman seeks something with all her heart. To find help in a time of change and confusion, a person laments to Wakan Tanka, the One Who Is Everything, suffering without food and water for several days awaiting a vision.

The vision quest begins, as all the sacred rites do, with the Chanunpa. The man or woman who seeks a vision brings a Chanunpa loaded with cansasa to a spiritual man and asks him to serve as an advisor. If the spiritual man accepts the request, he becomes responsible for the seeker. He must help with the preparations and then sit in prayer during the time the seeker is on the mountain lamenting.

Hanbleceya begins at the fire. The seeker purifies himself in the rite of purification, where the spiritual man loads his Chanunpa and calls upon the powers of the Grandfathers in the four directions and all the powers of the universe, the star people, the rivers and streams, the tree people, the stone people, all the four leggeds and wingeds, and the grasses and plants that grow on Grandmother Earth. Incense may be burned. The pungent smoke of sage offends evil beings and they move away from it. It is said they even fear the leaves themselves, and they never go where a sprig of sage is kept. An incense of sweet grass is a clean, fresh fragrance that pleases the good spirits. It smells of moist spring evenings when the dew settles on the prairie grasses. It is said to be offensive to evil spirits and able to bend their power. Cedar is pleasing to the Thunder-Being of the West. It is said that lightning never strikes a cedar tree. In the sweat lodge, the spiritual man asks the seeker how many days he will fast. He might pledge one, two, or four days, but however long he promises to fast, he is obligated to spend that time on the mountain even if his vision comes early.

The spiritual man leads the seeker up the mountain. The seeker takes only four things with him: his loaded Chanunpa, four chokecherry sticks, a blanket, and his prayer bundle containing a long string of 405 prayer ties. These prayer ties stand for all the good spirits who serve the One Who Is Everything and the Grandfather. When they reach the place where the seeker will cry for a vision, the spiritual man marks a rectangle about six by eight feet, placing the four long chokecherry sticks in the four directions and tying banners in black, red, yellow, and white to their tips. He wraps the 405 prayers around the sticks, beginning and ending in the West, then he goes to the sweat lodge or another quiet place to pray.

The one who seeks a vision may not move from the sacred ground marked by the

HANBLECEYA, CRYING FOR A VISION

cherry sticks and prayer ties. He may not eat or drink for the days he has pledged to spend on the mountain.

The seeker calls upon the four directions and the Above and all its wingeds and the Earth and all its growing things for their help. He prays all day, aloud and silently, for the Creator hears everything—even the thoughts in our hearts. He must keep his focus and not let his mind wander. He must be alert to any messenger the Creator sends to him, for the messenger may be a bird or deer or even so small a creature as an ant. Maybe none of them will speak to him, but he should remember each of them, for each tells a story. At first the animals are afraid of him, but as time passes, they come near.

The seeker cries for visions—and they come. He may hear stomping and feel the ground shake as though something huge is coming, but when he looks, he sees only a grasshopper. He may feel a thunderstorm blasting around him driving hail like stones, yet when he looks, his skin is dry. In this way, he is tested, and he must stand with a strong heart. For what he sees, he becomes—whether an animal or a bird or an element of weather. In this way, he feels its power to teach him.

The vision that comes to the seeker comes from a consciousness other than that which is human, often by way of an *akicita*, a messenger, such as a hawk or a meadowlark. It may come to him while he is awake or asleep. It may speak aloud so he can hear, or it may be a voice in his thoughts or a picture in his mind's eye.

When the seeker has lamented for the number of days he pledged, the spiritual man goes for him. Back in camp, the sweat lodge is made ready to receive him, the rocks are brought in, and the seeker tells his advisor what he has seen. He must tell the plain truth, but in fact, the spiritual man already knows what he will say for he has seen the visions, too. The spiritual man helps explain any signs and symbols, and he holds the visions up like a crystal so the seeker can see them from every direction.

After Hanbleceya, the seeker is bound to act according to what he has seen. For if he has seen a vision, he has received a gift brought through the Chanunpa by the Calf Pipe Woman. A true vision will work out. It'll never, never fail.

Mitakuye Oyasin.

Honoring the Fighting Men

IN THE LAKOTA Way, the red feather signifies the Tokala society, the warrior. The red feather is awarded to a warrior who has been wounded in battle—like a medal of honor. When a warrior returns to tell his story, the people present him with a red feather—that is, they turn an eagle feather red with their own blood in his honor. We honor our veterans because they are our guardians.

We Lakota know a person by what he does. His actions speak louder than words. We realize that when a man becomes a warrior, he is changed forever. We respect his dedication to his people. We respect his responsibility to protect and provide for the women and children and old men. My dad and uncle were there at the first red feather ceremony when the tradition was revived by Grandpa Fools Crow.

When a red feather drops during a ceremony, it means a warrior somewhere in this world has fallen. It takes another red feather warrior to pick it up or at least another veteran. If none are present, then a spiritual person with respect for these ways picks up the feather. The warrior who retrieves the red feather prays to the Great Spirit to help his brother. Everyone is quiet then, because they know a wounded warrior has gone beyond.

The yellow feather represents a man who is a leader. The Creator picks great men to great things, men don't pick themselves. Ordinary people have to accept who they are and go with the flow. But some of them claim to be a leader without taking responsibility for what is involved in it.

A great leader throughout history has been someone who provides for his people. His ability to be generous to people sets him apart from ordinary men. Nowadays people put yellow ties on their tipis believing that alone makes them leaders. But they don't have enough food to share with others. They only have enough for themselves. They don't understand what the yellow feather represents.

For a man to put yellow ribbons on his tipi, he should have big pots and pans. He has to walk the talk. People want to be regarded as a leader without really knowing what is required.

—*Thomas Dubray*

Bazooka, a Vietnam Veteran

I WAS RAISED Roman Catholic, but in Vietnam I had my spirituality cauterized out of me. I was taught that God was all-knowing, all-just, and all-merciful, and I couldn't balance that with my experience in war. I had more or less given up on spirituality.

HANBLECEYA, CRYING FOR A VISION

Once, I went to Sundance with Big Jim, and while I'm not sure what happened to me there, when I left South Dakota, I knew I had changed. For the first time since the war, I felt full. I felt like I had eaten a huge meal. I felt content. The Lakota people treated me differently than anyone I had ever met because they honored what I had been through in war.

When I came home from the service, I knew I was different than I had been. I wasn't the same young man who had left Cleveland, Ohio. I had progressed in my life along a different path than my friends and family. When our paths crossed again, there was a gap. I felt marked. I felt like a very old, old man. I went through the motions of a normal social life—marriage, family, job—but I had no feeling for it.

Big Jim and I were sitting with several men at Jimmy Dubray's house in Allen shortly after we went to Sundance at Green Grass. The men started talking about how the Lakota people understand the changes that occur to a man when he goes to war. The people know he isn't the same when he returns, but that's okay. It's a normal and natural thing, and because of his difference from a man who isn't a warrior, he has a new role as a protector, teacher, and role model.

I really connected with that. I am different now than before I went to Vietnam, but I'm okay. And among those people, I am honored. In Allen, I was given my first wiyaka, and to me it was a symbol of acknowledgment and acceptance.

I feel I owe the Lakota people a great debt because since that time, I've been much more at peace with myself and my experience in Vietnam. I've felt much, much better about myself and my future on this earth.

—Bazooka, the machine designer who helped design the mechanism for rotating the pedestal on which the Sacred Buffalo stands, is a Vietnam Vets Motorcycle Club member.

Veterans

NOWADAYS, EVERYONE WANTS to claim that they're some kind of warrior, some kind of veteran. But before, there was no such thing as a veteran because you were never "discharged" from service. In our way, once you're a soldier under the chief, you're a soldier until the day you are no more. You sleep with the sword, *mila wakan*, holy knife, as a pillow so you can protect and feed the people. Nowadays, everyone claims to be a war hero, and he can't even take care of his own family.

—Jimmy Dubray

> ### Colors
>
> WE USE FOUR colors basically—black, red, yellow, and white. When I was a young man, I saw these colors as representing natural things. To me yellow represents the sun coming up. Black represents the night and the mystery of life—the not knowing what will happen when it gets dark, but knowing that tomorrow when it gets light, we're going to be okay. Red represents the blood of the people, the blood of the buffalo, which gave itself so the Lakota people could survive. White represents the cranes flying north after the long winter, their white bellies overhead a sign of the coming hot weather.
>
> Green is the color of living things. Blue is being healthy, like a blue shiny day when the sky is healthy. A darker blue means a storm. It's frightening, a threat. Orange and dark blue represent the Thunder People. If you get those colors toward evening, a man has to pray and be plenty powerful to communicate with those things that could bring life or take life.
>
> We see these colors as being part of nature, and we accept them and always remember them in our everyday life.
>
> —*Thomas Dubray*

cousins danced all four days of Sundance. Stephen made it through all that dust and pollen and contact with other people and cigarette smoke. Today, he's a healthy man.

The next year, at the Sundance at Porcupine, I thought to myself, "I should be in there. I'm going to give thanks because the Great Spirit gave my son back to me. In exchange, I will give him what was his in the beginning—myself." So, you see, it took something special and very close to my heart to make me decide to get involved.

You don't go from sweat lodge to Hanbleceya to Sundance within a few weeks or a few months or even a year. It takes a long time. Some men prepare for four years or more. You have to have an advisor to help you get prepared. But most important, you have to have a reason.

A boy becomes a man through the sweat lodge, vision quest, and Sundance. He becomes a man when the Creator decides. It's not just that his body changes. When he begins to dream of hunting, his mind changes. He goes into the sweat lodge. In the sweat lodge, he takes his first step toward the vision quest. During a vision quest, he dreams of what he'll do at Sundance. In this way he becomes a man.

In the Lakota way, you're a child until you're eighteen or so. From eighteen to thirty years old, you're a young adult. From thirty to forty, you're on the verge of adulthood. From forty to sixty, you can think—you're not a baby who is having babies. From sixty on over, you're supposed to be a member of the big-belly bunch. People feed you good when you're that age so you can think and talk. They call the chief Old Man, yet in his mind and health he may be stronger than the young ones. Today, the United States government says you're a man or woman when you're eighteen years old, but what kind of man or woman?

Calf Pipe Woman taught the people many, many things, and Hanbleceya is one of them. The people came to this nation, and with the Chanunpa, as well as with the cross, they can survive. At Sundance, there are four chokecherry branches fastened onto the Sundance tree, and against the tree trunk, they form a cross. We're not saying that the Calf Pipe Woman is the same as the Virgin Mary, but she brought the Calf Pipe and said, "This is truly the way you pray." She taught us how to sleep and dream and see a vision, she taught us how to tell it and how to try it. A true vision will work out. It'll never, never fail.

You must become the living Calf Pipe. You must try to be at peace with everyone. Get out of the habit of judging people. Everyone is sacred. Greet and accept each person you meet knowing that you can learn a lesson from him. I try not to judge anyone, because how do I know that person isn't saying a little prayer for me right at that moment?

Do people judge you? Do they gossip and speak against you? Let it go. Words are like a winter storm. It snows one day, and the wind is icy. But even though it's cold, you can look forward two or three months to the warm days that will follow. Then you'll be looking for a little patch of shade to sit in. What people say about you is like the winter wind: it blows one way one day, and another way the next. Keep your course.

HANBLECEYA, CRYING FOR A VISION

Words don't hurt me. I have grown like the buffalo: when a storm comes, I turn my head into the north wind, and I am strong. Why does the buffalo face the wind? So he doesn't get buried in the snow and suffocate. Other people may stumble in the storm, and it hurts me knowing that they suffer. But I hold my head high above the snow and wait until there's sweet, green grass growing all around me.

To become the living Calf Pipe, you must become nonviolent. You must live in harmony with all creatures. I'd like to see a macho guy go out and catch a trout with his bare hands. No way, Jose! He can't because he's violent. There's violence in his heart. He thinks, "I'm a man, so I can kill." This is no good.

Once, in winter, Florine and I had nothing for supper and I decided to catch a trout with my bare hands. It was in the winter, and the water was like ice, but we needed food, so we prayed about it. Even though my hands are small, I caught us a good-sized trout. I felt him, and all of a sudden, I closed my fingers over him and jerked him out of the water. I made sure he was far away from the water, or he'd have jumped back in and we'd have missed dinner. I couldn't have done this if I had had violence in my heart. We must think and live like the buffalo. We must give thanks, just like they do.

When Great Waters Covered the Land

WE HAVE BEEN on this Turtle Island for thousands of years—how long no one really knows. Fossils show that this continent was once under water, and there is a story my grandmother told about this. Way back then, there was a young chief. When water began to flood over the land, he only had time to grab the hand of a young woman and help her climb up into a tree out of the flood waters. The water rose higher and higher into the tree, and it looks as though they might drown, but the young chief was determined to survive and to save the woman. And so he became an eagle, and he picked up the young woman and flew with her to higher ground. When all the water went away to the ocean, they came back down. They had children then, and he became the chief of the land. The children were our ancestors.

—*Jimmy Dubray*

The Thunder-Being

THE THUNDER-BEING is a great winged one that lives in the direction of the West. Its voice is the thunder. Maybe that great clap of thunder was the first word. The lightning bolts that come from its eye form the bridge between heaven and earth. The Thunder-Being brings the living water to us, it brings us life and the joy we feel after a rain. It brings the night that takes away our cares. Its messenger is the eagle.

—*Jimmy Dubray*

Chapter 14

Wiwanyag Wachipi, Sundance

> "When you're pierced to the tree, you're on God's time. You feel this unbelievable safety. And peace. Your prayer is so, so strong that you feel there's no one else in the world. Just you and God—talking things out.
>
> —BIG JIM DURHAM

IN THE SUNDANCE CIRCLE, we give the most precious thing of all back to the Creator—we give our flesh and our suffering. We recreate the crucifixtion once a year, using our bodies as the sacrifice. To be hooked to that tree is to be hooked by an umbilical cord to the Creator. I've never felt safer and more connected to him than when I'm pierced to the Sundance tree. It's the greatest gift we can give. It's the greatest thing we can do for our families. But it's a hard path to walk.

The Sundance is one of the sacred rites on the foundation of the Chanunpa and the Sacred Red Road. The Sacred Buffalo's front legs show the four days of the Sundance. The lowest bone of the left front leg shows the drummers and the singers at Sundance. When you're at Sundance, you hear the sound of the drum. Thum, thum, thum, thum. It's like a heart beating. To me, it represents the heartbeat of the earth, it has so much power. When you're laid down on that buffalo robe and you're getting piercing sticks pushed through the skin on your chest, the only thing you hear is the drum. It sucks you down into the earth so you don't feel the pain. That's what you focus on. Thum. That's one. Thum. That's two. If you understand that drum, you can bear the pain. Thum. That's three. On that drum bone, there's one mallet down against the drum and three mallets raised. There's just one beat at a time. Thum.

When I sing, I beat the drum to give the respect and power the words. "I am standing in front of you, facing you, hear my prayers. Remember the Chanunpa is first. Remember to load that pipe. Grandfather, Grandfather, this is what I'm doing. My prayers will come true." The drum helps me send that message home.

If you follow that lower bone up to the middle one, you find the people praying in the arbor. The arbor surrounds the Sundance Circle, and the women and children pray

WIWANYAG WACHIPI, SUNDANCE

> ### Cansasa
>
> OUR ANCESTORS TREASURED tobacco, which is why it is such a special offering. They didn't have a sports car to share—"Do you want to take my Porsche for a spin?"—but they did have tobacco to offer.
>
> Real tobacco as we know it is made from the red willow. You peel away the red bark until you reach the green inside. Once it's dry, that's what you smoke in the Chanunpa. It is offered to the Grandfathers before us with a prayer. It is offered as a sign of respect.
>
> Now we also use regular tobacco as a gift to show our respect or as an offering. We wrap tobacco in cotton cloth of different colors. We pray as we place a pinch of tobacco in the cloth and tie it closed. We tie the prayer in a tree as an offering to Spirit. Prayer ties can be very powerful.
>
> —*Thomas Dubray*

> ### Sundance Song
>
> Grandfather, I am going to pray, hear me.
> To the universe, I am going to pray, hear me.
> With my relatives I will live,
> I am saying this.
>
> —*A Traditional Song*

> ### Sundance Song
>
> Great Spirit, have pity on me.
> I want to live and that's why I am doing this.
> Help me.
> I am suffering.
>
> —*A Traditional Song*

there in support of their men who are at the tree piercing for them. I've looked into the eyes of those people and seen their pitifulness—their humbleness—as they raise their hands in the air, praying to God. If you let Tunkashila take you, you can hear them praying. They've come thousands of miles to stand in the circle and pray to Tunkashila for another year of life. That drum starts it. Thum. The drum brings the beat for the dance, the singers bring the words, and the people support it.

On that bone, four men are hooked up to the *cha wakan*, the sacred tree. It takes a real desire to get yourself pierced to the tree. You do it to thank Tunkashila for life and to ask for special help in your life—and to help your kids and your family. When you dance and pray and sacrifice yourself, you're proving to Tunkashila that you're willing to suffer for your prayer.

Once when I pierced the tree jerked my rope up in the top as I broke free of it. The powers that be tell me that I'm done piercing. The tree took my piercing for the rest of my life. That's a great gift. I may choose to pierce again, but that's between me and God. All I've got to give him is my body. Some people give from their wallets. Other people give of themselves. They love the great gift the Creator gave them—their lives—and that's what they give back. It depends on what you believe. If you believe suffering is what God requires of you, it's what you'll do. If you don't believe, it's impossible for you to do. Some people come to Sundance and pierce because the scars are honored among people who know the sacrifice. The scars on your chest and your arms and your back tell the story of your life. But there are shallow people in every tradition, and those who come for the scars end up drinking alcohol a couple of days after Sundance; I guess their prayers are answered in the same manner they are asked.

The four men shown pierced to the Sundance tree give back to all four directions. Everything on the Sacred Buffalo is shown as four and six and seven, but there's only one God. We all serve Tunkashila, Wakan Tanka, the One Who Is Everything.

That spiritual man holding the eagle wing fan on that leg is a servant to the Creator, too. The Creator gave him special power to be able to see things in people, to hear their prayers, to hear their dreams, but he's still a man. He uses the eagle wing fan to direct the dancers to go to the tree. They charge it four times before they try to break free from it.

Time is funny. When you're pierced to the tree, you're on God's time. There's a place that being pierced to the tree takes you—a beautiful, beautiful place. You feel this unbelievable safety. And peace. Because your prayer is so, so strong, you feel like there's no one else in the world. Just you and God—talking things out.

I remember once when I was pierced to the tree I hollered at God: "Do you hear me you son-of-a-bitch?" People were freaked out by that. I asked them, "How am I supposed to act? Can I be something I'm not?

WIWANYAG WACHIPI, SUNDANCE

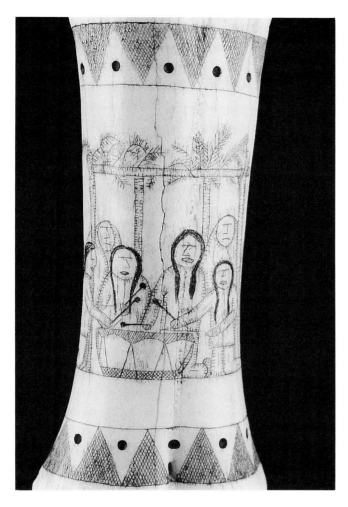
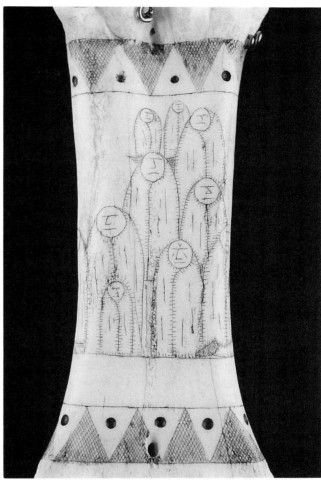

Do you think God doesn't know who I am? Do you think I can go out there for fifteen minutes and bullshit God?" Not hardly. For whatever reason, I am what I am, and I love Tunkashila. Whatever I might say, my heart is pure.

Why are people afraid to be what they are? I would like to paint a picture of how it feels to be really, really scared, and then all of a sudden be sitting in God's lap. Nothing can harm you there. You're safe. You have no fears. You belong to God. If you don't realize that when you're pierced up, you'll never understand it. Out there in the circle, when you're pierced to the tree, there's no place to run and hide. You're taken down to the very core of your being. If you can't get next to the Creator then, there's not much hope for you. It's such a really special time. Time stands still.

When you pull back against your rope, you can feel the force of the tree pulling against your body. That's when you go to that place in your core. You can feel it. You'll really feel it if you don't pray! When you get to your fourth charge at the tree, it reminds me of being in a situation you believe is going to cost you your life. When you think you're going to die, you get that surge that says, "Just do it." When you're pierced to the tree, you jerk back. You look up the rope and see that you're hanging there, and you think, "Just do it." So you pull back with all your might. If your prayers are good and your

Sundance starts with the drums and the songs. On the lowest bone of the left front leg, four drummers play the drum that is the heartbeat of the earth: three drumsticks up, one on the drum. Behind them are the singers.

WIWANYAG WACHIPI, SUNDANCE

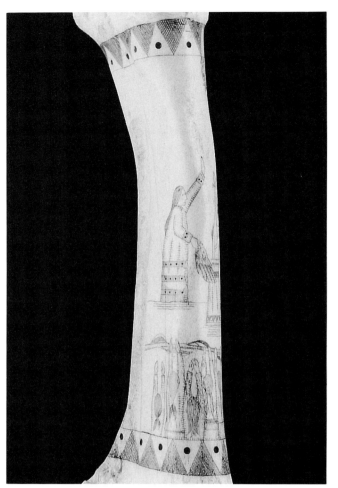 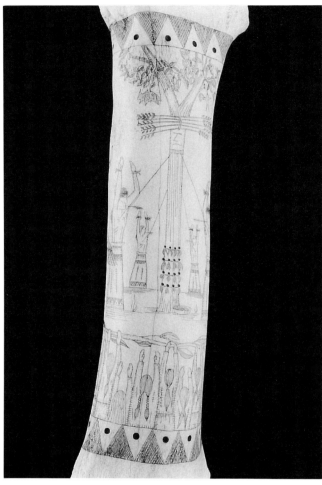

Four men are pierced to the sacred Sundance tree on the center bone of the left front leg. When the spiritual man directs them with his eagle-wing fan, they charge the tree four times, breaking free of it on the fourth. Their women, children, and friends support them from the arbor.

heart is pure, God helps you. Next thing you know, you're off the tree. You're really glad you got a chance to stand with Tunkashila. You think about the beautiful body he gave you to use for a little while on earth, and you just gave a little bit back to him.

Some years ago, I had a dream about the Sundance tree. So when Sundance time came, I took two of the leaders out to the previous year's tree before it came down to tell them what I saw. I told them at the Sundance tree so they'd know it was the truth.

I dreamed I was standing in the middle of the Sundance circle facing West with my arms outstretched North to South. While I was standing there, lightning came from the North and South gates and hit the Sundance tree behind me. I wasn't hurt at all. I saw one of the men I told my dream to standing by the West gate.

"I just want you to know what I dreamed, in case of something," I said.

The old tree was taken down and the new one brought in and prepared to stand in its place. The prayers ties were put on it and the figure of the buffalo and the man. And the men who were going to pierce tied their piercing ropes onto it. When the Old Man waved his fan, everyone began to pull the tree up. As they pulled it, it split in two. The two main forks just sagged, and it split in two a pretty good ways down.

WIWANYAG WACHIPI, SUNDANCE

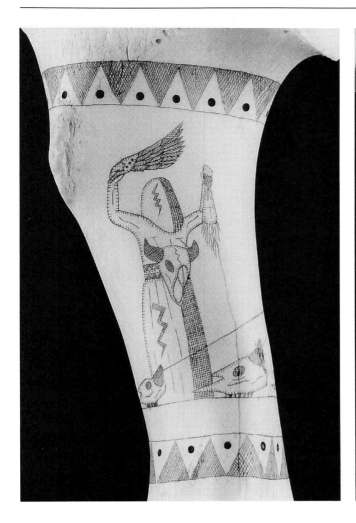
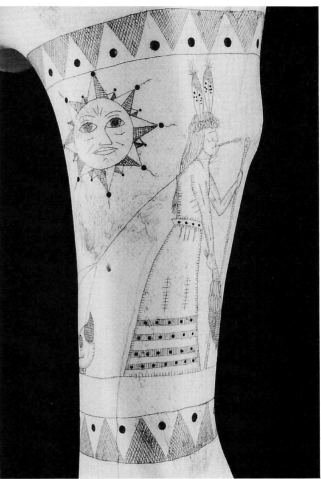

When the people realized what had happened, they came to me. They wanted me to tie it together. No one else was allowed to touch the tree. I put some good braces on it and tied ropes around it to keep it together. The bracing was real strong, and afterwards, the men even tied their piercing ropes to it. The ropes and braces held tight, and it stood all the way through Sundance and into the next year when it was replaced by a new Sundance tree. This is a true story.

I always look at the meaning behind every event, and I can't help but think the split was because the camp there had split in two. Before Sundance, some of the leaders had decided not to let non-Indians pierce. They felt that if they didn't let white men pierce, maybe the Old Man's health would improve. But they didn't tell anyone about this plan up front. They waited until after people had traveled hundreds or a thousand miles to be there and helped build the arbor and set up their camps. Then the day before Sundance, during the sweat lodge, non-Indians were told they couldn't pierce. Some of them came out of the sweat lodge and asked me, "What are we going to do?" I didn't know what to tell them. A few of them were on the fourth year of a four-year pledge.

Some of the people packed up and went home angry. Finally, the others were allowed to pierce on the last day. But those men who took it upon themselves to stop them from piercing played a dangerous game. The Sundance tree showed them that.

The Heyoka, a contrary man, pierces at Sundance with a buffalo skull on his chest (top bone of the left front leg). He wears a cloth over his head, and lightning adorns his robe. At Sundance, a man's back is pierced with skulls, which he drags until he breaks free—thus freeing himself from ignorance. He blows an eagle-bone whistle and holds an eagle-wing fan and a sagye, staff. A sage wreath with two eagle feathers encircles his head.

WIWANYAG WACHIPI, SUNDANCE

The inside surface of the left scapula shows the people carrying the sacred Sundance tree, traditionally a cottonwood. Led by the spiritual man, a little boy, and four virgin girls, the men carry the tree into the Sundance circle, never letting it touch the ground.

On the highest bone of the left front leg a man at Sundance drags three skulls pierced on his back. He drags skulls as a way of getting rid of his ignorance. When he breaks free, he leaves his ignorance behind. I saw one man drag seven skulls and then put a child on the last one and drag the child. I saw a veteran drag skulls all the way around the inside the arbor and outside and then behind the Sundance circle where the sweat lodges are before he broke free.

Three of the skulls on that bone are in the light, and one is pierced to the chest of a Heyoka—a contrary man who goes opposite nature. He's on a different side of power. The lightning bolt is a symbol of a Heyoka's power. The Heyoka always does everything in reverse. He says he hates you to mean he loves you. He goes into the sweat lodge backwards. He pierces backwards, hanging skulls from his chest and getting hooked to the tree from his back. He pierces wearing a bag over his head, and dances that way. When the lightning comes, he'll stand in the storm and pray without fear. A true Heyoka has the power to make lightning, to control a storm in a prayer, and to make things happen. But I've only known one true Heyoka.

With the skull pierced on his chest as it's shown on that bone, the Heyoka has to jump up and down until his flesh rips. It really hurts. It takes much longer than if the skull is pierced to your back because, that way, you have the weight of your body pulling against it as it rolls along the ground. But then, if Tunkashila wants the skull off, he'll get it off.

WIWANYAG WACHIPI, SUNDANCE

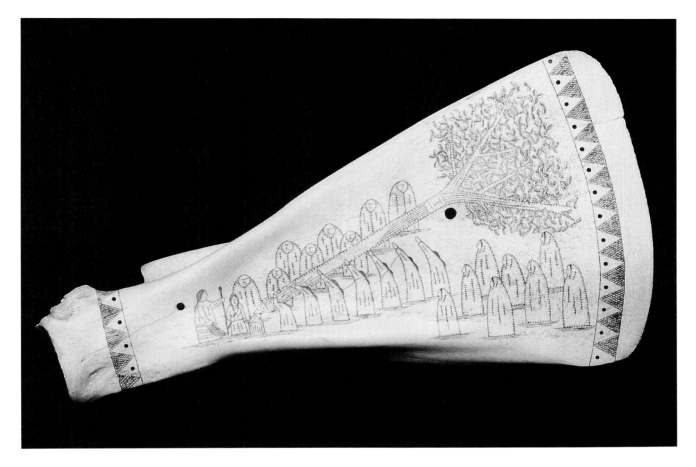

The day you cut and carry the tree is a good day. That ceremony is shown on the inside of both of the left and right scapulas. The Sundance grounds are ready. The arbor's done, and everything's fresh and beautiful. The old tree's down. The first sweat lodge fire has been lit. The rocks are in there. Everyone is getting ready to go get the tree. The whole camp waits.

Finally, the Old Man and the little boy and the four girls come with the axe. The Old Man has chosen the tree earlier, and everyone goes to where it stands. There's a ceremony for chopping the tree. The children chop the tree in the four quarters, and then all the pledgers get to finish the job. They all chop until the tree goes down.

When the tree arrives at the Sundance circle, you get excited because you know you're going to be hooked to it. You know the tree represents Tunkashila. You listen to the wind going through the leaves, and they go clicky, clack. You touch the tree like you caress your own child, showing it your love because for the next four days, it's going to help you. You tie your piercing rope onto it, and you're praying really hard.

Then the Old Man brings his fan up, and the tree starts to come up, pulled up by the pledgers. You can feel the tree pulling on your rope. When it's up, you can see the buffalo and man made out of buffalo rawhide up in it. You can see the prayer banners flying—black, red, yellow, and white. All the races are represented on that Sundance tree, and old men and old women and children are all in the Sundance circle. It doesn't get much better than that.

On the inside of the right scapula, the people go to chop the sacred Sundance tree the spiritual man has chosen. He sings to it before it is cut, blessing it for the sacrifice it is making. A little boy touches it before the chopping begins, making it innocent.

WIWANYAG WACHIPI, SUNDANCE

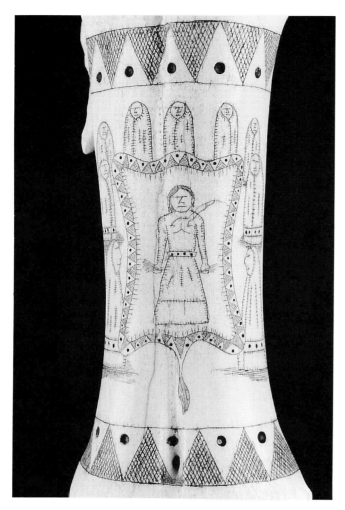 

On the lowest bone of the right front leg, a man ready to be pierced lies on a buffalo robe placed beside the Sundance tree. He holds sage in his hands. On the back of this bone, the spiritual man drives a man to the ground, putting him to sleep so he can receive the vision he needs.

Once Sundance has started, I've lain on the buffalo robe on the West side of the Sundance tree and been pierced. The West side is where the spirits come from—where help comes from. That scene is on the lowest bone of the Sacred Buffalo's right front leg—the West leg. At that moment, all of Sundance comes together. You're lying there, you feel yourself being pierced, you're praying, the tree is there, the Old Man is there, the incisors are there, the drum is there. You can feel the drum come up through the earth, and when the cherry sticks are being pushed through your flesh, its beat is all that keeps you from drowning in the pain. The Old Man waves his eagle-wing fan over your face and you feel eagles are flying by.

The Old Man has the power to see when someone's supposed to receive a vision. He can take his eagle-wing fan and wave it in front of you, and take you straight to the ground to bring you the dream. It's very heavy spiritually, but it's a blessing. The Old Man has the power of connection with the spirits, and in the Sundance circle, he feels them. I've watched Jimmy Dubray drop a man with his fan and seen the man stay out for fifteen or twenty minutes. When he revived, he crawled to the tree asking Tunkashila to help him. Who knows why the Old Man did that? Maybe he saw the man standing there in all his pride and glory and wanted to help him get into a vision.

I've seen men hang from the Sundance tree as shown on the middle bone on the

WIWANYAG WACHIPI, SUNDANCE

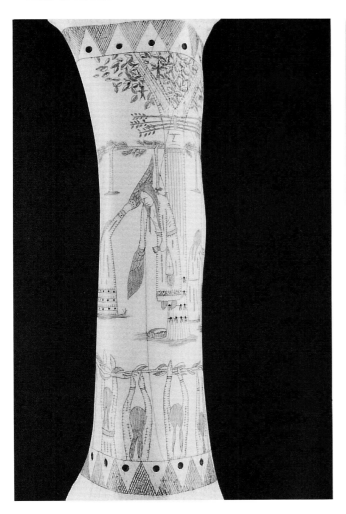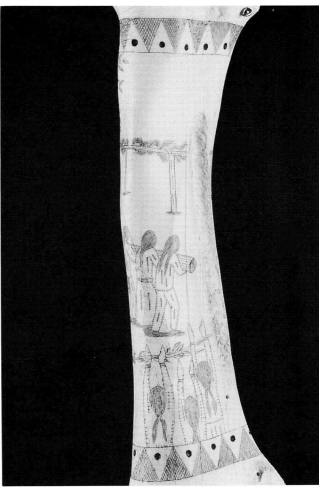

right front leg. I've been one of those men holding him up, but I've never asked a prayer so big that it required hanging from the tree. Once an Indian from Montana came to Sundance with a special vision. He and his wife wanted a son, but his wife couldn't have a baby. He asked to be hung from the Sundance tree so he could pray real hard and ask for the greatest gift of all—the gift of life. That's what that Sacred Circle represents and those prayers. Your sacrifice and suffering are for life. You're praying for your family to live. You're asking Tunkashila to have pity on you. That man asked for new life, so he suffered a lot for it.

The man was pierced in his chest, and I was one of the men holding the log as we pulled him up in the tree. I could feel the rope tighten, then I could feel the man's weight as his feet lifted off the ground. I could feel him kicking. I could feel him dangling. I could feel his life in our hands, just like a fish on a line.

The man hung up there in the Sundance tree for fifteen minutes or more before his flesh ripped. I could see him in my prayer; I could see how bad he was suffering. When he finally broke free, he had big holes in his skin—holes as big around as a cup.

The next year, he and his wife brought a new little baby boy with them to Sundance. They took him straight to the tree. The Old Man walked them out to the tree to pray with that little child. That prayer works. It really works.

A man who prays a huge prayer to Tunkashila is pierced to the sacred Sundance tree and pulled off the ground (middle bone of the right front leg). The spiritual man with the eagle-wing fan prays with him. The people in the arbor support him. Behind the tree on that bone, four men hold a log that lifts the pierced man off the ground and helps him in his prayer.

WIWANYAG WACHIPI, SUNDANCE

 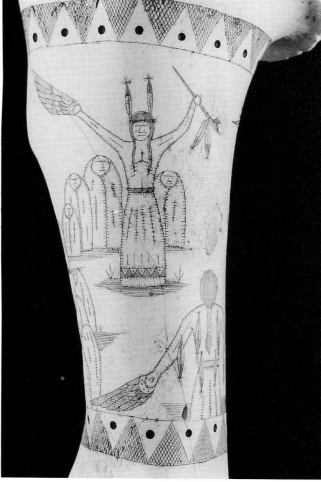

On the highest bone of the right front leg, a man carries his child out of the Sundance circle after praying with the spiritual man for the child to be healed. Other people bring their young, elderly, and sick to the sacred tree to be healed. A dancer at Sundance prays with his Chanunpa on the reverse of that bone. Another man, who has had the eagle dream, dances with eagle feathers pierced to his arms and back.

The third day is for healing. That's one of the scenes shown on the upper bone on the right front leg. On the third day, the people in the arbor who are sick come into the circle asking for help. They go to the tree, and the Old Man prays for them. I once saw a man carrying his dying daughter to the Sundance tree for healing. The Old Man said that sometimes people come too late—that the child was too far gone. She didn't make it. But Tunkashila always has a reason for taking a child home. Only he knows that. We don't.

On that bone, a man is dancing with his Chanunpa. He's singing a song to Tunkashila and raising his Pipe to the Sundance tree.

The man in front of him has had the eagle dream. He has asked to be pierced with eagle feathers on his arms, and he dances that way in the Sundance circle. The feathers spin and fall off as he dances, or they're pulled off, or his flesh is cut and put it in a prayer tie on the Sundance tree.

There are horses on all four legs of the Sacred Buffalo. When Jimmy Dubray blessed the project, and he predicted that the horse would become part of the Buffalo. We had no idea how that would come true, but one day, we just saw the horses on the legs, and after that, we could never look at the bones again without seeing them there.

WIWANYAG WACHIPI, SUNDANCE

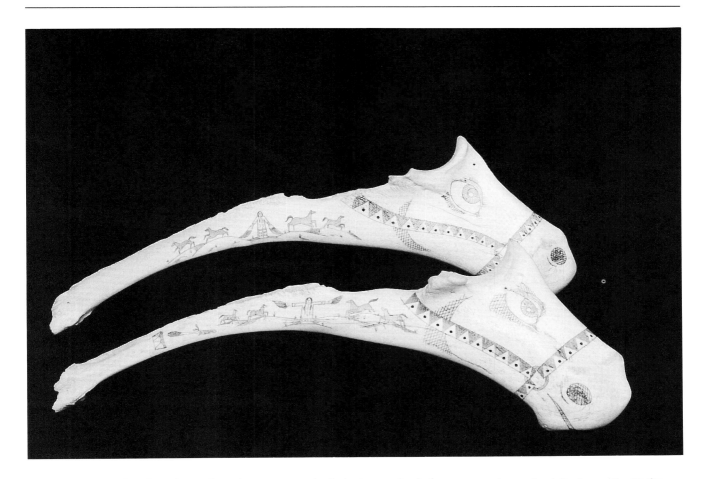

Shunka, the dog, has always been important to the Lakota people. A dog represents healing and loyalty.

Horses are called *shunka wakan*—holy or mysterious dogs. There's no doubt that they changed the lives of the Indians once they came. They represent the West, because their hooves sound like thunder. A long time ago, there were men who could direct a herd of horses with a wave of the eagle wing fan. That's what you see there on the horse bones: a holy man calling them to him with his eagle-wing fan and then directing them away. But this ability hasn't shown itself for decades now, and I don't know anyone who is qualified to speak from experience about that ceremony.

A spiritual man directs the horse dance on these bones on the front legs. He lifts his eagle-wing fans to call them to him and lowers them to drive them away.

* * *

Reporter: When did you first pierce?

Big Jim: Seven years ago, I gave flesh for the first time, but I saved being pierced for a special prayer—like I was taught. A lot of people say one thing and then do something else for self-glory. But I believed in saving being pierced for the first time for something special. When it came time I did it for a very special prayer.

Reporter: What was your reason?

Jim: I hung my Vietnam ribbon in prayer ties on my rope—I always have those men who were killed there and those men who are still unaccounted for there on my mind. But my main reason for being pierced was my prayer for my children to have an easy life. I prayed that they'd never have to suffer like I did. It was worth it to me to pierce for that prayer. I saved it because it's special, but I prayed on it for a long time first.

* * *

> **How Horses Came to the People**
>
> ONCE, A LONG time ago, a whole camp of people had nothing to eat. Elders cried. Women cried, and children cried because they were hungry. One young boy had a little puppy dog, and some of the people looked on it as something to eat. One evening, the boy said, "I'm going up the hill to talk to the Creator." He took his dog with him and he prayed. He fell asleep, and all of a sudden, he felt something on his face. He woke up, and his puppy was gone. But a large form was there, and it spoke to him. It said, "Look down." The boy looked down on the prairie, and he saw a herd of buffalo. The spirit said, "Now you get on me, and we'll go down there and your people will eat. They'll be hungry no more." The boy looked again, and he saw that his little puppy had become a horse. The boy hopped on the horse and went down to chase the buffalo. He drove them over a cliff for a massive kill, and he went back to camp and told his people. Everyone had their fill of food.
>
> —*Jimmy Dubray*

I AM JAMES DUBRAY, and I have served as the Sundance chief, the Intercessor, of the Fools Crow International Sundance in Kyle, South Dakota, since Grandpa Fools Crow died. We call the Sundance *wiwanyag wachipi*, which means "dance looking at the sun."

Only I don't dance to the sun, but the sun dances to me. I'll tell you how that happens: the drum beats its rhythm, and I dance at the sacred tree and look at the sun. I pray with all my heart. The sun is happy that a soul on earth has finally seen the light so it dances. It jumps up and down a little. My wife, Florine, and some others have seen that happen during Sundance. Many blessings come to us then.

Many people don't know how Sundance started. I was told that it started with a man and his wife. One day a man and wife had trouble between them. They had a family, but she left him and went from camp to camp crying. He stayed with his children and prayed every day that she'd come home. She didn't. Finally, he had an idea. He decided to go up on a hill and pray.

He was up on the hill praying, when he saw a tree. He said, "Maybe I'll pray to the sun for help. Maybe the sun is the eye of the Great Spirit. Maybe he's behind there, and he'll see me and answer my prayer."

The man stood in front of the tree and sang. He moved around as he sang, and he saw that the sun moved, too. He saw an eagle on the tree. The eagle was whistling, and it seemed like the eagle was helping, too. The man's prayer soared into the sky. He prayed for four days, with his children sitting there watching him.

About the fourth day that man was up on the hill, his woman felt lonely. She came back to the house, but no one was there. Some people told her that her husband was up the hill praying for her and that her children were there, so she went, too. She saw her husband standing under the tree singing and dancing. An eagle rose off of the tree and flew higher and higher into the sky. The sight of her husband out there sacrificing himself was a sorrowful sight to the woman. She hadn't known until then how much she loved him. But when she saw him, so pitiful, praying to God to bring her home, she sang praises. Today, the women sing that song at Sundance and raise their hands up. They sing, "Oh, how sadly I see my man. I love my man so. Look how terribly he's suffering there."

The man heard his wife singing and rejoiced. Later, they found a solution to their problems. That's how the Sundance started. That's one version, anyway.

Ever since, I can remember, the cottonwood tree has been the Sundance tree. Its leaves are shaped like a heart, and when it's cut, they tell me, sometimes there's the

WIWANYAG WACHIPI, SUNDANCE

shape of a heart inside. If you notice, the tree has a skin, like a human skin. It has sap, like human blood. Some say the tree of life is a cedar or a pine tree. Every tree is a tree of life. But the Lakota people use the cottonwood.

The tree sacrifices itself for us, so when I go down through Yellow Bear Canyon, I pray that I will find the right tree. Down at the creek, we tell the trees, "We're part of you, we're part of the water, we're part of the earth, we're part of everything." We ask forgiveness from the tree we've picked for the Sundance. We tell it, "You are picked today for the sacrifice. We'll use you to pray to the Almighty Creator." We sing to the tree, "Holy you stand." When I stand there with my eyes closed and touch the Sundance tree, it's alive. It's a living thing. It breathes. It moves. From outside, it may seem to be just a tree, but that's only if you don't know.

I try to find the smallest tree out of consideration for the people who have to carry it into the Sundance circle. But even then, it grows and ends up forty feet tall. Maybe it takes thirty people to load it into the truck, but when it's unloaded, it takes sixty or seventy people to carry it. We know then that it's a sacred thing. We don't ever let it touch the ground. Almighty God has blessed it, and every limb, every wood chip, has healing power. He created it, and he proclaimed it good. So we take it, and it's good for us.

Some books say that the tree is considered the enemy, and that we shoot at it and hit it to subdue it. But that's crazy. We sit under it in the summertime and rest in its shade. In the wintertime, we use it to keep from freezing. We use it to cook our food. There's nothing about a tree that is an enemy. We go to the tree humble. We tell the tree to forgive us for picking him. As Sundance chief, I go after the tree with a little boy and four virgin girls. We take the smallest, most innocent child, and he touches the tree first so the tree becomes innocent. The tree could be a woman. It could be a young man. We ask it, "Look around here. Look at these people below you. These people depend on you. They come to you to pray. They tell you what they need. Whatever the people ask, listen to what they need. The Creator will use you to bless the people." If the tree were an enemy, our prayers would never be answered.

Since I've come in as Sundance chief, every year, there's a little lightning and thunder all four days of Sundance. Sometimes, there are no clouds, but it thunders or there's a little drizzle. It's a blessing on the people from that tree. The tree has tears, and it washes the people in them.

Just as the tree is part of our family, so is the buffalo. We put the image of a buffalo on the tree. We put a man on there, too. They are made out of buffalo hide. Or sometimes horse hide or elk hide or deer hide. I ask someone to make the shape of a buffalo for the tree, and the shape of a man, and I don't ask questions about what they've chosen to make it from. When you look up in the Sundance tree, you see the image of the buffalo and the man, and with your belief, you see other

---

We Are the Buffalo

THE PEOPLE AND the buffalo are connected. Years ago, every minute of every day, my people prayed for survival. Especially when others came in and started shooting the buffalo. The buffalo were killed by the millions, sometimes only for their horns. When my people were attacked, they tried to stand up to defend themselves. Finally, they gave up and said, "Okay, I fight no more." At one point, my people were trophies. Every scalp taken from an Indian, every finger, was a trophy. But the buffalo survived, and by standing and praying, he's getting stronger. We are like the buffalo. As long as the buffalo is alive, the Lakota will live.

—Jimmy Dubray

Giving Back

WHAT WILL YOU give for wopila? If you get something from the spirits, you have to give something back. You might offer some tobacco. You might give some flesh. But if the spirit asks you for something in return over the course of your life, you have to give back or it will take something precious from you.

—Thomas Dubray

Looking at the Sun and Dancing

SUNDANCE IS A time when men thank the Creator for his blessings by giving of themselves. It is a time when they draw down his holy blessings on their families and all the people of the world through their prayer and sacrifice.

No one now alive can say how this sacred rite came to be. One story goes like this: One day, a man dropped his robe down around his waist and started dancing, raising one hand to the sky. The elders were surprised to see this and sent another man to discover what he was doing. The second man also dropped his robe to his waist and started dancing, raising one hand to the sky. So the elders went to see for themselves. The first man told them about a vision he'd had showing a new way to pray that would bring people back to the Sacred Pipe and strengthen their wills and their bodies.

The elders thought this over. They sent someone to ask the keeper of the Chanunpa for his opinion. He thought for a while and said, "We were told that we would have seven ways of praying to Wakan Tanka, and this must be one of them, for we were told we'd receive our rites in visions."

So the elders asked the man to instruct the people. He taught them songs. He taught them to blow an eagle bone whistle made from an eagle's wing. He taught them to cut rawhide in the shape of a man and his brother, the buffalo. He taught them that the cottonwood tree would become their Sacred Pole, and that it should be placed at the center of the great circle marked with the four directions so that they might draw down the power of the universe with their sacrifice and prayer to the One Who Is Everything.

And the people saw that it was good.

Today, as then, Sundance is held during the full moon of midsummer when the moon lights the night and the sun shines long. It is a rite that requires that every preparation and ceremony be done perfectly for four days and nights if the power of the Creator is to be called into the Sundance circle.

The Sundance circle has no end and no beginning—just as the bowl of the Chanunpa is a circle without end or beginning—but it does have a center. And that is where the Sundance tree is pierced to the earth. The circle has four directions, too, and the doorways are marked with black, red, yellow, and white flags to honor those four Grandfathers that can answer prayers in the name of the Creator. The area is smudged with sage and sweet grass, and in this way the Sundance circle is made sacred.

It is the cottonwood that serves as the sacred Sundance pole. It is sacred, people say, because its leaves taught man how to build a tipi and because inside its upper limbs is a five-pointed star—the shape of the Morning Star, that bringer of wisdom. To get the tree, the holy man goes with a little boy and four virgin girls. When the tree has been cut, the people carry it to the Sundance circle, never letting it touch ground. They stop four

WIWANYAG WACHIPI, SUNDANCE

times to pray. They thank Grandmother Earth for the tree, and they pray for the people of the world. They pray that the powers will come inside the circle. And they pray that they will all walk the Sacred Red Road together.

In the circle, many things must be done before the tree can be put into the hole dug for it. First, the women put sacred food of jerky, fat, and chokecherries into the hole, along with seven stalks of sage. Before the tree goes up, the people tie the shape of a buffalo and a man in its branches. They tie four prayer ties with long banners there, too. Four cherry branches are tied onto the trunk to make a cross. And then the ropes of the men who will pierce are tied to the tree beneath the cross.

With this, the tree is pulled upright—ready for the four days of Sundance.

Each morning of Sundance begins the same way: the men who have pledged to dance and pierce get up in time to see the morning star and purify their hearts in the sweat lodge before dawn. It is wood from the old Sundance tree that heats the grandfather rocks for the lodge. Each pledger thanks Tunkashila for his blessings, and asks for what he needs. He ends with a prayer of thanks, knowing that he will receive what he has asked for.

In a separate sweat lodge, the women pledgers also pray in preparation for the day.

When it is time for Sundance to begin, the man who carries the buffalo skull—which represents the sins of the people—leads the way. Behind him is the Sundance leader and the keeper of the Chanunpas. The male pledgers come next, and then come the female pledgers—all of them carrying their pipes. They walk outside the circle first, stopping to pray to the powers of the West, the North, the East, and the South. The powers aren't called to come into the circle; their forces would disturb the Sundance.

Following the man carrying the buffalo skull, the people pass through the east doorway and circle sunwise to the west to the altar. The West is the home of the Thunder-Being that watches over the correct use of the Chanunpa. On the altar, there's a pipe rack made of cherrywood and a bed of sage. The man who carries the buffalo skull places it on the sage facing east. The pledgers lean their Pipes side by side against the rack.

The men who will dance and pierce wear wreaths on their head of braided sage. The wreaths of sage represent the circle that contains the heavens and the stars. They wear sage wreaths on their wrists and ankles. Their hair hangs long, and their feet are bare. They wear long skirts to honor the women who brought them into the world. And they wear a long cord with an eagle bone whistle on it.

Women pledgers wear dresses. They do not pierce to the tree.

The Sundance leader takes the pledgers sunwise to each of the four quarters. The drummers beat, beat, beat, beat a rhythm. The singers raise their voices in song. "Grandfather, have pity on us. We have come here and are doing this so that everything will be right with us." This is what the pledgers might pray as they dance and pray and blow their eagle bone whistles.

There are four rounds that first day.

At the end of the last round, the pledgers are given back their Pipes. The Pipe carrier offers their Pipe to them four times, giving it to them only on the fourth. The first time asks the unspoken question, " Would you tell a lie if I were to give this Pipe to you?" "No, I would not." The second time asks, "Do you believe with all your heart that this Pipe is holy?" "Yes, I do." The third time asks, "Do you believe this Pipe is an instrument of the Creator?" "Yes, I do." The pledger takes his Pipe on the fourth time, and the men shake hands.

On the second day, the pledgers again rise with the Morning Star and purify themselves in the sweat lodge so they become clear enough and strong enough to be touched by God. Again, the drum beats, and songs are sung.

Some of the pledgers touch the sacred Sundance tree. They walk up to it four times like they're going to touch it, but only on the fourth time do they put their hands on it. It feels warm to them and as soft as human flesh. Prayers have been tied on the tree, and bits of flesh offered to Tunkashila buried at its base. The dancers see these prayers of the people and pray that they be answered.

On the third day, the drum beats, and songs are sung. The pledgers dance in place at each of the four directions, toe-heel, toe-heel, toe-heel, toe-heel, head back and chest thrust forward. They blow their eagle bone whistles. They look into the tree and into the sun. The sun is not God, but it is said that it was created by the one true god. The sun watches over the world and bestows its gifts on it.

There are visions seen and voices heard as the pledgers pray for help from the powers that be. Help comes into them like a fire bolt. And in that one moment, they feel they are one with the Creator.

Women and children come then to the circle to be healed. The pledgers and the Intercessor pray for them and sometimes lay hands on them.

There are four rounds, and between rounds, people give testimony about the power of a healing, or they give thanks for help. There are giveaways of great gifts to strangers. Babies' ears are pierced so they can learn to listen.

It is on the fourth day that the men pierce to the tree. The day starts like the others—up with the Morning Star and the rite of purification before dawn. The pledgers enter the Sundance circle. The piercer's ropes are stretched out from the tree ready for them.

The piercing takes place beside the Sundance tree on a buffalo robe placed in the West on a bed of sage. The man lies with his head in the North. There are circles

WIWANYAG WACHIPI, SUNDANCE

drawn on his chest show whether he will pierce on one side or both.

The drum beats, and songs are sung.

The flesh of the man's upper chest is pinched hard and a sharpened stick pushed through it. Or the flesh may be cut with a knife—and the sharp stick threaded through. The man is helped to his feet and a rawhide thong is tied to the piercing stick and to the rope. In this way, he is hooked to the tree.

He is led out to his place—untouched by human hands for he is holy now. He stands there until all have been pierced.

The Sundance leader waves his eagle wing fan, and the piercers go forward to the tree and back again. He waves it again, and they charge the tree again. The fan is the sound of eagle wings beating, and when the men have touched the tree for the fourth time, they walk back and pull hard against the rope. Some of them tear their skin quickly and break free of the tree with a jolt. Others are pierced deeply and lean backward with all their weight, blowing their eagle bone whistles, pulling against the tree. It takes what seems to be an eternity.

If a man has been pierced deeply, the force of his body on the rope throws the rope far on the rebound. If he has not been pierced too deeply, the rope falls.

The women in the shade of the arbor cry for the men. They sing for them. They know their suffering and pray for it to end.

The last man still hooked to the tree pulls back hard; his skin rips, and he breaks free.

Later, after the last round, the Intercessor will attend to their wounds, seeing that they bleed little and heal quickly.

On this day, other men drag buffalo skulls. The skin of their back is cut and a stick pushed through. Skulls are tied to the piercing stick, and they walk the circle dragging one, four, seven, or even fourteen skulls. Each skull weighs nearly twenty-five pounds. The skulls tumble behind them, the horns digging into the earth. The flesh represents ignorance, and as they break the flesh, they break the bonds of ignorance.

One man has seen himself pierced with feathers, and a dozen eagle feathers are sewn into the skin of his arms.

Sundance is a circle—it has no beginning and no end. The tree stands for a year before it is replaced by another. The blessings renew each year with the new Sundance tree. And always, there's the Chanunpa.

Mitakuye Oyasin.

WIWANYAG WACHIPI, SUNDANCE

Women at Sundance

THE MEN go to get the Sundance tree, but before they bring it into the circle, we women put sage all around. The sage purifies the ground and keeps all the bad things away from the tree. Then, before they stand the tree up, we feed Mother Earth. A virgin girl or some old lady puts into the hole a mixture of cherry juice and meat pounded with tallow. We pray that we'll have food to feed the people in the year to come. We pound cherries and save them for the winter to make pudding. We dry meat and save it. We pray so that the people don't starve. When the men pull the tree up to standing, Jimmy sings. He sings toward the West, then the people sing and shake hands, and everyone dances around. We're happy because we know our prayers will be answered.

—Florine Dubray

MANY PEOPLE misunderstand a woman's role at Sundance. Traditionally, women don't pierce. But some women say they've prayed for the people and promised to pierce for them. If they'd prayed about it... well, who am I to say anything different? In that case, they pierce to the tree through their upper arms. Women go to Sundance to support the men. A woman breaks water and gives blood for the child to come into the world—she has suffered enough. The women make sure that all things go well at Sundance for the good of the men who have come to pray. They do this through their work and prayer. They are the witnesses.

—Jimmy Dubray

things. Some of the people become a buffalo because of seeing them. Some become an antelope. Some become an eagle. A hawk. An owl. An elk. A bear. One of the brothers sounds like a buffalo when he calls out during Sundance.

The man is there in the tree to protect the family, just as the buffalo protects the females and the young. He's a warrior. Usually, one man from each family is picked to sacrifice himself during Sundance. He pledges to stay for those four days and fast and pray, pray, pray, and pray for himself and his family for the year to come. When we used buffalo rawhide to hook ourselves to the tree, you could hear blood pumping back and forth from the tree to your chest. The Bible tells about how Jesus sacrificed himself for the many. At Sundance, I sacrifice myself for the misses, the family, the *tioshpa*—the clan, and for everyone and everything in the world. No one is left out of my prayers. We as warriors protect our youngsters and our elders. Why sacrifice them when we can go to the tree and sacrifice ourselves?

Four tobacco ties with long banners go up into the tree. The four seasons are there in the circle. The twelve months. If all goes well, you come back the next year and give thanks. And before you know it, your brother or sister will go into the circle to help the family. Gradually, all your family members come to the circle. I say, "Try it, you'll like it."

You have to have a strong reason to go to Sundance. People come to me with their questions and problems. I tell them, "Pray for understanding." If they've done something wrong, I just say, "Well, you tried that, now try this. Maybe it will be better." They come to Sundance so they can have a better life. That's what we all want, isn't it? We may seem to have different problems, different personalities, but we all want to have health and healthy, strong children; a good, loving mate; somewhere to live; and food to eat. We want a strong connection with the Creator so our lives will be holy. All these desires bring us to the Sundance circle.

Before the tree goes into the ground, we put spiritual food in the hole where we'll place it. We use jerky, beef or kidney tallow, chokecherry juice, and corn. The women pound these together—some people put in tobacco, too. They put seven sprigs of sage in the hole, too. Before the tree is placed in the Earth, the grandmas put the food in there and pray that when the tree stands, she will accept the gift of the food. They ask, in return, that the harvest will be plenty. They pray not only for their families, but for everyone all over the world. They ask that people will not go hungry. They ask for plums, cherries, and crabapples. We don't have bananas, so they pray for those people where bananas come from. The blessings go out to everyone. Notice that they don't ask for gold and silver.

We offer the spiritual food to our Grandmother, to Mother Earth. But man is greedy. He knocks down trees. He mines coal and uranium. At first, this was done to keep life going, but now it's become so much that it's a lot of waste. We say, "No, no, don't do this. You're disturbing

WIWANYAG WACHIPI, SUNDANCE

some things that you shouldn't." But man goes on ahead. We pray at the Sundance tree for peace, yet man makes war. Men who pray in this circle are supposed to make peace and carry peaceful things—not rifles, not weapons, not throwing knives, not throwing hatchets. But man is violent; he's not yet human. His first thought is to kill something. Many years ago, you were banned from the tribe if you killed someone. To us, all of life is precious. Each person has a soul. If you kill a person, that soul is gone, and we've lost the usefulness of that person to perform good for the people. So when we pray with the Chanunpa, we have to put all violence away. We have to put away greed.

Big Jim Durham draws pencil lines on a Sundance bone.

Some of this teaching is hard to really apply in your life. The earth holds things that bless us and that we can use in the right way. But if you play with its power, later you become nothing. That's what the Calf Pipe Woman said, "Use it wisely." She said to remember that your main brothers and sisters are the air, the earth, the trees, and the water. The fire keeps you warm and cooks your meal. It can do other things, too. It can give you life, and it can destroy you. It depends on how you work with it. It all starts with the fire.

Sundance starts with the fire, too. Two days before it starts, I'll ask the fireman to bring the old tree down. He takes it out of the ground with the prayer cloth and everything still on it and burns it for the sweat lodge. Its coals are put in the smudge can and sage or cedar put on them to smudge the circle. For twelve months, the tree has stood there with those prayers in its arms. During that time, many of those prayers have been answered; many people have received a blessing. Then the tree goes to the fire, and the ashes go back to dust. Ashes to ashes, dust to dust, everything must return to the earth. And another tree comes up to give itself in sacrifice. People come to dance and pray. That is the circle of life.

Evil is at Sundance, too, and sometimes, it starts working on your mind. One time a Canadian woman came up to me and said, "Grandfather, you're a very attractive chief." I'm pretty sure the evil got into her. I said, "Do you see that man standing there?" It was her boyfriend. I said, "I think they're going to tie him here to stay overnight." She said, "My God, so that means I have to be out here to support him."

Awareness

BE AWARE OF the decisions you make in each and every moment. Your life is made up of moments, and every single moment, you're faced with making a decision about what you'll do. The road forks in a Y in every moment, and you're constantly being forced to choose which road you'll take: will you pay attention or let your mind wander? Will you distract yourself by smoking, or will you go deeper into the meaning of what's happening? Whichever way you choose to go, you can never come back to that original fork in the road. You'll be past it, and you'll be faced with another fork. That's why it's important to stay awake in every single moment.

—*Jimmy Dubray*

WIWANYAG WACHIPI, SUNDANCE

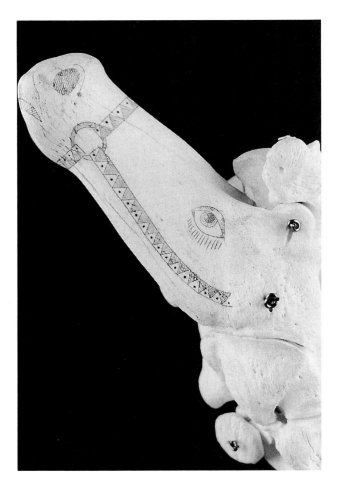

The horses on both of the back legs appeared after Jimmy Dubray said that they would come to join the Sacred Buffalo.

Her boyfriend had been praying, and after awhile, he came over and said, "Brother, tonight I'm going to stay out here in the circle. I'm going to have them pierce me, and I'm going to pray all night."

So the woman had to stay out there, too. Right there, she got her lesson. So while good things go on at Sundance, evil is moving, too.

Let me explain one last thing to you: before we ever pull the Sundance tree to standing, before we ever pierce to it and suffer, before we ever begin to pray around it, we tie four cherry branches up there on it, and this makes a cross. Sometimes the cherries are still on the branches, and that represents the blood of communion. How did this tradition of making a cross occur? We're not saying that the Calf Pipe Women is the same as the Virgin Mary, but she did bring the Calf Pipe, and she said, "This is truly the way you pray to the Creator."

When Christians talk about communion, they say that Jesus gave his body to us, which is the bread of life. He gave his blood, which is the blood of life. In the Lakota Way, we give of ourselves to the Creator. Our flesh and blood are the only things we have that are 100 percent ours. At Sundance, we give them back to the Creator. Sundance is our holy communion with him. He said, "If I can't, you can," and the Lakota has been doing it for centuries.

We Lakota believe that the spirit of God is with us always. You don't have to look clear up to heaven for paradise. He's right here with you. He comes to you, he stands with you, and he listens to you. He sees everything you do or think. From the day you're born, he knows everything you're going to do. So when your job is finished, he says, "Well done."

Or not. When we start giving an account to the Almighty, some people are not going to get that pronouncement, "Well done." He's going to say, "You fool. You're like a billy goat trying to work with the Calf Pipe."

That's why we Sundance. We put our prayers into our mind and our heart, and we let our words come out. We go to the tree, and we have Holy Communion with Almighty God. We have taken the flesh and blood of God, and we give our flesh and blood back to him. It's as simple as that.

This is the teaching of the buffalo, and the buffalo is always in there.

Chapter 15

Carving the Buffalo

"We have lived a piece of history."
—BIG JIM DURHAM

DEPENDING ON HOW YOU view it, the studio looks supremely spacious or devastatingly empty. The posters and newspaper clippings, the art supplies, and the jumble of electrical appliances have all been boxed and shipped East. Jim's drafting table is gone—replaced by a simple sheet of plywood screwed to sawhorse legs. It and Beemer's table are the only signs that this was the studio where the Sacred Buffalo came to life.

A cheap, old clock radio with lousy reception sits on the floor wheezing out music laced with static. The coffeemaker remains—coffee being the fuel of artists and veterans—but mineral deposits have hardened its arteries to the point where it takes an hour to spit out a pot of generic java. Even the red phone is gone—replaced by a black one with the numbers worn off. Jim's sagye is gone—a sentinel is no longer needed. All that remains of the spiritual work that went on here for a year is the circle marked by sage, four prayer ties, and Jim's buffalo skull.

The living room is equally bare. Two flimsy yellow-and-white lawn chairs face the television. A Coleman cooler holds four cans of Diet Coke and a quart of one percent milk souring in the summer's heat. Jim and Beemer now sleep on the floor.

"We've come full circle; we're back to where we started—no furniture, no refrigerator—just me and Beemer," Jim says. "Except that a magnificent Buffalo is finished and ready for the people of the world."

The Sacred Buffalo itself has been packed in its traveling crates and carted downstairs to the gym where it will be reassembled one last time in South Dakota.

Friends and relatives—and the people who helped out with money for the project—have come to see it, and Jim and Beemer have a bad case of nerves.

They sleep restlessly for several days before it's due to be reassembled.

"I woke up in the night, and the fear of failure hit me. I kept thinking, is it good enough? Could I have done it better?" Jim says.

In fact, the bones have been carved and inked and washed and reinked with care and prayer. Jim and Beemer have gone over every bone with a magnifying glass, making detailed lists of any lines that need to be repaired. It was a major task: each bone contains several thousand lines—the scapula showing the carrying of the Sundance tree, for example, has 6,776 individual cuts. The men looked for cuts missed in the inking process or cuts having dust that caused the ink to drop out. The lists were cross-referenced to catch everything.

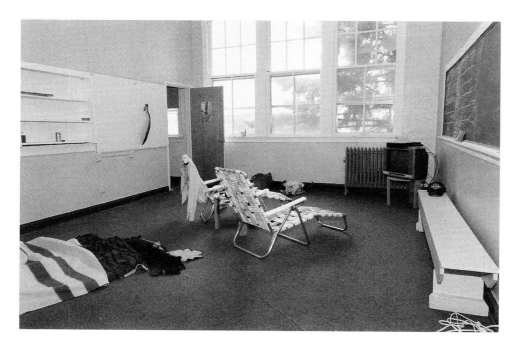

With work on the Sacred Buffalo complete, the studio is stripped down to the bare-bones necessities. Big Jim sleeps on the floor on a buffalo robe.

"Some bones were as close to perfect as you could expect," Beemer says. "Others had little things that happened during the wash."

Once the lines were redone, the bones were polished with steel wool. Then, in a final step, Beemer replaced the original copper wire put in at Ohio State University with steel wire on the larger bones and aluminum for the smaller ones.

The air is charged with tension during the final assembly in preparation for the closing ceremony. Time is tight—the men have two days to do it and need four, and working with the Buffalo on the finished stand has added another element of the unfamiliar. The men's voices are often tight, and their jaws clench.

"Beemer, I had a dream last week that you broke a bone," Jim says.

Beemer looks up from making notes on a yellow notepad. He doesn't speak.

"I just thought you'd like to know," Jim adds.

Beemer still doesn't say anything.

"It really worries me anytime you use that electric drill on that brittle bone," Jim continues.

A few minutes pass before Beemer responds: "How'd you see it happen? The bone breaking, I mean."

"You dropped it."

"I dropped it?" Beemer's voice ratchets up a notch. His disbelief is evident. "Which one?"

"The Heyoka bone. You split it."

"The Heyoka, huh?"

Beemer gets up and goes to where the Buffalo bones lie in their packing crates.

CARVING THE BUFFALO

When he returns, his face is relaxed. "As uncareful as someone was during the months of carving, the little attachment point on one of the foot bones on the Hanbleceya leg got cracked almost all the way through. It broke yesterday so I redrilled it top to bottom and fixed it."

The bone is on a different leg than Jim had thought, but he knew nevertheless that something had happened.

"Hmm," Jim muses. "Sometimes it scares me that I can see things. How can I know?"

Jim smiles.

Beemer smiles, too. The tension has evaporated.

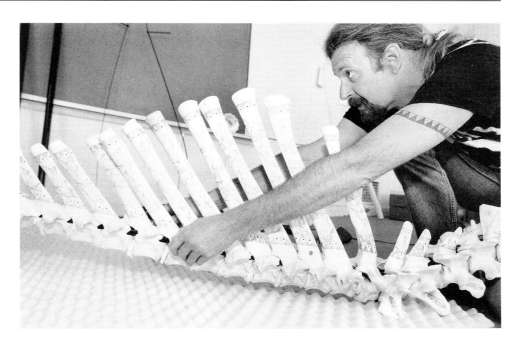

Beemer aligns and tightens the bones of the hump before he removes it from the studio.

On the evening before the Sacred Buffalo is assembled on its stand in the gym, Jim stands in the bare studio drinking coffee from his sacred fly fishing cup. Beth gave it to him when he started the project.

"You know," he says, "on a stream near where I'm going back East, there are 1,800 fish per mile."

The Buffalo completed, he's leaving South Dakota to be closer to Beth, Nick, Crystal, and his dad. He admits he's going to miss the big sky over the plains and the emptiness where nothing stands between you and the sun from the time it first cracks the Eastern horizon to its last orange rays in the West. He's going to miss the lots-of-land-few-people spaciousness of the Black Hills where in just a few minutes' drive you're out where the deer and the antelope play and you can fish all day without seeing another two-legged creature.

He's not going to miss the constant pits in his windsheld from errant gravel. "South Dakota is brutal country," he says. "Windshield replacement is a major business. It's raw, raw."

His completion of the Buffalo is an end and also a new beginning. He has no regrets that the work is done. He has done something few men do—he has made history.

"I never had any doubts that I'd create it," he says. "I even prepared for my own untimely death. I wrote instructions for every phase of it, exactly where the drawings went, how the stand was supposed to be done. I laid it out bone to bone, joint to joint. But I always knew I would finish it."

He pours another cup of coffee—this the lowly stuff of the used-up coffeemaker, his Cadillac of the espresso makers having gone East.

"It's been a wild ride," he continues. "I went from dancing at the Sundance at Green Grass, where the original Pipe is kept, to carrying the skull at the Fools Crow

Mike Riss and Steve Riss

IT'S SUNDAY WHEN Mike Riss brings his stand for the Sacred Buffalo to the school gym in Whitewood.

He's been working on it five to six hours each night after putting in nine-hours days at his job as co-owner of a custom-cabinet shop. On weekends, he's been working thirteen hours a day on it. He's alarmingly thin—he's lost twenty pounds. Dark circles pool under his eyes.

"But I did it," he says with a smile. "I brought it on time."

Big Jim Durham calls the stand a monument to the Sacred Buffalo. It's size alone is phenomenal. The twelve-foot diameter base—which breaks down into halves—weighs 750 pounds, and the pedestal on top of it another 300. It takes six men to haul it into the gym from the truck. They groan under its weight, careful not to scratch its gleaming, polished-furniture surface.

An eagle plays a breeze above them as they work.

Once inside the gym, the men push the two halves of the base an inch this way, three-eighths of an inch the other way, an eighth of an inch back until the circle goes together. The pedestal is placed on top.

"It's a good fit, especially considering that it was done from a cardboard template," Mike says. "This is the first time it's been together."

To build the stand, Mike chose seven types of wood native to the areas bison roamed. The base is wormy maple from Colorado. The medicine wheel is white and dark hickory from Wisconsin. Birch makes the plywood frame. The feathers are made of Western poplar, and the medallions on the medicine wheel and the buffalo skull are the cottonwood of the Great Plains.

It was Vietnam Vets Motorcycle Club member Floyd Winegar who first intrigued Mike with the idea of making the stand and then helped him to complete it. Both men donated their time to the project.

"This project has got me awestruck," Mike says. "My goal has been to do a job worthy of the Buffalo that'll be standing there on top of it."

Mike laminated the circle for the medicine wheel himself, going through 2,000 board feet of white hickory to get enough high-quality material that he could cut into strips, glue, and bend into a circle. He stained the four quarters black, red, yellow, and white.

Mike Riss spent months crafting a pedestal worthy of the Sacred Buffalo. His brother, Steve Riss, carved from cottonwood the buffalo skull in the center and the medallions that mark the four directions.

CARVING THE BUFFALO

He hand-finished the feathers—twenty-eight in all, seven per quarter—that pierce the medicine wheel to the cottonwood buffalo skull in the center. After Floyd hit them with the orbital sander, Mike finished them by hand late at night at home on the couch—about the only time he saw much of his family for several weeks.

"I've got fifty-six hours into the feathers alone," he says.

Steve Riss, an older brother, worked weekends and nights after his job as a hairstylist in Gillette, Wyoming, to carve medallions for the four directions of the medicine wheel: lightning in the West, a buffalo in the North, a deer in the East, and an eagle in the South. The eagle, with seven distinct points on each wing and its tail, also has seven total points. Steve styled it after an authentic stone eagle found on the bank of the Cheyenne River. Like his brother, he volunteered his time.

Steve also carved the cottonwood buffalo skull in the center of the pedestal.

"Something very strange happened with that," he says. "When I got that wood, it was bowed three inches in the center. It was a shame, because Mike was to the point where he really needed it for the pedestal or it was going to hold up the project. I couldn't carve it in that condition, but for some reason I decided to put it in a vise overnight. The next day the bow was completely gone. So I carved it—which took me awhile. Later when I gave it back to Mike, it was bowed again three inches. I can't figure it out—you tell me."

Mike, left, and Steve share their pride in having worked on the Sacred Buffalo project.

International Sundance in Kyle. I'm the only breed to do it, and I did it in seven years. I've had to ask myself, why did I do this?

"My philosophy for contribution in this life is based on knowing that you can do what you want, and be what you want, and still help other people. Take the Buffalo: you can look at it in two ways. It's itself, and it's me. Someone once asked me, 'Why is your life more valuable than mine?' The words were yelled in anger. My life isn't more important than anyone's; in fact, my life is less important than a POW's life. I'd trade my life for that feeling—that one second—when a POW would step off a plane and touch his kids for the first time in thirty years. That sensation of joy would blow up in him. I can feel it, and I'd trade my life for it. I just think my convictions are different than most people's.

"Why is it important for me to know how a veteran feels waking up in a box over a subway vent in Washington, D.C.? He's covered with snow, he's filthy, and the first breath he sees is a white one. Why can I feel the way he feels when he draws in that cold breath? Why can I feel him, as he puts the wine bottle to his lips to fix his sick feeling? I don't know.

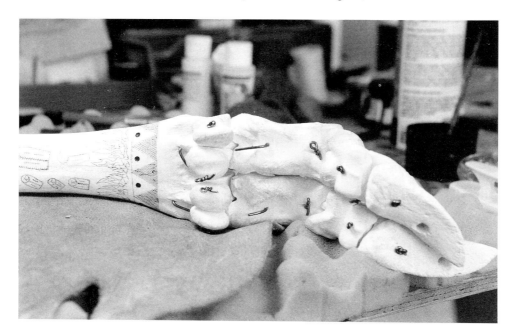

All of the Buffalo's bones are individually wired. There are about 180 bones.

"How can you put a price on men's lives? I see good men—veterans—who are suffering, and it's for them that I made the decision to do what I've done. I've taken their flesh offerings, I've staked them out at Hanbleceya, I've carried the skull at Sundance. Now they call me and tell me how much they enjoyed a good sweat lodge. But I remember when things weren't so good for them. One man's wife would call in the middle of the night, crying into the phone. 'He's crawling down the stairs and has his gun loaded,' she'd say. 'He thinks the (Viet Cong) are overrunning the bed.'

"I remember another man lying in a field crying because he wanted to die.

"I've asked the Creator, why did I come here? I was chosen. I came here to do this project. And I came to help men. Many of these men have suffered from fits of depression, from bouts of anger. Yet recently I heard one of them praying with the Chanunpa, 'Thank you, Tunkashila, for giving me this day. My life is so full.' My heart ached when I heard that. How much is that worth?

"I've changed a lot in this last year. I've given up completely. I don't want to fight with the Creator any more. I've learned some tolerance and patience. I've tried to deal with my anger. I've learned to have pity on people. Now it seems I'm constantly praying. Before, I'd pray during the day several times, but now, every day is very spiritual. I feel more protected. Remember how I described the feeling of safety and comfort of being a kid sitting in your grandpa's lap? That's how I feel the Creator has me now."

CARVING THE BUFFALO

* * *

Reporter: What will people want from the Sacred Buffalo?

Big Jim: Some people will want healing from it. It might have that power.

On the most superficial level, people will be in awe of the sheer magnitude of the work—this is the first time in Native American history that the story of a people has been scrimshawed onto a buffalo. And, certainly, this is the largest and most complicated work of scrimshaw that's ever been done. People'll see in it our dedication.

On a deeper level, people will be touched spiritually by the Sacred Buffalo. From the beginning, people have commented that they feel small in front of it. That's a response to the profound spiritual nature of the seven sacred rites of the Lakota and to all those people carved onto those bones who are suffering for the Creator. Some people cry spontaneously when they stand with it; others double over with emotion.

Reporter: You've expected criticism about showing all these sacred rites. What would you say to those people?

Big Jim: I'd say, first, that the Sacred Buffalo originated from a little boy's vision in the sweat lodge. It was born in innocence because little children are innocent. All we've done is to bring that vision into the three-dimensional world so that people can see it and touch it. Second, I'd say that all of us who worked on the project for over a year suffered to bring it into reality. I'm not full-blood Indian, I'm not Lakota, but I walked the Lakota Way for seven years before doing this project. I've given flesh and pierced, and I've carried the buffalo skull into the Sundance circle—which means I've

Teri, Beemer, and Jim align the pelvis on its mount in the gym in Whitewood, while Ki, a friend from Oklahoma, looks on. The hooves are placed on a drum until they are fitted onto the feet.

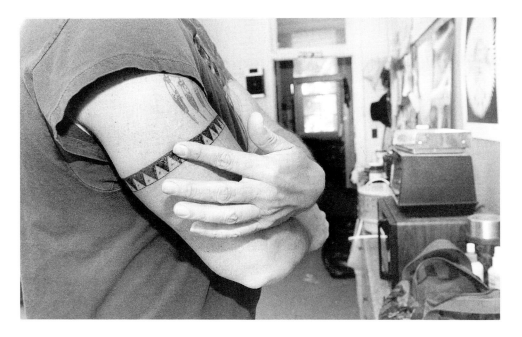

Jim examines his tattoo. He, Beemer, Teri, and Joe are tattooed with the mountain-and-sun design that adorns the Sacred Buffalo.

carried the sins of the people. I'd say this is a truly magnificent work—not because of me, I was just the tool, but because of the suffering of those people you see on those bones.

The Sacred Buffalo only requires that you look at it from an open-minded heart. Like Old Man Frank Fools Crow once said, "Don't look at me, look in me." Don't look at this Buffalo, look into it from inside of you. Its spirit will dictate what happens.

Reporter: What will people want from you?

Big Jim: Maybe people will think I have power, and they'll come to ask for prayers. Some people have expressed concern about this. But I never wanted nothing from nobody. Someone powerful once said to me, "I want to take care of you, Big Jim, to give you something." I said, "I want only one thing: to be able to catch the biggest trout in history on four-pound test line and play it all the way to the end. And that you can't give me."

You see, I can't be anything other than what I am. I don't know what people will want from me. I don't know if I've got it. I don't know if helping lots of people is my road. If it is, then I'll walk it. If it's meant to be, the Creator'll make that road the only one I can walk. I never saw myself in that role, but my dad says my life has changed forever. So I guess it has.

* * *

Teri has flown in from Florida for the ceremony in the gym. Jim is going to close the hochoka, and she and the others will be taken out of it. She sweeps the gym in preparation for the ceremony, her long hair swinging as she moves the broom.

Jim and Beemer are sitting on a bench in the gym smoking cigarettes. Jim, Beemer, Joe, and Teri each have tattooed bands on their biceps that bind them to each other and to their memories of the Sacred Buffalo. They wear the same mountain-and-sun, triangle-and-circle design that borders all of the Buffalo's bones.

"Teri has changed so much since she first came here that it makes my heart hurt," Jim says. "She's as sober as a judge. The people around her who drink are giving her a hard time. What they don't know is that they're giving her strength. They think they're tearing her down, but they're making her stronger. How does one fly so high so fast?"

Beemer stubs out his Camel Light. "Every time I've watched someone else get sucked in by the Buffalo, I remember when it happened to me. It's like if you get caught in the riptide—the only way is to relax and let it take you."

"Like the eagle feather Steve Riss gave me," Jim says. "He's had it for seventeen

CARVING THE BUFFALO

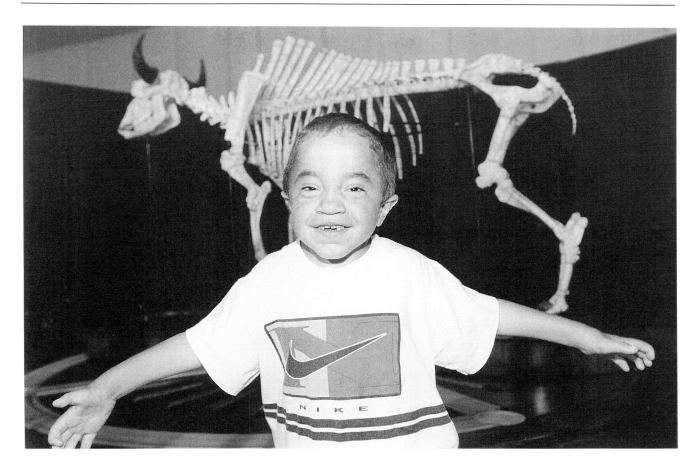

Matt Kristensen and the Sacred Buffalo.

years. Why did he go and do that? His passion for this is so great that he carved the medallions for the medicine wheel from a place he's never been before in his heart."

"They're the best thing he's ever done," Beemer says.

Jim nods. "We're touching something we can barely imagine."

Little boy Matt and his parents and sisters, Cassy and Cari, come to see the Sacred Buffalo standing in the gym. Matt gives Jim back the Sacred Buffalo robe.

"You need it now," he tells Jim.

But the child hangs on to the animal's cape—the fur that covers its head. The head is his *kola*, his friend, and he shares something with it.

"Washte," Jim says. "For as long as you need it, little man."

Jim sings a song for the boy in parting. He had hoped to be able to translate the Lord's Prayer into Lakota and sing it for Matt, but a man and woman had stopped by the studio seeking advice and left him with too little time. His voice is high and clear as he sings, and it shakes like an old man's voice. It's not his usual singing voice, and later he thanks Tunkashila for blessing him with it for the song. People in the circle sniffle and wipe away tears.

In the end, Jim gives Matt his white-and-black eagle feather—his favorite.

"I've carried this feather many places to give me strength," Jim says. "It will help you at night. You hear words in your dreams that are very hard for a young man like you. I've seen your dreams, I know. So just remember that the man who walks with the spirit of this feather will be there to walk with you when you need him."

Jim smudges the feather in the smoke of sage and hands it to Matt in the traditional way—holding it out four times—before he gives it to him. Man to man, they shake on it.

"I didn't want to give him my feather," Jim says later. "I thought, 'Oh no, not that. I really like that eagle feather.' It's one of only two, and my brother has the only genetic match to it that exists in the world. But Tunkashila said, 'Give him the feather.' So I did."

Friends in from Oklahoma for the Sacred Buffalo ceremony have brought their three young daughters and a boy fourteen years old. Jim enlists them to help move the hochoka from the studio to the gym downstairs. The boy, Brian, carries Jim's buffalo skull, while the girls, Ki, Annie, and Maya, carry the four prayer ties and the ring of dried sage that make the sacred space around the Buffalo. They walk downstairs single file. In the relocated circle in the gym, Jim plays the Old Man's drum and sings.

"I see all these children," he says, " and I remember that this project was started by a child and it is being finished by children. How fitting."

Jim's son, Nick, was seven when he passed out in the sweat lodge and saw his father talking to the Buffalo. Now, Nick is fourteen, and the Sacred Buffalo is ready.

The day dawns clear when the Sacred Buffalo is scheduled to stand in the gym—the start of its journey into the world. The weather report predicts a high of 85. A bruising rain during the night has scented the air with the moist fragrance of crushed sage and pine. About noon, Beemer is assembling the skeleton in the gym when a cannon shot of thunder rolls across the sky. There's just one, single resounding clap of thunder. It rattles the windows of the gym. No storm follows.

An hour later, Jim comes downstairs from the studio.

"Did you hear that Wakinyan, Beemer?" he asks.

Beemer nods. "I heard it."

"It's the Old Man coming back," Jim tells him.

The cavernous gymnasium is cool, its foot-thick stone walls a barrier against the summer heat and noise. The interior is a bilious green, the wooden floor shiny pine. It seems somehow like the belly of a ship with its light coming from bare bulbs mounted on the twenty-foot-high ceiling and high-placed windows. The sky beyond the windows is an early-summer blue. The blue of robin's eggs. The blue of prayer ties made for Wakan Tanka. The blue of pale eyes.

Someone has set up a good sound system and put on Robbie Robertson's *Music for the Native Americans* CD. His voice splashes against the walls: "Crazy Horse was a mystery, he knew the secret of . . . "

Center court in the gym, Mike Riss's sumptuous pedestal awaits the Sacred Buffalo it was built for. A black backdrop twelve-feet high stands behind it.

Beemer slowly and carefully lifts each scrimshawed bone from its packing crate and mounts it on black support rods invisible against the black background. Slowly, an animal takes shape in the void.

The stark bones of the half-assembled animal look like a prehistoric mammal swimming the dark void of time. Or a dolphin leaping against dark water. Or a star-ship gliding through galaxy-studded space.

* * *

CARVING THE BUFFALO

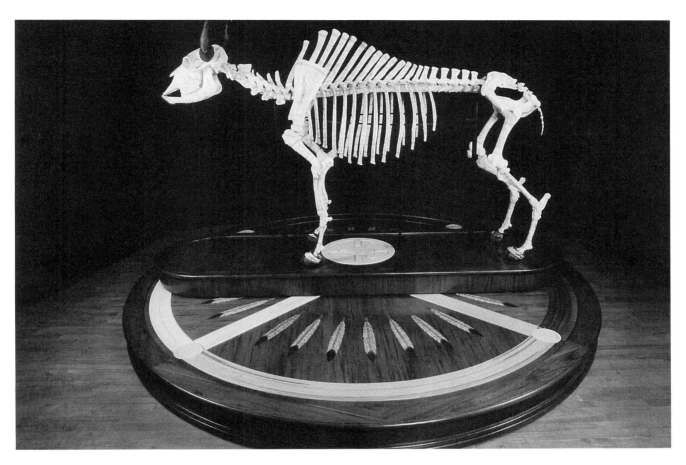

In the last scene of Jim's dream about the scrimshawed Buffalo, he's sitting on a plain, old metal chair wearing his old boots and a straw hat. There's an odd, little curved window off to his right. Ahead of him stands the magnificent carved and inked skeleton of a giant bison. A bright light shines down on it, illuminating the bones that tell the story of the suffering of a people.

In the dream, as he marvels at the Sacred Buffalo's beauty, the majestic beast turns to him and says, "Pilamayapelo."

"Han," Jim replies, acknowledging the word of thanks.

With that, the skeleton turns its head to look forward forevermore.

Jim gets ups and leaves—and awakes.

On the eve of summer in 1995, the end of the dream becomes real. Big Jim sits alone in the big gym of the old Whitewood elementary school on a metal chair. He wears jeans and old lizard-skin boots and a white straw hat. It's the room of his dream—there's a funny, little curved window where a ticket-taker for school plays once sat, and the ceiling is studded with bare-bulb lights.

In front of him stands the magnificent Sacred Buffalo, proud and powerful, head erect. In the strong light, its bones gleam under the sacred ceremonies of the ever-proud Lakota. Big Jim Durham has done what he set out to do. He has touched his dream.

"Power like this hasn't been seen in a long time," he says. "It'll flat out walk tomorrow. It'll walk around the world."

The Sacred Buffalo, completely scrimshawed with the seven sacred rites of the Lakota, takes its message to the people of the world. Its pedestal is a medicine wheel with a buffalo skull in the center, the Thunder-Beings at the West, buffalo in the North, deer in the East, and eagle in the South. The twenty-eight feathers pierce the medicine wheel to the Sacred Buffalo.

CARVING THE BUFFALO

The last scene from Jim's dream: just him and the Sacred Buffalo in the gym in Whitewood before the Buffalo begins its journey to the people of the world.

Chapter 16

Beginning of Time

"I am the Buffalo. Look upon me. I am sacred. You are all my children. Don't hide from me. Follow me down the Sacred Red Road, and the Creator will hold your people forever."

—SONG OF THE SACRED BUFFALO BY BIG JIM DURHAM

PEOPLE ASK ME WHY the Sacred Buffalo came now. It came now because we need a way to get back in touch with the Creator.

You've heard me say that man and the buffalo are related. We're spiritually bound together. The buffalo used to feed the people, and when the buffalo became nearly extinct, we fed it and brought it back. The buffalo helped us, and we helped him. Mitakuye Oyasin. We're all related.

But times have changed, and now that role is fixing to reverse itself again. The buffalo is going to feed the people spiritually. This Sacred Buffalo will feed people spiritually for generations. That's what the spirit of the buffalo must do—care for his brother, man. With the Sacred Buffalo, we're giving him back his power.

Since the beginning, the Sacred Buffalo has stood inside a hochoka marked by black, red, yellow, and white prayer ties. Throughout this project, I kept waiting for the Buffalo to pull the four races together. Full-blood Lakota had come to stand and work and pray with it. Full-blood white people had worked on it and prayed beside it. But I wondered when the others races would show up. I knew they would. Things happen around the Buffalo.

Some of the fittings in the supports for the skeleton were made in Asia, and I honored them as being the representatives of the Asian people's contribution to the Buffalo until one day the stones for the sweat lodge told me something different: the Asian people gave us their ancestors to pray with during the time we carved the Buffalo. While we worked on this project, we had a sweat lodge in the Black Hills, and we pulled all the rocks for it from the piles of mine tailings there. It was Asian men who

Seven bears on the tail stand for the power of the bear and the seven generations.

BEGINNING OF TIME

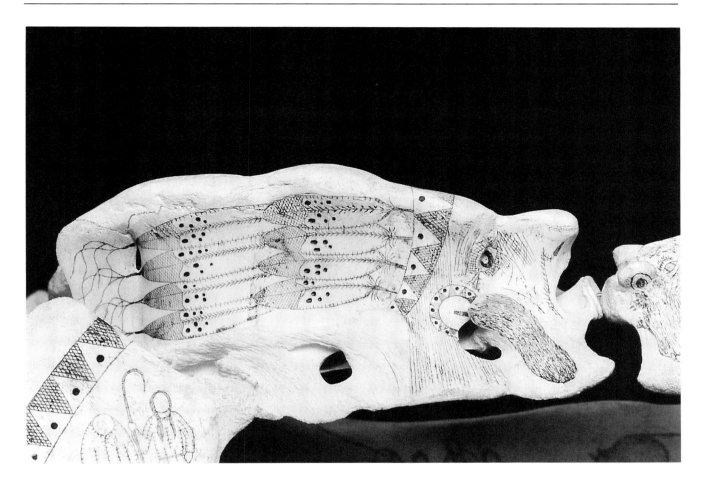

worked their hands to the bone digging all those rocks we used in the sweat lodge. It was through those men's suffering that we had those rocks to use in our prayers. Men died doing that work and they prayed to their ancestors doing that work, and when we took those stones into the sweat lodge to purify ourselves, we took the Asian race in with us. They helped us all during the project; we just didn't realize it.

The black race came to us in the form of a sister. One day when I was checking on the wooden stand for the Buffalo, I met a half-black, half-Indian woman. We had a long talk, and something told me to ask her to the sweat lodge. She agreed, and we were both surprised. At the sweat lodge—with my son and my brother John and other brothers present—I made her my sister according to the Hunkapi ceremony. I even gave her the eagle feather off of my Chanunpa. Her people are my people, now, and all animosity and misunderstanding between us has been cleared. This will last until the end of our lives and beyond. I didn't plan to do this. It chose its own time.

That Buffalo Calf Woman warned us, "Don't kill each other," but we went ahead and slaughtered each other. She told us to live in peace and respect the Chanunpa and each other and the Earth. But the Wounded Knee Massacre and Custer Battle on the Buffalo's hump show that we've failed to do as she said.

We must come together now and follow our belief in goodwill toward other people into peace, or we can continue to hate each other and end up with nothing at all—no identity and no faces like those people carved onto the Buffalo pelvis. We'll end up

Tunkashila, shown on the backbone over the pelvis, is over all life—including the faceless people.

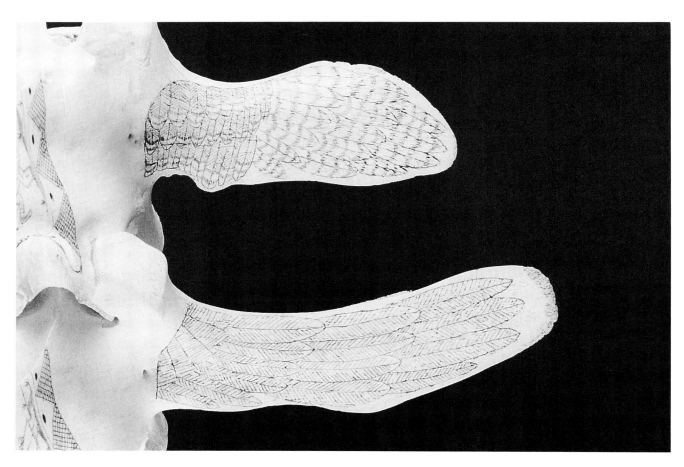

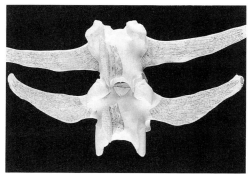

The owl wing, shown at top, leads the eagles through the darkness, away from the end of time toward the Chanunpa. Below, a detail shows two of the four eagles.

with no life. Even babies are born without identity. These are truly the last days of time.

But Tunkashila is giving us another chance. The Sacred Buffalo has come to fill us spiritually. And during the production of it, a little white buffalo calf was born to remind us of the ancient wisdom: "Use the teachings wisely." It has turned dark—as the original one did—and later it will be red and yellow.

On the Sacred Buffalo, the coming of the Chanunpa is the skull, and the sacred rites of the Lakota are on its legs—they are the foundation on which it stands.

At the very beginning of time—at the tail—are seven bears. Bears are power. The spirit Bear taught the medicine man how to treat diseases.

They say a bear lives on Bear Butte. I saw him the day Fools Crow died. We were sleeping out on the ground down near the ravine under a big gnarly tree. We had come out for the funeral. I took my sagye and drove it into the ground near the sweat lodge. Sometime during the night, I woke and saw a girl run by in a windstorm. I thought I was dreaming, but the wind sucked her sleeping bag up and threw it over by my sagye, and she was running after it. I sat up, and when she came back, I talked to her, so I know I wasn't asleep. The wind was blowing everything around, but my staff was standing straight up.

I had laid back down when I heard a rustling coming from up the hill. It sounded

BEGINNING OF TIME

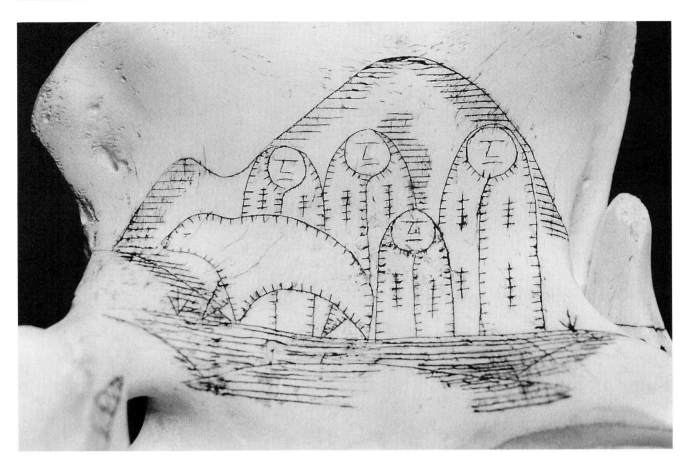

like a train coming down. I stood up and picked up a branch. In the dark, I could see a bear come running down off the mountain. He ran right across the feet of the two people I was with, and when he got by me, I slammed the branch down over the back of his head. He rolled over and over into the ravine. Then he got up and ran back up the mountain. Years later when I spoke of the incident, people said the bear offered me his power, but I wasn't ready to take it. All I know is he wasn't going to give it up easy.

Over the Sacred Buffalo's pelvis is Tunkashila, Wakan Tanka, the One Who Is Everything, as he is over all life. He is over all time. He is over the baby white buffalo and her mother carved inside the pelvis going back toward the Chanunpa on the skull.

They are going away from the end of time. And with them are four wise men from the four races. These four men have the wisdom to realize the power of the sacred.

Leading them toward the Chanunpa is the owl. The owl has the power to fly through the darkness, so it's the owl that leads people away from the darkness of death.

Following the owl are the four eagles from the four directions. They are the messengers of the Grandfathers, and they carry the prayers of the four wise men.

Finally you see the white buffalo calf and her mother on the neck bones just behind the skull, approaching the Chanunpa. Beside them on the neck, the Chanunpa supports seven wiyakas from the Wanbli gleska, which represent the seven sacred rites.

Four wise men—men with faces—follow the white buffalo calf back toward the teachings of the Chanunpa (top). Below, the white buffalo calf and her mother and the four men inside the pelvis.

SACRED BUFFALO **173**

BEGINNING OF TIME

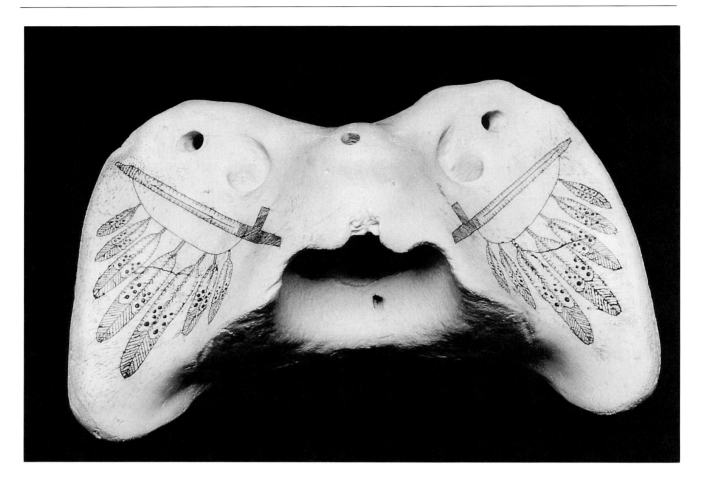

The Chanunpa, with the seven sacred rites, on the neck.

Final Words

The Reporter: You like a piece of art for what it makes you feel. But more than that, art gives you a window into the artist. You look at a man's art, and you see the man. And in seeing him, you feel yourself.

Beemer: The day I assembled the Sacred Buffalo for its first public showing was on June 19, 1995. That was the twenty-third anniversary of the day I left Vietnam.

Teri: I think about the Buffalo every day. It's a big part of my life because of what it's done for me. My friends who are still drinking say I look ten years younger. I don't tell them I think they look ten years older.

If you sit and look at the carvings on the Sacred Buffalo, you'll begin to comprehend a story that will still be emerging a hundred years from now. There's the story of the seven sacred rites and the story of each person carved there. But there's a deep, deep meaning that no one will discover during my lifetime. I'll just tell you this: numbers, always think about numbers—the seven rites, the four directions, the way everything is placed based on those numbers. Like the owl and four eagles and the white buffalo calf and her mother walking forward. And the four men with faces inside the pelvis.

No one will be able to figure out the meaning for a long time. But then a child will know. And he or she will know this is the work of Tunkashila, not of a man. I'm just a worker who brought to life the vision of a boy.

I'm waltzing with God.

And I say, "Father, thank you for the dance."

Mitakuye Oyasin.

Lakota Glossary

The following list is, at best, an approximation of the spellings of Lakota words used in the text. Lakota is a living language that has only recently been written. The written versions are based largely on phonetics, therefore allowing for several acceptable variations. This list indicates variations in spelling where appropriate. Some words have been spelled first in a way to give non-Lakota speakers the best clue as to common pronunciation, with the more formal spelling also shown.

akicita — n. A warrior soldier or veteran.
cansasa — n. The bark of the dogwood (sometimes called red willow) that is smoked in the Sacred Pipe.
cante — n. Heart.
Chanunpa — n. Pipe; herein used for Sacred Pipe. (Also cannunpa.)
doksha — Term used in parting to mean "I'll see you later" instead of good-bye. (Also doksa.)
han — adv. Yes, an affirmation.
Hanbleceya — n. To cry in the prayer of seeking a vision, one of the Lakota sacred rites.
Heyoka — n. A clown or contrary man who goes opposite of nature.
hochoka — n. center; herein used as sacred circle. (Also hocoka.)
hokshila — n. Boy. (Also hoksila.)
hunka — n. A relative or an ancestor.
Hunkaka lowanpi — n. The making of relatives, one of the Lakota sacred rites. Sometimes shortened to Hunkapi.
Inipi — n. A steaming or sweating. Ini means to take a vapor bath. Herein used for the rite of purification, one of the Lakota sacred rites.
inyan — n. A rock or stone.
kila — adj. Awesome.

LAKOTA GLOSSARY

kola — n. A friend.
mastincala — n. A rabbit.
mila — n. A big knife.
mila wakan — n. A holy knife. (Miwakan is a sword.)
Mitakuye Oyasin — All my relations. Refers to the interrelatedness of all life.
mni — n. Water.
mni wiconi — n. The spirit of the living water.
ohanpi — n. Boiled food, as in soup.
pejuta — n. Medicine.
peta owihankeshni — n. Fire without end.
pilamayapelo — n. To make glad.
pte — n. A female bison.
ptesan — n. A grayish buffalo cow.
Pte Oyate — n. Buffalo Nation or Buffalo People.
sagye — n. A staff or cane.
shunka — n. A dog. (Also sunka.)
shunkawakan — n. A horse. (Also sunkawakan.)
Tapa Wanka Yap — n. Throwing of the Ball, a sacred rite of the Lakota. Also, tab wanka yeyapi.
tatanka — n. A male buffalo.
tipi — n. A house.
tiospaye — n. A band or clan or party under one chief.
toka — n. An enemy.
Tunkashila — n. Grandfather, here in the sense of the Supreme Being. (Also Tunkasila.)
wagmu — n. A gourd.
wagmuha — n. A rattle.
Wakan Tanka — n. God, the One Who Is Everything; the Great Mystery.
Wakinyan — n. Lightning. Thunder-Being of the West.
WaLakota — n. Peace.
wanagi — n. A soul when separated from the body, a ghost.
wanbli — n. An eagle.
Wanbli gleska — n. A spotted eagle.
Wanbli gleska wiyaka — n. A spotted eagle feather.
washte — adv. Good. (Also waste.)
wasna — n. A mixture of dried meat, marrow, corn, and chokecherries.
wazilya — v. To burn as incense.
wichasa — n. Man. (Also wicasa.)
wiyaka — n. A feather.
winicala — n. A little girl.
wiwanyag wachipi — n. The Sundance, or dance looking at the sun. A sacred rite. (Also wiwanyank wacipi.)
wopahta — n. A prayer tie. (Also canli wapahta.)
wopila — n. A gift, talent; a food offering given out of respect.
wotah — n. A stone with a spirit.

References

Alexander, Hartley Burr. 1953. *The world's rim: great mysteries of the North American Indians.* Lincoln and London: University of Nebraska Press.

Black Elk, Wallace and Lyon, William S. 1991. *Black Elk: the sacred ways of a Lakota.* New York: Harper SanFrancisco.

Brown, Joseph Epes. 1953. *The sacred pipe: Black Elk's account of the seven rites of the Oglala Sioux.* Norman and London: University of Oklahoma Press.

Buechel, Rev. Eugene, S.J. 1970. *A dictionary of the Teton Dakota Sioux language*, ed. Rev. Paul Manhart, S.J. Pine Ridge, S.D.: Red Cloud Indian School.

Densmore, Francis. 1918. "Teton Sioux music." *Bureau of American Ethnology*, Bull. 61. US Government Printing Office.

Hodgson, Bryan. 1994. "Buffalo back home on the range." *National Geographic.* Vol. 186, No. 5: 64-89

Jensen, Richard E., R. Eli Paul and John E. Carter. 1991. *Eyewitness at Wounded Knee.* Lincoln and London: University of Nebraska Press.

Keith, Sidney. 1989. *English-Lakota dictionary.* Spearfish: Black Hills State University.

Lame Deer, John (Fire), and Erdoes, Richard. 1972. *Lame Deer, seeker of visions.* New York: Simon and Schuster.

Mails, Thomas E. 1979. *Fools Crow.* Lincoln: University of Nebraska Press.

Mails, Thomas E. 1978. *Sun Dance at Rosebud and Pine Ridge.* Sioux Falls: Center for Western Studies and Historical Research, an Archival Agency of Augustana College.

Miller, David Humphreys. 1957. *Custer's fall.* New York: Bantam Books.

Sandoz, Mari. 1942. *Crazy Horse: strange man of the Oglalas.* Lincoln and London: University of Nebraska Press.

Walker, James R. 1980. *Lakota belief and ritual*, ed. Raymond Demallie and Elaine Jahner. Lincoln and London: University of Nebraska Press.

White Hat, Albert, Sr. 1983. *Lakota ceremonial songs.* Rosebud, S.D.: Sinte Gleska College.

Acknowledgments

■ **David Bjorkman**—I dedicate these photos to my late mother, Frances Bjorkman, whose spirit was with us during this project. I want to thank Uncle Ray Huebner, one of Walt Disney's finest, for his artistic excellence and inspiration; H. Morgan Smith, the quintessential explorer long before there was an Indiana Jones, for bringing my wife, Virginia, and me together for the first time in the Darien Jungle of Panama; and the Lakota people.

■ **Jim Durham**—This book merely skims the surface of all that has gone into the creation of the Sacred Buffalo. The project itself is the culmination of all of my talents and beliefs as well as the strength of character in those I know and love. Without them, I would not be that which I am and the project would not have been possible. I want to acknowledge and thank the following people for their sacrifice and support: First and foremost, I extend my love and thanks to my children, Nick and Crystal, for the many times it may have felt as if they had no father at all—this is a sacrifice that goes beyond all others. I thank Nick for his vision that changed my world. I give my love and prayers to Matt Kristensen, whose man-sized spirit reminds me what it means to *truly* live. My undying gratitude goes to my father and to Jim Dubray, whose simple philosophies and complex beliefs have given me direction in life. Possibly the most difficult acknowledgment of all goes to my wife, Beth, whose Navy enlistment has dragged us through hell and high water and acted as the catalyst for change. Beth's belief in me and the project served to strengthen my resolve in order to make that change take place.

■ **John T. Durham**—I would like to thank my mother and father for all that I am and shall be.

■ **Joe M. Durham**—I want to thank my family—Lora and Whittany—and my father and mother.

■ **Teri Krukowski**—I thank my family for always being there—my mom; my sisters, Sheri and Keri; my brothers Roy and Rod; and my dad, Pat. I thank my old man, Mike (Rambo) Schaffer, and my dear friends, Jocko and Wanda, and the Vietnam Vets Motorcycle Club, Chapter O. Also Joker, Pappy, Gunner, Phrog, Breeze, Sarge, Candyman, Kathy, Chip, Stalker, Kim and Dave, and Sherry and Stanley for years of encouragement. In loving memory of Sandman and Lou, you are not forgotten. And most of all, to the Spirit above.

■ **Harry Lindsay**—I wish to thank my wife, Marilynne, whose sacrifices during my absence sometimes exceeded my own, for her love. My son, Scott, for being the man of the house while I was away. My dad and Nilda for their love and support. The memory of my mother. My brothers and sisters of the Vietnam Vets Motorcycle Club for their assistance to me and my family. My many friends in South Dakota and the Lakota Nation for making me feel at home away from home. My brother Big Jim for the opportunity to take part in this project. His son, Nick, whose vision made all this possible. And above all, Tunkashila, God.

■ **Michael Riss**—First, I would like to make a special thanks to my father. He instilled in me the ability to trust in myself. He taught me that I can do anything I wanted to do. He also taught me most of the skills it took to do a project of this nature. For all that, Dad, I thank you. I would like to thank Jim and Harry for having such faith in me and my abilities to do such a project. Jim, your thoughts about life were very uplifting for me. You have a side I only wish and dream I could have. I have much to learn. I wish you both good luck in life. I would like to thank Riss Brothers for letting me use the shop and the materials. If it weren't for that, this stand wouldn't have been possible. Thanks to John Hazucha for the great draftsmanship—your blueprints were great. Thank you to Andy Vig of Woodstock Supply. Your materials were a pleasure to work with. Thank you to my family. My wife, Leticia, whom I love very much. I know I must have driven you nuts! You were always there for me in many ways. To my children, Heath, Jenny, and Rebecca. You have all given me a feeling of pride. Thank you all for being with me and behind me and the project. Thank you to my brother, Steve Riss. Your carving is of impeccable quality, and your commitment equal to the task. Thank you to Floyd Winegar. If it weren't for you, I wouldn't have made my deadline. Even after a hard day's work, there you were. I am "Crooked Face."

■ **Steve Riss**—I would like to thank my brother, Mike, for getting me involved in this project and for his exceptional skills in preparing the cottonwood for my chisel; Jim and Harry; and Gene Potter—a gentle man in a rough world—for the cottonwood. Thank you to our son Justin, who has the critical eye for getting the right proportions on my carvings, and to our son Keith, for his help in drawing the small carvings—you are both a great joy. Thank you to my wife, Dee, who was supportive throughout the project—she was especially patient, and her love always inspired me. Thank you to Doug and Sheila for the buffalo skull I used as a model. Finally, thank you to Matt—it was because of you that I'm in the pure state of mind and health. There are angels among us.

■ **Virginia Thomas**—I thank my family for their love—my father and mother, Ray and Velma Raleigh, Meigen, Jennifer, Stephen, and Susan; my friends Valerie McBride and Lola Bravo for listening; Peder for the opportunity; Big Jim for his brilliance; Harry for his quiet compassion; Jimmy Dubray and Verdell Red Cloud, and the Lakota people for teaching me; David for walking with me always; and the Power of the Four Times Four.

The Drawings

Buffalo Calf Woman presents the Chanunpa, the Sacred Pipe, to the chief of the people, who has summoned his spiritual leader, healer, and herald to honor it.
Skull: front
Page: cover, 38, 39, 40, 41, 42, 43

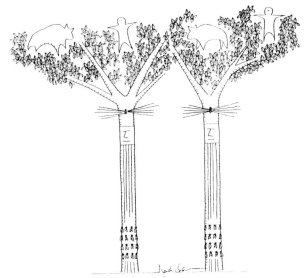

The sacred Sundance tree—a cottonwood—holds the images of a man and a buffalo. Chokecherry branches are tied near the branches, and prayer ties are on its trunk.
Skull: front
Page: 40, 41

THE DRAWINGS

The rite of purification takes place in the sweat lodge, where men drum and sing, calling the Grandfathers. Heated rocks sit in the center rock cradle. The bear robe on top is for healing. Spirits rise from the fire without end.
Leg: back right (North), bottom bone
Page: 67

Through the rite of Hunkapi, the little boy (top) is being made a relative. The ceremony includes drumming and singing (center), and then the little boy is just like his new family, except for the eagle feather he has been given.
Leg: back right (North), middle bone
Page: 76

180 SACRED BUFFALO

THE DRAWINGS

In the rite of keeping of a soul, a child has died—the body is on the scaffold—but to comfort the parents, the spiritual man promises to walk with the soul for a year. He puts the child's spirit in the bundle on the tripod in front of the tipi where he will live with it. He raises his Chanunpa high. At right, the spiritual man purifies a lock of the child's hair in the smoke of sage.
Leg: back right (North),
top bone
Page: 94

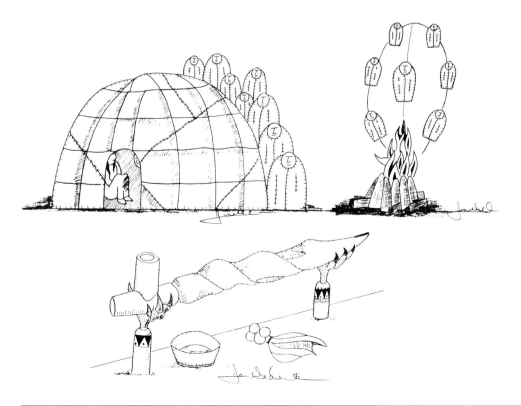

The rite of Hanbleceya, crying for a vision, starts with the Chanunpa and the sweat lodge with its fire without end. Eagle claws hold the Sacred Pipe.
Leg: back left (East),
bottom bone
Page: 125

SACRED BUFFALO **181**

In crying for a vision, four men follow the spiritual man, with the eagle-wing fan, to the top of the hill where they will fast and pray four days. They carry their Chanunpas, chokecherry branches, and blankets. Their families follow in support.
Leg: back left (East),
middle bone
Page: 126

Below left: during Hanbleceya, a man wearing a buffalo robe sees the buffalo spirit come for his dead mother. Below right: a man prays inside his hochoka, a skull on his back.
Leg: back left (East),
top bone
Page: 128

THE DRAWINGS

The rite of Sundance begins with the cutting of the sacred tree. Then, led by the spiritual man, a little boy, and four virgin girls, the men carry the tree to the Sundance circle, never letting it touch the ground.
Leg: both front legs, inside the scapulas
Page: 142, 143

Sundance starts with drumming and singing. Four men play the drum that is the heartbeat of the earth: three drumsticks up, one on the drum.
Leg: front left (South), bottom bone
Page: 139

SACRED BUFFALO **183**

THE DRAWINGS

Four men are pierced to the sacred Sundance tree. When the spiritual man directs them with his eagle-wing fan, they charge the tree four times, breaking free of it on the fourth. Their women, children, and friends support them from the arbor.
Leg: front left (South), middle bone
Page: 140

The Heyoka, a contrary man, pierces at Sundance with a buffalo skull on his chest. He wears a cloth over his head, and lightning adorns his robe. At Sundance, a man drags skulls pierced to his back until he breaks free—thus freeing himself from ignorance.
Leg: front left (South), top bone
Page: 141

184 SACRED BUFFALO

THE DRAWINGS

At Sundance, a man ready to be pierced lies on a buffalo robe beside the Sundance tree. He holds sage in his hands.
Leg: front right (West),
bottom bone
Page: 144

The spiritual man drives a man to the ground, putting him to sleep so he can receive the vision he needs.
Leg: front right (West),
bottom bone
Page: 144

SACRED BUFFALO

A man praying a huge prayer to Tunkashila is pierced to the sacred Sundance tree and pulled off the ground. The spiritual man prays with him.
Leg: front right (West), middle bone
Page: 145

Below left: a man carries his child out of the Sundance circle after praying for the child to be healed. Others bring their babies to be healed.
Below right: a dancer prays with his Chanunpa, while another dances with eagle feathers pierced to his arms and back.
Leg: front right (West), top bone
Page: 146

THE DRAWINGS

The Yuwipi ceremony is performed for healing or to find lost items. The Yuwipi priest is wrapped in a blanket and tied, and when the room becomes dark, he is freed from his bonds. He calls upon the spirits.
Leg: left scapula
Page: 98

In the rite of throwing of the ball, a young girl holding a ball stands with her grandmother. Men stand at the four quarters ready to catch the ball. He who catches it receives its blessings for all the people.
Leg: right scapula
Page: 102

Men and women have disrespected life and Buffalo Calf Woman's teachings, and they are faceless, identityless, and spiritless as a result.
Pelvis
Page: 50, 51, 52

The white buffalo calf, with her mother, leads four wise men back toward the wisdom of the Chanunpa.
Inside Pelvis
Page: 173

SACRED BUFFALO